Praise for *Kill the Gringo*

"Before there was Indiana Jones there was Jack Hood Vaughn, the fearless Peace Corps executive plunging into some of the most dangerous territory on earth to spread the story of American values.

Jack's life story is at once inspirational and terrifying, such a compelling combination for this modest man who looked like a country doctor and lived like a poster for a Harrison Ford movie."

—**TOM BROKAW**, journalist and author of *A Lucky Life Interrupted*

"...engaging eyewitness history...and a textbook for those seeking a career in public service. You must admire a man whose career advice included, 'I often say it's a gift to be fired at least once,' and 'it is always better to be rumored to work for the CIA than to actually be employed there.'"

—*Kirkus Reviews*

KILL THE GRINGO

KILL THE GRINGO

THE LIFE OF

JACK HOOD VAUGHN

with Jane Constantineau

This is a Genuine Vireo Book

A Vireo Book | Rare Bird Books
453 South Spring Street, Suite 302
Los Angeles, CA 90013
rarebirdbooks.com

FIRST TRADE PAPERBACK ORIGINAL EDITION

Set in Minion
Printed in the United States

Photographs are courtesy of the Vaughn family collection unless otherwise noted.
Photograph of Vance Rogers on page 110 courtesy of Sue Higbee
Photograph of Bob Avery on page 112 courtesy of Sue Higbee
Photograph of Warren Wiggins on page 121 courtesy of Richard Irish
Photograph of Spencer Beebe on page 350 & 376 courtesy of Ecotrust

Design by STARLING
10 9 8 7 6 5 4 3 2 1

Publisher's Cataloging-in-Publication data
Names: Vaughn, Jack Hood, author | Constantineau, Jane, author.
Title: Kill the gringo : the life of Jack Hood Vaughn / [Jack Hood Vaughn] ; with Jane Constantineau
Description: First Trade Paperback Original Edition | A Vireo Book | New York, NY; Los Angeles, CA: Rare Bird Books, 2017.
Identifiers: ISBN 9781945572173
Subjects: LCSH Vaugh, Jack Hood. | Diplomats—United States—Biography. | United States—Foreign relations—1963-1969. | United States—Politics and government—1963-1969. | Panama—Politics and government. | Dominican Republic—Politics and government. | Peace Corps (U.S.)—Biography. | Iran—Politics and government. | Planned Parenthood. | Conservation International. | Ecotrust. | BISAC BIOGRAPHY & AUTOBIOGRAPHY / General
Classification: LCC E748 .V33 C66 2017 | DDC 327.2/092—dc23.

To Leftie,

You are the best bet I ever made—by far.

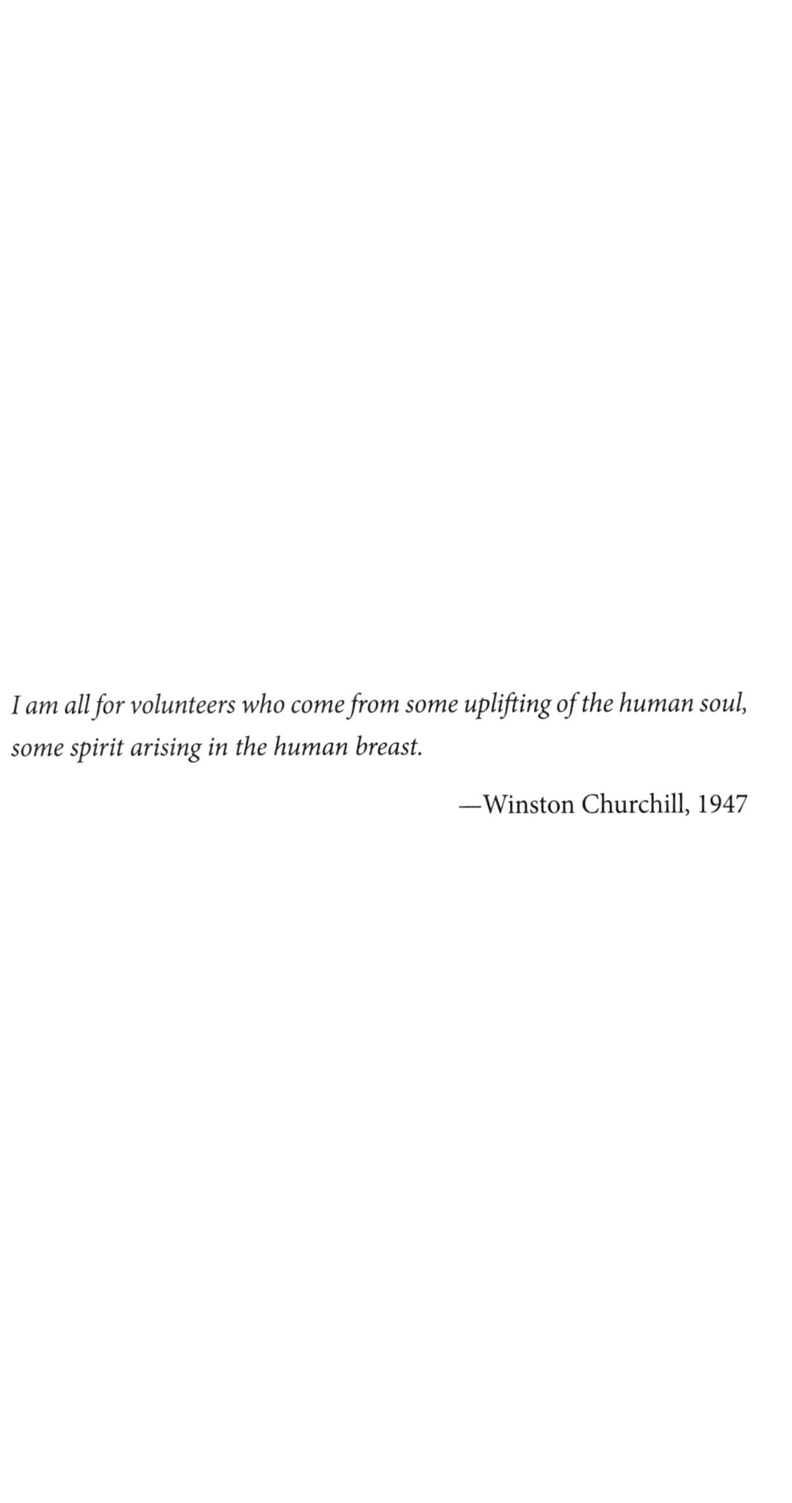

I am all for volunteers who come from some uplifting of the human soul, some spirit arising in the human breast.

—Winston Churchill, 1947

1

1966–1969

Easily the most important single item the international traveler can pack in his luggage is dental floss. It's light and strong and can be used in dozens of ways—for shoelaces and clotheslines and fishing line and all-purpose string. It's also good for cleaning between your teeth, and for subduing antiestablishment staff members.

—Guest article in the *Saturday Review*, circa 1969

I BECAME THE SECOND director of the Peace Corps to the rumble of thunder across Southeast Asia and the roar of antiwar protests across American college campuses. More than 385,300 US troops were deployed in Vietnam when I inherited roughly 12,000 American volunteers working for peace in forty-six countries. As I moved into Peace Corps headquarters in 1966 to begin what was then one of the highest-profile jobs in the State Department, young

Americans were raising their profile as the leading antagonists of our foreign policy.

That year, the Peace Corps had more volunteers than any time in its history. The University of Wisconsin, Madison was second only to the University of California, Berkeley as a source of volunteer recruits. I made Madison one of my first stops after I was sworn in as director. Addressing students on the steps of the Memorial Union, I congratulated them for their robust response to the call for peace. Hecklers in the crowd repeatedly interrupted me, criticizing my record in Latin America, denouncing the government's role in Vietnam, and accusing the Peace Corps of terminating volunteers who protested the war.

I returned to Madison on a recruiting trip in early November 1968. Some professors let Peace Corps staff take over their history and political science classes to talk about what it meant to be a volunteer—at once a thrilling, joyous, maddening, and disease-ridden adventure. This time in Madison, we encountered an even more cynical tone that bordered on hostile among student activists. To these young people, the Peace Corps was a government program under the aegis of a State Department that was murdering civilians and napalming children in Vietnam.

"How dare you talk about peace when you're killing people in large numbers every day," they charged. "We can't work for the US government, take money from the US government, or represent the US government while America is at war with Vietnam." It had been an especially tumultuous year; in addition to the war, the assassinations of Martin Luther King Jr. in April and Senator Bobby Kennedy in June contributed to the sense that the country had lost its way.

Capping off the week of recruitment events was our usual all-campus assembly, where I was to deliver a talk geared to inspire and entice students (and some professors) to peaceful service abroad. These speeches were normally well attended, as was the case in

Madison that day when I arrived at the auditorium with four of my staff.

We entered the building to find most seats already taken, the audience on its feet, and the noise thunderous. Students holding placards and standing along either side of the center aisle quickly closed in on us, shouting and pumping their anti-Peace Corps signs in the air. A couple of signs called me the "Hood of the Peace Corps," playing on my middle name and referencing my controversial year as assistant secretary of state.

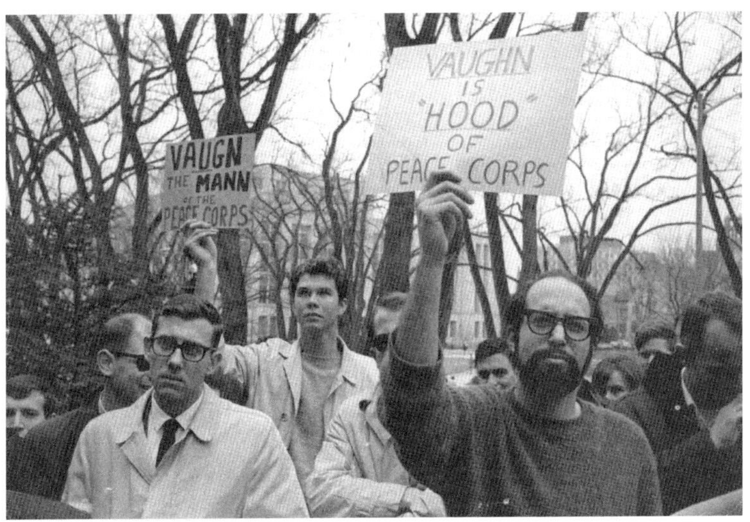

Protesters at the University of Wisconsin, Madison

With hundreds of people in the auditorium looking on and shouting, the students squeezed and jostled us down the aisle as we struggled to keep our footing, unable to communicate with each other over the din. Instead of ascending the stairs to the podium, our aggressors pushed us to stage left and out the side exit to raucous jeering and applause.

Once we were outside, the students grabbed and shoved, knocking down two members of my staff. A former football player recruiter and I began to throw some elbows and punches to get free of this mob. We finally broke loose but were blocked from reentering the auditorium. I was relieved that no press had documented the melee outside the building: "Peace Corps Director fights students at recruitment event."

The experience at Wisconsin prepared me for the scene a few months later at UC Berkeley, where guests were invited to speak for thirty minutes on the mall in the center of campus. I was told that the previous week's speaker had been a striptease artist named Miss Twin 44s; she had drawn a large crowd and been very well received.

The students assembled before me sported beards and bandanas, looking not unlike banditos. Normally I feel right at home in a group like this, but the shouts and vulgarities they hurled made it challenging to pull off my warm-up jokes. When a young man sprinted toward me and lunged for the microphone, my fast-moving colleague tackled him. I managed to stand my ground for the full thirty minutes, but my performance did not generate the positive buzz of Miss Twin 44s'.

•••

By 1966, I had already visited more volunteers than anyone alive—with the possible exception of Sargent Shriver, the Peace Corps' first director, and its hero. When I worked for Shriver as regional director for Peace Corps–Latin America after the organization's founding in 1961, I had shared volunteers' floor mats and their dysentery in almost five hundred cities and villages.

I watched as those first volunteers realized that, beyond any skill or trade they possessed, their most valuable asset was their attitude, and their greatest challenge was to master the art of the possible. Seeing how the Peace Corps opened minds and changed paradigms, I understood that peace had no utility if countries like ours didn't share their abundance with those less fortunate. Volunteerism seemed the ideal vehicle to deliver resources, technology, and labor.

The Peace Corps' mission is threefold: to provide trained manpower at the request of foreign governments; to allow the people of foreign nations to know Americans; and to allow us to know foreigners. Volunteers serve at the invitation of the host country on its terms, live among its people, and speak the native language. It is a simple mandate demanding no tangible results, yet it amounts to the most powerful foreign policy tool we have. The approach is so different, so disarmingly earnest, that it changes the attitudes and lives of local hosts, as well as volunteers; it is impossible to determine who gains more.

The idea of peaceful engagement with the Third World has always appealed greatly to idealists of all ages; the Peace Corps attracts the cream of the crop from every walk of life. In 1960, the average age of a volunteer was twenty-four, although we had an eighty-year-old nurse serving in Turkey.

Volunteers work as experts in more than three hundred professions, from agronomy to carpentry to teaching. One volunteer from Arizona conducted Bolivia's National Symphony Orchestra; another worked on Liberia's five-year economic plan. Ninety percent of volunteers have university degrees when they enter the Peace Corps. Recent liberal arts graduates, known at the Peace Corps as "AB generalists," teach in schools and work in healthcare clinics, agriculture co-ops, and fisheries, to name a few. In every instance, volunteers work alongside locals.

An impoverished Jamaican man in a tiny seaside town created a successful fishing cooperative with Peace Corps volunteers' help. When I visited him, he told me in awe, "This is first time anybody come to work for *us*."

Almost 20 percent of volunteers decided to extend their Peace Corps tours beyond two years—something I encouraged, as it always seemed a shame to bring volunteers home at their point of maximum understanding. Among those who extended their tours were volunteers in a Chilean town that flooded every winter after an earthquake struck in 1960. The residents were waiting endlessly for government assistance. Peace Corps volunteers convinced the townspeople that they could do something for themselves, and together they built a new town at a higher elevation.

When I came to the Peace Corps the second time, as its director, I had just finished a fraught tenure as assistant secretary of state during a time when President Lyndon Johnson sent Marines into the Dominican Republic. Beleaguered after defending our highly controversial military actions, I was relieved to be rejoining the peacemakers.

I thought that one luxury of the Peace Corps assignment was the ability to be unconcerned about war. I soon learned how wrong I was, as the Peace Corps became entangled in war both on the home front and abroad. On the day of my swearing-in, President Johnson pulled me aside to ask if I would consider sending Peace Corps volunteers to "safe zones" within Vietnam. Even then I knew that having volunteers and American soldiers on the same soil would create conflict, confuse the Vietnamese, and alienate our pool of potential recruits at home. I told the president the timing was wrong. Indeed, the timing in Vietnam would always be wrong, because our volunteers should have been there long before our troops.

In July 1967, President Johnson doubled the number of men drafted each month from seventeen thousand to thirty-five thousand. Many war supporters claimed that young men were joining the Peace Corps only to avoid going to Vietnam; in truth, some of them were. Peace Corps service did not substitute for military duty, but some state draft boards could be persuaded to give volunteers II-A (national interest) deferments.

Making the case for military deferments for volunteers became one of my more consuming duties as Peace Corps director. These cases started in a trickle in 1966, but by the middle of 1968, I was writing as many as one hundred letters a month in support of delaying volunteers' military duties. I visited the office of General Lewis Hershey, director of the Selective Service System, twice a week. Hershey was a generous and gentle man, but he had little control over the Selective Service Board. The state directors who made up the board were the type you might expect: largely conservative former colonels who saw nothing but righteousness in achieving peace through war.

The heated, scorn-filled sessions with row after row of assembled state directors took place just a block from the Peace Corps headquarters. A typical exchange started with a state director saying that seven Peace Corps volunteers from his state had been called up and he wanted them brought home immediately; he didn't care if the volunteers had one month left in their tours, or twenty. My arguments were laden with references to service, investment, sacrifice, and cost. The board always countered with accusations of draft dodging. Despite my best efforts, during my three years as director, about one hundred volunteers were forced to return for military duty before completing their Peace Corps service.

Volunteers facing a draft notice often contacted their representatives in Congress for help, with mixed results. The politicians who didn't see the unique contributions of the Peace Corps as a pillar of our foreign policy (the majority of Congress) viewed volunteers as resources better suited for Vietnam.

The topic of draft-eligible volunteers came up whenever I appeared before Congress. I argued to the budget-conscious legislators that our monetary investment alone—anywhere from $8,000 to $20,000 depending on length of service—justified keeping a volunteer at his site through his tour. The fiscal argument came back to bite me when a group of patriots in Congress threatened to stop payment of my $28,000 annual salary if I continued to make my case for deferments before the Selective Service Board. Happily, that idea never found traction.

A few in Congress understood the importance and the sacrifice of Peace Corps service, and it was always thrilling when one of them had the courage to make my case for me. This happened memorably during a Senate budget hearing in 1967 when volunteers' motives were called into question, and Senator Gale McGee of Wyoming enthusiastically defended them: "The Peace Corpsmen are already on the firing line, [but] they have no weapons with which to defend themselves, except their own personality and the ingenious devices that they develop by their own means. If he wants a little easier life he ought to go to the Selective Service and line up, because there he has a whole platoon with him; he doesn't have to stand alone."

Volunteers came to the Peace Corps with a wide range of motives: adventure, idealism, self-interest, selflessness, romance, and postponement of military service. I suspect, too, that some had no idea why they joined the Peace Corps. Virtually all of them understood five years later, though, that it was the most important thing they had ever done.

In a nationwide poll in 1966, high school seniors listed the Peace Corps as their number-one career ambition—and it doesn't even qualify as a career. In 1967, the Peace Corps was the largest single employer of new college graduates, despite our accepting only about 20 percent of applicants. Peace Corps recruitment teams tirelessly fanned out across the country to visit college campuses, spending three or four days talking to students, hosting events, and usually reaping a flood of volunteer applications. More than a fifth of the graduating class of Swarthmore College applied to be volunteers in 1967.

By 1968, however, the recruiters' messages became submerged under growing waves of anti-Vietnam protest, and our applications took a nosedive. If it were true that young men entered the Peace Corps to avoid the draft, applications would have soared in 1967 and '68. In fact, the number of volunteers and volunteers-in-training peaked at 15,556 in September 1966 and never reached that level again. The gross contradictions between peace and an endless surrogate war—between Peace Corps service and military service—muddied our waters. As a government entity, the Peace Corps in a time of war amounted to hypocrisy and dishonesty in the eyes of outraged American youth.

•••

FERVENT DEMONSTRATIONS AMONG VOLUNTEERS abroad matched the pace and tenor of the antiwar movement at home. Volunteer protests outside US embassies in their host countries always resulted in threatening phone calls to me from ambassadors, members of Congress, and the White House. In one instance, a large group of volunteers had picketed the US embassy in a far eastern country, provoking Marvin Watson—one of the meanest and toughest enforcers on Johnson's staff—to call me. "Goddammit!" he shouted, almost without need of a phone, "can't you get those Goddamned volunteers to grow up and shut up? If you can't, maybe we'll just bring 'em all back to face the draft!"

Though I sympathized with the antiwar protesters, I couldn't let volunteers politicize the Peace Corps. Volunteers were meant to operate on a person-to-person basis, quietly encouraging social revolution, not meddling in foreign policy. I didn't begrudge the volunteers their freedom of speech among themselves, their friends, and the American media. But their comments were damaging when published in their host countries' local newspapers, especially when volunteers tied their message to the Peace Corps. The US media loved reporting the antiwar comments and letters of our volunteers overseas, and our ambassadors and members of Congress became apoplectic when those stories broke.

Ugliest by far of the sometimes pompous and usually lightweight members of Congress who objected to the volunteers' free speech was Louisiana Rep. Otto Passman, the Democratic chair of the House Appropriations Subcommittee on Foreign Aid. At a hearing in July 1968, Passman said that volunteers should be held to the same standard as Foreign Service officers and be required to support American foreign policy.

"If you do not advocate that all Americans who go out of this country represent the US and support our foreign policy, then I am thoroughly disappointed in you." Passman described volunteers as "spoiled or disappointed in love," and liable to destroy our country with their free speech. After much too long a conversation on the topic, I told him, simply, "This indicates to me how totally you misunderstand the concept of the Peace Corps and what it is setting out to do."

Our most notorious war protest case came out of Chile, where a volunteer named Charles Murray wrote a letter to the editor of the Chilean newspaper *El Sur* describing how the Peace Corps had discouraged local volunteers from publishing their antiwar petition. Our ambassador to Chile, Ralph Dungan, was furious, and I agreed that Murray had crossed the line by taking a public, political stand in his host country. I felt he had made antiwar activism his profession, when we had sent him to do a different job. We ordered him back to Washington, and I told him his tour was over.

He sued the Peace Corps and the Selective Service Board, which had immediately called him up for duty when he returned home. The court ruled in Murray's favor, saying that the Peace Corps had violated his First Amendment rights. The ruling granted him a draft deferment until the originally scheduled end of his Peace Corps tour and—icing for Murray—the Peace Corps had to refund the cost of his plane ticket home.

When these incidents came up at Secretary of State Dean Rusk's Monday morning meetings with senior people from the State Department, Pentagon, and CIA, Rusk would always say, "Vaughn, we like what the Peace Corps is doing. Don't pay any attention to the critics—go ahead and God bless you." Rusk never varied from this stance. Vice President Hubert Humphrey, too, provided unconditional support. Johnson never personally weighed in on his vocal critics among our volunteer ranks, but he continued to suggest sending Peace Corps volunteers to Vietnam, and I continued to turn him down.

The Peace Corps staff walked a tightrope between our rabblerousing youth and those blustering politicians. If we cracked down too hard on volunteers, we would lose the interest of many bright young potential recruits. If we gave the volunteer protesters free reign, we would alienate the diplomatic community, Congress, and some of our host countries.

Ultimately, we encouraged the volunteers to protest quietly and keep their Peace Corps affiliation off their angry letters and signs. I witnessed one of the more successful demonstrations at a dinner for President Johnson at the ambassador's residence in San José, Costa Rica. Volunteers stood silently along the driveway holding placards as the cars of diplomats arrived, then put down their signs to come in for an uncontroversial dinner.

The volatile antiwar climate created a constant sense of unease among headquarters staff that, somewhere in those sixty Peace Corps countries, volunteers were writing letters to the local media or cooking up something even splashier. The atmosphere was so touchy among diplomats and politicians that even a small comment from a volunteer could trigger a political firestorm.

Our ambassador to El Salvador, Raúl Castro, followed the usual custom of inviting new volunteers for a meal at his residence. Castro, who went on to become governor of Arizona, had been a vocal critic of the Peace Corps in its first years. When one young volunteer asked him how many CIA agents worked on his staff, Castro blew his stack. He called me to demand that the volunteers be removed from the country. I talked him down, explaining how typical these comments were of our establishment-loathing youth, and the volunteers stayed. But I'm guessing invitations to the residence were harder to come by.

With the Cold War as their backdrop, the founding fathers of the Peace Corps—President Kennedy, Sargent Shriver, and Warren Wiggins—had taken pains to set the organization apart from the bureaucracy, culture, and constraints of the US Foreign Service. An important element of that independence was a strict standard of separation from the CIA. Any applicants with prior CIA affiliation were disqualified from the Peace Corps, and former volunteers were barred from joining the CIA.

My staff and I were reminded regularly of the reasons for this strict separation of agencies. All of my overseas press conferences began the same way: "Mr. Vaughn, how many of your volunteers in this country are CIA agents?"

When it became known that my predecessor, Sargent Shriver, was preparing an overseas trip, the Soviet propaganda machine would target all the counties on his itinerary, calling Shriver "the FBI millionaire butcher from Chicago." When I traveled abroad, the advance notice on Radio Moscow hailed me as "the CIA multimillionaire from the Eastern Establishment." I assumed the Russians were referring to eastern Montana, and had not bothered checking my tax returns.

To ensure the mutual exclusivity of the Peace Corps and the spy agency, I met periodically with the head of the CIA's planning directorate, Cord Meyer, in a nondescript Navy building across from the State Department on Twenty-Third Street. I was thrilled to see Cord at our first meeting; I had last seen him looking near death at an aid station on Guam, where we had both fought as Marines. Even more impressive now with his grisly war scars than he had been back then, Cord was a great intellectual and man's man. The gist of our quarterly huddles was reconfirming that we had nothing to confirm.

On only one occasion did Cord and I discover a coincidental overlap of operations. The Peace Corps staff found it a wonderful insurance policy to reserve guaranteed hours of emergency helicopter services in remote corners of the world. In one instance in Asia, I discovered that the helicopter company we had hired was covertly run by the CIA to assist our forces in Vietnam. We had been fortunate enough never to need the service, though, and we changed companies immediately.

The Peace Corps public affairs and legal teams devoted uncounted hours to debunking Communist rumors and flights of fancy. We tracked down every half-baked, trumped up, or incredible charge of CIA taint right to its source. During my six years with the Peace Corps, first as regional director for Latin America and then as worldwide director, no violation of that faith was ever recorded, nor can I recall even one suspicious hint of it. The slogan came naturally to me: "No intelligence!"

•••

Because the Peace Corps reached into virtually every troubled spot in the world, we not only dealt with the ripple effect of our Cold War policy, but also ran headlong into other conflicts abroad, most frequently in Africa. That continent in the 1960s bubbled with both promise and strife as so many of its nations gained their independence. The climate proved extremely ripe for the Peace Corps, but also politically volatile and unusually challenging for volunteers. Communists infiltrated large swaths of Africa as the colonists retreated, Muslims clashed with non-Muslims, and warring tribes found themselves uncomfortably close within new boundary lines and under new governments.

In Nigeria, a large and populous country in West Africa, two revolutions brewed in the summer of 1966. Violent discord among the ethnic and religious groups in the recently independent British colonial country had spurred military coups and counter-coups. Tens of thousands of Nigerians had been killed in riots. Quietly embedded in this violence were 699 Peace Corps volunteers fomenting their own revolution. The program in Nigeria suffered from vacant field positions and high staff turnover—volunteers felt frustrated by a lack of support and communication. Despite the challenging and at times dangerous living conditions, the country staff had proposed a decrease in volunteers' living allowance.

Nigeria was one of the Peace Corps' first countries, started under the good auspices of Brent Ashabranner, a former USAID education officer and, later, my deputy director. Sam Proctor, a renowned black minister, took over and guided the program for six years. Brent and Sam's leadership had made Nigeria one of the Peace Corps' successes.

After Sam left and Nigeria fell into political turmoil, the Peace Corps program began to unravel. In a moment of misguided empathy, someone at Peace Corps headquarters had authorized the creation of as many as seventy-six hostels throughout Africa where volunteers could congregate on weekends and vacations. Hostels provided a decent bed and a social outlet to combat the isolation and hardships of the volunteers' posts, but occasional getaways had turned into longer and more frequent weekends. Instead of being isolated from each other, volunteers had become more distant from the people they were sent to serve. Before I became director, I had never heard of a Peace Corps hostel; when I ran the Latin America program, they didn't exist.

An attendant problem was the volunteers' dependence on motorbikes. Instead of walking a mile to see a friend, they could ride ten miles to visit friends or stay at a hostel. In 1964 and '65, eighty-one volunteers around the world were involved in motorbike accidents, two of them fatal.

Shortly after becoming director, I shut down the hostels and extended a ban on motorbikes ordered by Proctor in 1965. I did this to preserve the spirit and mission of the Peace Corps and to protect volunteers, but it gave volunteers the impression that I didn't understand their challenges and needs. Those in Nigeria, who faced particularly difficult circumstances with tribal warfare roiling the country, felt unsupported and unheard. When I received a telegram from the volunteers requesting that I come to address them immediately, I was happy to go.

A Washington staffer and former volunteer in Sierra Leone, Kevin Lowther, accompanied me to Nigeria. When we landed in Lagos, I met with the office's skeleton crew, who appeared less than thrilled to see me. I encouraged them to find more work for these disgruntled volunteers, most of whom were teachers or teacher trainers, typical of our Africa programs. I rarely received angry telegrams from volunteers busy doing something.

I spent three weeks visiting with roughly six hundred volunteers over the course of twenty-six meetings. I preferred visiting them in small groups where I could make eye contact with each one. I listened to their complaints, many of which were valid, and disputed them when their arguments strayed from the mission of the Peace Corps. Admittedly, we had let them down on the programming side, but I asked them to take responsibility as well.

The communication between the staff in Nigeria and Washington had broken down. The volunteers were demoralized by the deaths of their Nigerian friends in the civil war, and many felt ineffective in poorly planned jobs. Yet I knew that countless resourceful volunteers before them had faced and surmounted host country violence and spotty programming.

I told one group, "The Peace Corps is only one thing: trying to promote change. I have never made a decision that was responsive to convenience or comforts. If my decisions are misguided, however, you must tell me." Banding together at hostels was not the answer. "Stay where the Nigerians stay! Better yet, spend the weekends in your village practicing your Igbo and Yoruba—it will make you better at your jobs."

The volunteers rallied and got back to work, typical of volunteers faced with the toughest circumstances. They served admirably through the summer of 1967, until the government of Nigeria could no longer ensure the safety of 250 volunteers assigned to the midwestern and eastern regions of the country. Of that group, 197 opted to continue service in another African country.

While in Nigeria, I also met with the emirs who wielded influence in the vast Muslim regions of the country. I was most impressed by the Sultan of Sokoto, Siddiq Abubakar III, spiritual leader of northern Nigeria. He dressed much like the rest of the Muslim leaders I visited, with a white turban and cloth draped under his chin, but he demonstrated unusual, irreverent humor, and we developed an instant rapport.

He pointed to a decrepit old man, "This is the minister of health; he's probably the sickest man in the region!" He went on to the next, "Meet our minister of finance. Look how fat he is! I wonder where he gets his money?" Abubakar became the longest-serving Sultan, surviving fifty years of British rule, independence, and civil war.

My trip to Nigeria wasn't a complete success, thanks to a group of slum dwellers in Onitsha who thought they had found an easy target in a short American tourist. It was 2:00 a.m. when I wrapped up my conversation with volunteers in their little shack and headed back to my hotel. After a couple of blocks, four or five young men surrounded me and began groping my pockets for cash. I carried just a handful of Kleenex, some dental floss, and a roll of Tums. I escaped with a torn shirt pocket and sore knuckles from several uppercuts to the jaw delivered in quick succession.

Many staffers in Washington saw my trip to Nigeria as a showdown between disgruntled volunteers and an untested new Peace Corps director, but I didn't see it that way. I found it an education in the challenges facing the agency in its sixth year: we had understaffed in-country offices, uneven programming, inadequate planning, and poor communication between volunteers and staff. Our biggest assets, as always, were our intrepid volunteers.

In a Senate hearing about the Peace Corps' budget, my Nigeria trip came up. I told the senators about my commitment to visit any group of volunteers who wanted a meeting. Senator Al Gore Sr. was incredulous. "You really mean that any time a group of volunteers wants you to come halfway around the world that you will do that?"

"Yes, sir, I certainly will. I have no excuse for not doing it. Any time a volunteer overseas wants to talk to me, I can be there in forty-eight hours, and I plan to be there when that request comes." I also made a mental note to buy more stock in Pan Am and TWA.

I thrived on the travel demands of my job, finding trips to visit volunteers fascinating and invigorating, with a few exceptions usually involving pickpockets or the local cuisine. One of those occasions was a visit to the Ivory Coast, where I went to see a group of eight volunteers working on vegetable crops for the lucrative Abidjan market.

As a chief from Washington, I was to be treated to a special luncheon in my honor. When I arrived in the village that morning, the volunteers pointed out the pièce de résistance bubbling away in a large black pot hanging from a primitive tripod over an open fire. With a stone tied between its feet to keep it upright, the skinned monkey bounced slowly, neck-deep, in boiling water.

Touring the volunteers' vegetable fields and inspecting their beautiful, leafy cassava plants, the disquieting prospect of my noontime meal loomed large. When the time came, I was proudly presented a large wooden bowl containing a monkey shoulder and attached arm resting anatomically correctly on a mound of rice soaked in monkey gravy. I made an effort to eat a sliver or two of the slick meat but had trouble swallowing. I ate a great deal of rice under the smirking stares of the surrounding volunteers. The Peace Corps volunteers I visited, though smart, fun, and sympathetic, always seemed to take enormous pleasure in my encounters with the hardships of their posts. I couldn't blame them.

If only undercooked monkey had been the Peace Corps' biggest problem in Africa. Our volunteer teachers in Somalia faced a crisis unlike any we had encountered. Though many issues in the program were familiar—weak staff, rapid turnover, and harsh living conditions—in Mogadishu the devastating twist was the school children's tradition of throwing stones at their teachers. When one volunteer was badly hurt, I told the minister of education that this practice needed to stop or we would leave. The stoning continued, so we left, and never went back. Knowing now what I know about Somalia, we should never have been there.

When we received a request from Libya for secondary school teachers, we found the government rigid and uncooperative. They wouldn't allow us to operate as the Peace Corps: the volunteers could not be known as volunteers, only as contract workers, and we weren't allowed to set up a program office. When we tried to explain the Peace Corps approach—living like the locals, organizing community projects, teaching adults on the weekends—government officials seemed confused. The ministry of education wanted free English teachers, period.

We finally persuaded them to allow us one staff representative with the first fifteen volunteers in the fall of 1966. The volunteers performed exceptionally well in Libya, gaining the trust and friendship of the people in the communities where they taught. Even during the highly charged war between Egypt and Israel that caused unrest throughout the Muslim world, the volunteers managed to stay and thrive. In 1968, the Libyan ministry of education shocked us by requesting five hundred more volunteers. Obviously, they now understood the Peace Corps advantage.

Despite our excitement about this development in Libya, cool heads at Peace Corps headquarters settled on a more manageable expansion to 150 volunteers for round two. The new teachers arrived to a warm reception, with the Libyans even referring to them as Peace Corps volunteers and allowing us to send along a few more staff. A year into that tour, General Muammar Gaddafi took control of Libya in a coup, and Arab nationalism swept the country. Teaching English was now anathema to the government's mission, and the Peace Corps volunteers were asked to leave.

The Arab-Israeli conflict affected our programs in several Muslim countries in North Africa. Locals hassled volunteers, and our relationships with host governments suffered due to America's strong support of Israel. The most dramatic response to these tensions occurred in Mauritania, where the government ordered that all Americans, public and private, leave the country within forty-eight hours. The Peace Corps staff and volunteers quickly loaded everything they could fit into and on top of jeeps and drove in caravan down the coast to Dakar, Senegal.

In cases where the Peace Corps' relationship with a country broke down and volunteers were asked to leave, the reasons were almost always political. In the 1960s, the Peace Corps left Ceylon, Indonesia, Libya, Gabon, Guinea, Tanzania, Mauritania, and Pakistan.

Sargent Shriver had felt that the Peace Corps should feature prominently in countries with leftist governments. He had courted Tanzania, where President Julius Nyerere leaned Marxist, as well as the more openly Communist Guinea. I had worked in Guinea with the International Cooperation Agency when the country first gained independence and Sekou Tourey became president. I knew how brutal a dictator he was, and how anti-American. Guinea banished the Peace Corps in 1966 and again in 1971; it became a joke at headquarters that we specialized in getting thrown out of Guinea.

On the other hand, Shriver had shunned right-wing dictatorships, where I felt the Peace Corps could be most useful in exposing people to American democracy. When I worked for Shriver as regional director for Latin America, I had unsuccessfully lobbied to send volunteers to Paraguay and Nicaragua. After I became director, the Peace Corps sent hundreds of volunteers to those countries to live among some of the most hospitable and capable people in the world. My interest in bringing the Peace Corps to countries with military dictatorships and my reluctance to deal with the Communists was the only real difference between Shriver's and my philosophies.

Due to Shriver's enthusiasm for Tanzania, the Peace Corps had been there since the country's first days of independence. President Nyerere—intellectual and warm—was considered by most European leaders to be the kind of president Africa needed. By the time I visited as director, more than five hundred volunteers were teaching in schools and working in agriculture there. Still, I arrived in Dar es Salaam in November 1967 expecting the worst; our embassy had reported that Nyerere showed every sign of taking his country down a Communist path, and I needed to assess what kind of role, if any, the Peace Corps could continue to play.

I had never met President Nyerere, but he treated me like family, thanks to the wonderful relationship he'd had with Sargent Shriver. We spent all day and evening in his modest home and garden talking tomatoes, communism, and other garden insects. His message was clear: after years of analyzing political and economic theories, he had decided to go Communist, choosing a narrow course between Russian and Chinese models.

Nyerere made it gently plain that he saw no role for the Peace Corps or other foreign volunteers beyond the Chinese construction gangs already taking the country by storm. "Capitalist, free-market Americans here under our new system would confuse my people," he said. When Nyerere left office in 1985, eighteen years after our meeting, he had bankrupted his country and set it back many decades.

Coasting into Africa on Shriver's reputation proved helpful on many occasions, and I'm sure I came up comparatively short on charisma and diplomacy by comparison. During Shriver's first visit to Ethiopia he had spent a few days touring rural volunteer projects before his meeting with Emperor Haile Selassie in Addis Ababa. Word reached Shriver at the last minute that the meeting, though in the afternoon, required formal attire. Sarge had not packed a tuxedo. After considerable scurrying around, an aide located a tux that turned out to be about two sizes too small. Shriver squeezed his way into the outfit and took short steps over to the palace.

Uncomfortably bound, Sarge kept trying to stretch the tux, bending forward and then slightly back, giving the impression of bowing and scraping. It pleased the emperor greatly. Shriver spoke somewhat breathlessly in praise of the emperor's country and people, completely charming him, as Shriver could do with any head of state. The meeting amounted to "cross-cultural communication in its highest form," according to a smitten Selassie as he circulated a large, signed photo of Shriver among the members of his court.

Several years later, in mid 1967, I received a call from the US ambassador to Ethiopia, Edward Korry, reporting that Haile Selassie was anxious to meet with me about a very sensitive matter. Uneasy with the idea of an anxious emperor, I jumped on an early flight to one of my least favorite cities, Addis Ababa. In spite of knowing that something serious was bothering Selassie, I arrived confident in the afterglow of Shriver's warm, friendly, and reverent visit.

I went to the palace with Ambassador Korry, our country director, Don Wilson, and his deputy, John Coyne. After we made our way past the mangy lions guarding the entrance to the throne room,

Selassie began by telling me how much he liked Shriver and how much he missed President Kennedy. Then, surely noting my inferior genuflection, the emperor said, "I am so angry, I almost don't know how to express it. When I'm this angry I prefer to speak in French."

"*Allons-y*" ("Let's go"), I replied.

With Emperor Selassie

Selassie teed off in the most aggressive way about his recent discovery that Peace Corps volunteers teaching secondary school were promoting democratic principles. At the time, we had about five hundred volunteers in Ethiopia, constituting well over half of the teachers in the country. Selassie was outraged that the volunteers would teach children to think for themselves and question authority. "This must stop."

I explained that these volunteers were university graduates there to teach in an open and honest way. Their democratic philosophies about life and government could not be censored. Selassie came back at me in even harsher terms, and I noticed Ambassador Korry beginning to fidget. I am fairly good at sensing when I'm being bullied, and this seemed like a classic case of dictatorial intimidation. Selassie surely knew that the highly educated volunteer teachers we had sent him composed the backbone of his country's school system.

Summoning the rhetoric of our mutual friend Sargent Shriver, I told Selassie that the volunteers were "the point of the lance" of modernization in Ethiopia. "They are here as your guests to serve you. If you can't agree to our standards of openness and if you find their performance unacceptable, I'll take them all home. In so doing, I will make it known to my government and media, and to yours, exactly why the volunteers were asked to leave."

Selassie grimaced and began mumbling something I couldn't understand as I sat waiting for an answer. Finally he told me he would gather more intelligence and make a decision in the next few weeks. I suspected, correctly, that the emperor was bluffing. Our volunteers in Ethiopia, including Paul Tsongas, later a senator and presidential candidate, stayed. They did their usual wonderful job as friends and advisors, quietly and sensitively facilitating change.

Eventually the Communists got to Ethiopia, too; the Peace Corps left the country in 1977, a few years after a Marxist junta deposed Selassie. It was always terribly deflating to pull volunteers from countries like Ethiopia, Libya, and Tanzania where the Peace Corps had brought so much good and showed boundless potential to do more.

One country stands out as a place where the government tolerated our presence for years, but we probably shouldn't have tolerated it. In Iran, I took my normal five-day spin, visiting volunteers, sharing meals, and touring projects. Our biggest success story was a televised English language educational program taught by volunteer Lynn Meena, who had achieved near-celebrity status in Iran. I noticed that, compared with volunteers in other countries, those in Iran had fewer local friends, but otherwise I detected nothing untoward.

On my last morning in Tehran, I found a letter slipped under my hotel door signed by all the female volunteers. It detailed the persistent, demoralizing harassment of the women by Iranian men. The men made obscene gestures, pinched, goosed, and patted the volunteers in outrageous ways, and then leered at them after committing these indecencies. I extended my stay to talk with the women about their situation, and I got the gut feeling that the Peace Corps would not work in this culture. Dealing with difficult working and living conditions was par for the course in the Peace Corps, and it was our policy not to remove volunteers unless their lives were threatened. The women showed tremendous courage and stayed on through their tours, but I was delighted when the Peace Corps finally left Iran in 1976.

•••

I HAD (AND STILL have) an abiding love for the Peace Corps—a passion I shared with Shriver—that manifested in many ways. I enjoyed bumping along for hours in a shock-free jeep across rocky terrain to reach remote volunteers. Arriving in Katmandu, Nepal, after thirty hours of flying only to be escorted to a trailhead for a two-day trek to a Himalayan village thrilled me. I couldn't believe how lucky I was.

I often spoke about love as part of the Peace Corps formula, and I received some ribbing for it—such talk didn't become a bureaucrat in those days. I equated love with commitment, the kind of dedication that volunteers needed to work compassionately and productively with human weaknesses, societal flaws, and bureaucratic ineptitude.

Shriver's and my affection for the Peace Corps was a tough love. In 1964 when Panama City exploded in anti-American riots that spread throughout the country, some Peace Corps volunteers and staff took refuge in the Canal Zone. Shriver ordered that they either return to their posts or lose their jobs.

We made sure, with frugal allowances, that volunteers lived in conditions little better than the people they served. Volunteers could not travel home during their tours. In addition to abolishing hostels,

I banned beards—a wildly unpopular move in the sixties—and required that volunteers dress respectfully. I had zero tolerance for any staffer or volunteer who gave the Peace Corps a bad name.

In most cases, the volunteers went above and beyond the demands of their jobs, and our role at headquarters was simply to back them up. When Omar Torrijos and his coconspirator, Boris Martinez, overthrew Panamanian President Arnulfo Arias in 1968, a series of protests erupted across the country. The most violent reaction occurred among pro-Arnulfo peasants in Chiriquí province, where a number of Peace Corps volunteers lived.

Torrijos sent his brutal enforcer, Manuel Noriega, to silence the protests. Noriega had no peer when it came to suppression: his draconian methods ranged from pistol-whipping and beating with cattle prods to slow beheadings and tossing clergymen from helicopters. The vicious attacks against peasant protesters in Chiriquí quickly got the attention of several Peace Corps volunteers, who stood up as defenders of their abused friends and hosts. Major Noriega arrested two of them, a young Peace Corps couple from Minnesota named Susan and John Freivalds.

Since their rural road had been washed out, it took Noriega's goons two days to march the handcuffed Freivalds twenty miles in the mud to a jail in the provincial capital of David. John said later, "You don't argue with a man wearing four hand grenades on his chest." When word reached me that the couple was being held incommunicado and without charge in a Panamanian jail, I was livid. I called Boris Martinez and told him that President Lyndon Johnson wanted to know what the jailed couple had done in violation of Panamanian law.

"There are no charges against them. We just want them out of the country immediately, and the problem is solved." The harder I pushed Martinez, the more arrogant and evasive he became. When I insisted on speaking to Omar Torrijos, an acquaintance of mine, I was told that he did not wish to become involved in such a petty matter.

"Petty, my ass," was my reply, in Panamanian Spanish.

The Panamanian government had interpreted the Freivalds' stand for their tortured friends as intervention in Panamanian affairs, and indeed it was. Though they had violated protocol, I would have been disappointed in the volunteers had they not acted as they did. After a couple of days the Freivalds were released unharmed—except by prison vermin—and allowed to return to their village. When I spoke with Torrijos about the incident later, he replied dispassionately that Noriega had been instructed to pacify the countryside, a mission supported by the US Army. The Peace Corps was expelled from Panama three years later.

Occasionally, strained relations with a host country arose for completely apolitical reasons. In the Philippines, a volunteer fell in love with the mayor's wife in the town where he taught English, and they decided to elope. They had barely made it out of town when the mayor caught wind of the plan and set out in hot pursuit. There arose a flurry of debate at our office: Should we get involved? What was the embassy's role? Even President Marcos became aware of the situation as the mayor tried desperately to prevent the two from leaving the country.

After speaking with our ambassador to the Philippines, we decided not to intervene. To the consternation of a distraught mayor, the couple boarded their flight to San Francisco. I don't know if they lived happily ever after, but I did know that we could never send another Peace Corps volunteer to that town.

Episodes like the Philippine romance brought the diplomatic community's attention to the Peace Corps, and I always felt that any attention, no matter how scandalous or petty, was an opportunity to educate people about the work we did. In Venezuela, volunteers served in extremely remote mountainous regions with a horse or mule as their only means of transportation. One day a telegram arrived via the State Department from the Peace Corps director in Venezuela asking:

1) how much allowance should we provide for horse feed? 2) should we rent saddles or buy them? and 3) do we have the funds to build a stable? It was a routine cable, but very illustrative of the conditions and challenges our volunteers faced every day.

Immediately sensing the educational value of our exchange, I told the director in Venezuela to continue this cable dialogue with me through State Department channels in the most detailed way, including every conceivable question about volunteers financing their horses and mules: insurance, veterinary care, routes to and from the village. Our correspondence went on for weeks, and many eyes at State followed it with great interest. It was a wonderful way to educate Foreign Service officers who had no clue about the Peace Corps experience.

Despite the pressure on volunteers to perform under the toughest conditions and some volunteers' impression of Washington as demanding and out of touch, the staff at headquarters was truly devoted to them. When a young volunteer in India became sick with infectious hepatitis in the summer of 1968, the staff sent him to Breach Candy Hospital in Bombay. Shortly thereafter, the volunteer slipped into a coma, and the Peace Corps went into overdrive to help.

Our medical director, Stan Scheyer, immediately called one of our National Advisory Council board members, Dr. David Rutstein, at Harvard Medical School. David told us about Dr. Charles Trey, a colleague who had developed a treatment for liver failure involving exchange transfusion—removing all of the patient's blood and replacing it with donor blood. When we asked, Dr. Trey said he would fly to India immediately.

We booked Dr. Trey on Pan American's flight 1 from New York City, stopping in Calcutta on its around-the-world trip. At the airport, Pan Am informed the South Africa-born doctor that he would not be granted an Indian visa. Since our ambassador to India, Chester Bowles, was a friend of the Peace Corps, we asked the Pan Am officials to board Dr. Trey and promised we would resolve the issue in-flight. Ambassador Bowles pulled the right strings in New Delhi and our doctor landed in Bombay just two days after we had received word about the sick volunteer.

By the time Dr. Trey arrived at the hospital, the volunteer had lost 90 percent of his liver function, and his chances were grim. Peace Corps volunteers in India donated the necessary blood, but Trey couldn't do the full transfusion with the primitive equipment at the Bombay hospital. He performed a partial transfusion, but the volunteer's condition worsened.

Washington staff scrambled and discovered that the hospital ship USS Hope was anchored off the coast of Sri Lanka, (called Ceylon in those days.) We wired the ship to ask if they had facilities to perform a complete transfusion. The answer came back, "Yes." We chartered a Viscount four-engine plane and flew the volunteer with Dr. Trey from Bombay to Colombo, Ceylon. Trey performed the procedure, and it worked: the volunteer's liver function improved, and eventually he flew home to California to recuperate. It was a hair-raising experience for all of us, but ultimately a good one for the Peace Corps. It showed volunteers who may have doubted the commitment from Washington that we could and would go all out for them.

My worst moments were the cases of volunteers we didn't have the opportunity to save. The death of a volunteer abroad usually resulted from an accident, most often a car or motorbike crash. Thirty-three volunteers died during the three years I was director, each one a terrible blow. Parents worried constantly about their children in the Peace Corps; in 1966 an internal report showed that one-third of Peace Corps dropouts could be attributed to "parental distress."

I was flip about worried moms when I began my recruiting trips in the spring of 1966, saying that the only thing mothers had to lose "was their apron strings." But I sobered up quickly after my first phone call to the parents of a volunteer who had died abroad. There was nothing worse than that, and we took great pains to prevent it whenever we could.

•••

If the rough-and-tumble volunteer interactions were the joy of my job, the annual hostility of congressional budget hearings was the pain. I could not duplicate the political performance of Sargent Shriver, who could sway even the biggest ignoramus without seeming argumentative and bear any insult with a smile. I angered quickly, was offended easily, and generally lacked patience for the legislative process.

Regular sessions with Congress, usually dealing with budget approval, almost always became contentious due to one or another strongly biased or misinformed politician. Many of the members of Congress at that time had little knowledge of the Third World—they didn't travel there and didn't understand the cultures, the living conditions, or the mentality.

One of my dust-ups with Congress came as a result of a 1967 *New York Times* article about husband and wife volunteers assisting doctors at an Indian vasectomy clinic. They were helping to reduce the clinic's infection rate by ensuring standard aseptic practices. The article stated that the wife had assisted in more than four hundred vasectomies, alarming many members of Congress who felt that the US government should have no involvement with family planning, and certainly not sterilization. My refusal to recall the volunteers, as many had demanded, enraged Rep. Clement Zablocki of Milwaukee, Wisconsin. In one budget hearing he ranted, "I am afraid if you do bring them home you will promote them!"

The family planning incident reminded us at the Peace Corps, an organization only seven years old by then, how little some members of

Congress still understood or agreed with our mission and philosophy. As I wrote to Rep. Zablocki at the time, "India's great problems are too little food and too many people. The Peace Corps has always taken pride in being the one United States government overseas agency that is responsive to the maximum extent possible to host countries' requests for assistance. The Indian government's request for help in family planning was genuine and persistent, and I think the Peace Corps was right in responding to it."

The program in India had begun under Sargent Shriver. A devout Catholic, he had agreed to help the family planning operation because the Indian government had made such a compelling case for it. Within the Peace Corps, however, Shriver prohibited the distribution of contraception to volunteers. Most of the Peace Corps doctors discreetly provided it anyway. When I became director, I allowed contraception for volunteers, and, if an abortion was indicated, it was provided.

Eunice Kennedy Shriver, Sargent Shriver's wife and President Kennedy's sister, strongly objected to our work in the vasectomy clinic in India. After the *Times* article came out, Eunice began a campaign with her brother, Senator Robert Kennedy, to remove me from the Peace Corps. They made a good team; Bobby and I had an acrimonious history, and Eunice had never warmed to me. At a party the Shrivers gave for me when I became director, Eunice had described me to her children as "the man who is going to undo all the good your father has done at the Peace Corps."

Shriver, as usual, saved the day by talking his relatives down from their fury over the India program. Though the Peace Corps never admitted wrongdoing, the volunteers were reassigned from clinic work to training and education.

Family planning battles with Congress provided me with a wonderful opportunity to have a little fun with Rep. Otto Passman. Ever since we met in 1966, he had addressed me as "Shriber." When

Passman asked about any ongoing volunteer projects involving birth control, I told him that we were distributing a breakthrough new contraceptive pill, a sulfur derivative called "sulfa denial." The joke got some chuckles from the room but went right over Passman's head.

A standard complaint from Congress was that the Peace Corps robbed America of fine young teachers at a time when our inner cities needed them badly. The fact is that the Peace Corps returned to our country four or five teachers for every one it took. The typical volunteer with a bachelor of arts from an outstanding school had at the beginning of service a pretty low opinion of teaching secondary school—no future, no money, no excitement. After teaching children in the slums of Bogotá, that volunteer returned inspired to earn a certificate to teach in the US.

There was no greater favor we could do our country than to bring these bright, experienced, high-thyroid young adults back from the Peace Corps to teach in secondary schools at home. While I was director, 50 percent of returned volunteers went back to school for an advanced degree, and 40 percent went on to serve their country in education, the nonprofit world, or the Foreign Service.

Seeing the need to build support and understanding for the Peace Corps in high places, including Congress, Sargent Shriver had created an outside body of informal advisors and advocates called the Peace Corps National Advisory Council. The council was first chaired by Vice President Johnson and later by Hubert Humphrey; both men were adept at keeping the diverse and prestigious group engaged and proud. One early board member was the famous IBM President Thomas Watson Jr.

The council convened at Peace Corps headquarters once or twice a year for a sweeping update on volunteer heroics and a glimpse of political celebrities who dropped in for photo ops. After five years of standard beltway fare, and after losing Shriver, some council members grew restless. Eager to get them out of Washington and closer to the volunteers, we organized a trip to the Peace Corps' Puerto Rican Outward Bound training camp. Two full days of intensive exposure to the staff, trainees, and mosquitoes gave the council a taste of the real thing.

One of the trainees present for a Q&A with council members was the future senator from Connecticut, Chris Dodd, bound for the Dominican Republic. Even then a confident and opinionated orator, Dodd launched into a tirade that I sensed he'd been preparing for days. He criticized in the most brutal way every aspect of Peace Corps training: the skills training, the quality of staff, and the language instruction.

Despite his deficient training, Dodd excelled in his post at Benito Moncion as a community development volunteer. His first project was organizing the prostitutes in his province. Legend has it Dodd's project slogans included, "You don't have to take it lying down anymore! Better prices and better beds equal greater dignity."

The idealism, indignation, and ingenuity displayed by Dodd and other volunteers really turned me on—this was how the world would be changed. For all those fervent protesters of war who greeted me on college campuses, I could think of no greater outlet than the Peace Corps. Here was an opportunity to do something important and difficult, to put their skills and talents where their rhetoric was.

Working for an agency of peace during one of the most turbulent and hostile periods in our history seemed, in a way, perfect for a lover and fighter like me. From my youth as a muskrat trapper in Michigan to my discovery of French in high school and my devotion to the sport of boxing, my life's path has pulled me between the violent and the romantic. From fighting in the Pacific as a marine in World War II to touring the world's remotest corners with the Peace Corps, I came from war to peace.

In Mexico as a professional boxer I learned Spanish and became a lifelong lover of everything Latin—not to be confused with a

Latin lover—which led to a lively career with the Foreign Service in Central and South America. In my later years, I stumbled into one last battle of greater proportions than any before it: environmental conservation. Turning green took me back to Latin America and also to my Midwestern farming roots.

Never planned or calculated, my career's trajectory does owe something to my talent for getting fired. Its length I attribute to daily shadowboxing and good luck surviving assassination attempts. Though seemingly indiscriminate, my jobs—more than twenty-five of them—have always kept me close to the fight, which is right where I like to be.

2

1920–1944

I didn't know enough Spanish at the time to tell whether the agent said I would get sixty pesos for four rounds or four pesos for sixty rounds.

—Interview with Cobey Black of *The Honolulu Advertiser*, 1975

At my birth in Columbus, Montana, in 1920, my dad hung a pair of miniature antelope-skin boxing gloves from the headboard of my crib. But he didn't mention the sport to me until I was thirteen and some teenage bullies in our new hometown of Albion, Michigan, stole my prized marble collection. It was then that my mom confided the origin of my name: Jack Dempsey, the world heavyweight champ. Dad created a makeshift gym in the basement with a punching bag and jump rope. I worked out there religiously, using techniques gleaned from books about boxing and making up the rest.

By the time I started high school, I felt confident enough to enter tournaments in Albion and nearby Jackson, a tough town called Prison City because it was home to the world's largest walled prison. I adopted the nickname "Chopper" for my right-hand punch that swung over and down. When done with the right timing and velocity, the "chop" could be extremely effective.

I started my sophomore year setting my sights on the Golden Gloves. I entered the Jackson tournament in the bantamweight division—115 to 118 pounds—and won my first three fights. After losing the championship match to a brute it was discovered later weighed too much for the class, I was instated as champion and inherited a trip to Grand Rapids for the state amateur championship. I lost in the third round of eliminations by what the local sports reporter called a "hairline decision."

My performance at the Golden Gloves drew the attention of veteran coach Everett Wilder from Jackson's Sparta Gym Club. He was a stocky, heavily accented Bostonian with a dry sense of humor who had trained a heavyweight champion. When he offered to coach me, I was thrilled.

Wilder drove over from Jackson every week to put me through the paces. He schooled me in all the classic pillars of boxer training: shadowboxing, rope skipping, heavy-bag punching, and road work. He was a bear on balance and getting distance to my punches, which we achieved by hitting an old mattress secured to the wall while I inched slowly backward. Wilder gave me the sense of rhythm and timing that allowed me to duck and weave my way out of dicey situations—especially helpful in fights where I was clearly outmatched.

By my next Golden Gloves tournament, I felt even more overconfident than I had my first time out. I won the Jackson Novice Featherweight Championship, this time cleanly earning a trip to Grand Rapids in four fights. Then I had the misfortune of fighting twice on the night of the championship. In the championship match, I sore-muscled my way through three rounds with Jim Monroe of Flint, only to lose on a split decision. I was seventeen and utterly crushed.

At the Tri-State Tournament of Champions, I was scheduled to box internationally-known Earl Reid, a student at Michigan State University who was one of the top two or three amateur bantamweights in the world. In the first round, I was in complete control. Keeping Reid off balance, I staggered him several times with left hooks. So confident was I after going through round one virtually untouched that, to begin round two, I foolishly reached out with both hands to touch gloves. Reid's response to my magnanimous gesture was a thunderous overhand right flush on my nose. I have always been a profuse bleeder, especially from the nose, and Reid's dead-on blow opened up the floodgates. I was barely able to stagger out of my corner for round three.

I put in a smarter performance at a carnival in a small resort near Duck Lake, Michigan. Both on paper and in person, my opponent appeared formidable. Justin "Duke" Hunter, recently paroled from Southern Michigan Prison, had for several years held the prison's featherweight championship title. Duke was about twenty-five. I was eighteen and almost ten pounds lighter. A ten-pound spread in the lower weight classes usually makes a crushing difference.

Duke was built like the brick prison he had just vacated. He had an ever-forward, buzz-saw style. I, on the other hand, possessed a build once described by a Kalamazoo sports writer as "reminiscent of a skinned muskrat." I refused to fight at the middle, street-fighter distance with Duke. As Wilder predicted, that was Duke's only range. My opponent spent a hot August afternoon fanning the air and grunting while I systematically circled, feinted, danced, and jabbed. I not only frustrated his efforts but floored him in each of the last two rounds.

When I wasn't chasing Golden Gloves or Diamond Belt titles, my Sparta Gym stablemates and I boxed at smokers. Usually sponsored by Moose and Elk Lodges, the standard fare for the evening was three semipro boxing matches followed by a fully professional striptease or wrestling match. The wrestlers, Gorilla Gruboney and Alex Kasabowski (aka The Pitiless Polack), traveled with us.

Semipro boxer in those days meant discreetly paid amateur. The pay was five dollars if you won, three if you didn't. Often the hat would be passed to reward especially lively combat, and quarters and half dollars poured in, sweetening the purse. The smoker audience was amenable to shenanigans of all kinds, and boxers frequently fought twice or more on the same night under different names. One evening, I fought three times against the same opponent. The outcomes: a win, a loss, and a draw.

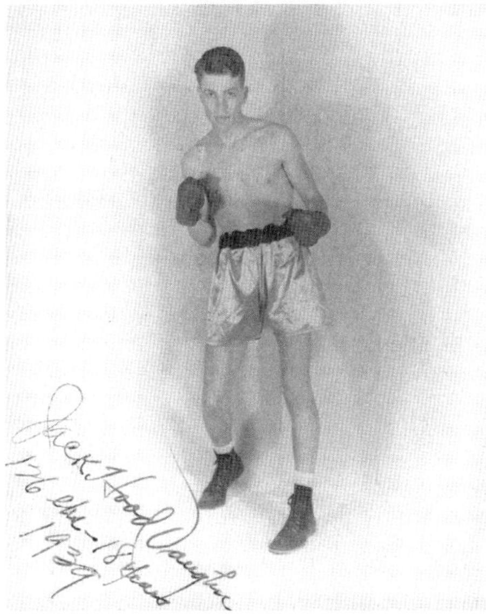

The smoker fights were usually not fixed, but there was a congenial showmanship that made them great theater. My favorite smoker rival was Johnny Gallegos, a swarming club fighter type. We sometimes enhanced the drama of our encounters using the capsules of reddish food coloring that were sold with white margarine to make it look more like butter. We put them in our mouthpieces and, in the last round bit, down hard, sending streams of "blood" trickling down our chins.

Senior year brought my third opportunity to try for Golden Gloves glory. This time I could enter the competition as an "open" fighter rather than a novice, recognition of my greater experience and an entrée to much better opponents. I won the Albion title in two fights and went on to win the Jackson Championship again to earn a trip to Grand Rapids. There was something about Grand Rapids. This time I came down with a nasty head cold. I made the trip, trying to cure myself en route with horehound lozenges and orange juice, but on Wilder's insistence I withdrew myself from competition.

The state glory that eluded me in the Golden Gloves was mine during summers in the Civilian Military Training Corps (CMTC). The program at Fort Custer, a US Army base near Battle Creek, Michigan, seemed tailor-made for me. It fed my boyhood fascination with the military and also hosted a robust boxing program. We lived a boot camp-style existence every morning with marching, saluting, rifle cleaning, and mastering military courtesy. The payoff was the afternoon, completely devoted to athletics. I relished the chance to train intensively and fight guys from all over the Midwest. I won the featherweight championship that first CMTC summer after my junior year.

During the school year, my boxing schedule got me out of much of the work on my family's farm—a sore point with my dad—so in the summers he made a point of pinning me down for hay duty. I did the arduous and hot job of putting hay up in the barn. I stood on top of the hay rig and loaded it, flattening it out evenly as it came up on the conveyor at the back of the wagon. If the hay was dry, I worked a twenty-hour day to get it in. Tough as it was, I viewed hay duty as a great boxing workout.

When not boxing or working as a farm hand, I developed my own side business as a muskrat trapper. My good friend George "Shooey" Schumacher and I set up trap lines along the Kalamazoo River, several miles away. Muskrat fur matures to its silky prime in December. The shallow swamp waters where they lived were frozen, but the muskrat followed trails under the ice to find food. We used steel foothold traps that we chained to a stake that kept the muskrat from swimming away and also served as a marker for us when we returned.

The trapping season lasted from November through February, and sometimes into March. On a good week, we'd catch four muskrat, throw the carcasses over our shoulders, and jog the several miles back to my house. We skinned them and stretched the skins on a wooden shingle. The local junk dealer was our best and only customer; we sold our skins to him for a couple of dollars each.

•••

In my senior year, high school was an inconvenient obstacle to my boxing career. The only academic subject that captured my interest was French; it was love at first mispronunciation. Over four years with Madame Olga Hicks, I seriously considered a future as a professor of French literature. The French Club became my only legitimate after-school activity. My father occasionally wondered aloud about the starting salary of French professors.

As I pondered my post-graduation options, the one I considered most earnestly was turning pro. I was faring increasingly well during my sparring sessions with the journeyman pro boxers who were fixtures in Midwestern gyms. I found them much easier to hit and outmaneuver than the better amateurs. I was also unhappy with the petty semipro purses of three to five dollars. I was brought to my lowest point at a resort on the shores of Lake Michigan. After having promised me eight dollars for a five-round fight, the promoter left the premises early with instructions for an assistant to distribute ice cream popsicles in lieu of cash to his amateur performers.

By the second semester of senior year, in early 1939, my growing fascination with the idea of turning pro hardened to resolution. I had been slowly preparing my parents, telegraphing my career punch every week or two. They usually smiled or exchanged glances. Once in a while they casually offered a counterproposal. Their ideas struck me not so much unrealistic as truly unexciting. My mother suggested studying medicine like her esteemed late father. My father, a businessman and farmer who had gotten his start in Montana, stressed the wisdom of choosing a profession like forestry or geology that would keep me outdoors.

My plans for a pro boxing career were unexpectedly sidetracked that spring by another kind of professional sport—subsidized college athletics. The opportunity came at a benefit boxing match held in East Lansing, a college town some fifty miles from Albion. I had scored an unexpectedly flashy and dominant victory over a star boxer from Saginaw named Al Kirchenbauer. It was the feature bout of the evening, taking place right under the noses of the Michigan State University coaching staff. Like bankers, they occupied most of the ringside seats.

When a well-dressed Spartan coach came into my locker room after the bout, I sensed immediately that what he was carrying in that large duffle bag was for me—whether I said yes or not. "We'll need a good featherweight by next year. From what you showed us out there, you're better than any featherweight we have seen recently in our conference. I was amazed that Kirchenbauer couldn't land a solid punch after the first round. But you'll have to learn not to punch in a clinch, and not hit and hold the way you do on the ropes."

He said that if my grades checked out, I would have a free college education, plus a few bonuses. The duffle bag revealed a Spartan warm-up suit and parka in my size. I'd had no idea college recruiting was this classy. He made his pitch, and I accepted in less than fifteen minutes. I was dazzled when shortly thereafter he invited me for a snack with the university's athletic director. Their hook was set deeply.

My parents were stunned by this turn, but relieved that I had been enticed into a college education. Wilder, my coach, was furious. Clearly he had been counting on making a little money when "we" turned pro. My four sisters thought it was odd I would choose a "cow" college, the term applied to Michigan State as a land-grant college in those days. Most of our friends were going to the University of Michigan.

Less than a month before I graduated from high school, I received a Dear John letter from Michigan State. For reasons beyond the control and wishes of the Spartan Athletic Scholarship Board, the letter read, my gold-plated boxing scholarship had to be cancelled. It could not be renegotiated or revisited. Just like that, my sweetheart deal collapsed.

Responsible for my body blow was an NCAA ban on the recruitment of professional amateur boxers. College boys were being killed in campus rings by semipro fighters. In just six months, three students had died in bouts against those seasoned "amateur" boxers, who in many instances had fought one or even two hundred bouts before going to college. In retrospect, the policy change was necessary, overdue, and surely lifesaving. For me, it resulted in even greater ambivalence about the idea of going to college.

I took my high school diploma and ran to the best possible training site I could think of for launching my professional boxing career: Fort Custer's CMTC program. Determined to recapture the featherweight title, I started picking off opponents on my way to the championship. In my semifinal bout against a tough professional fighter from Chicago, I suffered a serious injury to my right eye. After winning the decision, I went to the hospital, where doctors offered no conclusive diagnosis. They suggested taking a "wait and see" approach, which in my case took on a whole new meaning.

Flaunting my immaturity and stupidity, I kept my appointment in the tournament finals the following week. I won the title with one eye and a lot of luck. In the weeks following, my eye pain disappeared but my vision continued to trouble me. Knowing that my professional debut would have to wait until my eye improved—and seeing all my buddies prepare for their college debuts—I began to reconsider my plans.

Encouraged by my older sister, a recent transfer to the University of Michigan, I became interested in going to a "better" college, especially one with a strong romance language department. In August, Dad said he thought he could handle the sixty dollars per semester of in-state tuition at the University of Michigan. A semi-injured semipro with a penchant for French verb conjugation, I was suddenly college-bound.

•••

I ARRIVED IN ANN Arbor the same day Hitler's army spilled across Poland's borders. Hauling my possessions through campus in my father's ancient Gladstone bags, I felt like an alien. In the West Quad dormitory where I was assigned, I knew only one person—Albion classmate Bud Lonergan. My roommate was Robert Morrow, a platinum blond from Nyack, NY. He was shy and self-conscious, and I thought a rechristening was in order. I dubbed him Blackie, a name that brought him affectionate recognition from much of the student body, and we became great friends.

Shooey Schumacher came to the University of Michigan the next year, and we took up where we left off. The big dances, called J-Hops, brought fabulous musicians to campus. When Count Basie came, Shooey and I double-dated. I joined a fraternity, as virtually everyone did in those days, and made lifelong friends among my Phi Gamma Delta brothers. I thrived in the U of M's world-class modern languages department. At one point I was taking courses in French, Italian, Thai, and German—and developing a stutter.

Boxing briefly took a backseat as I settled into school, my vision still improving, and my senses soaking up the wealth of things to do, people to meet, and new words to pronounce. But after I was introduced to the U of M's remarkable head boxing coach, Martin Levandowski, I knew boxing would become a central part of my college career. After winning the US amateur light-heavyweight championship in 1929, Marty had turned pro. In his prime, his problem was simple and painful: he was too big to stay at the 175-pound level and too small to cope with full-fledged heavyweights, even though, incredibly, he defeated future heavyweight champion Jim Braddock in 1932.

When I met Marty my freshman year, I was a defensive fighter. Under Coach Wilder, I had been getting by on offense with a long left jab and right cross. Marty scorned defense. He taught me his famous left hook to the jaw in close. It was most effective when thrown in or coming out of a half clinch. In essence, it was a winding up and uncoiling, disguised as a harmless maneuver to extricate oneself from a clinch.

Marty's windup started with shifting one's weight from right foot to left with feet wide apart. Concurrent with the weight shift came the twisting of the torso to the left, together with the cocking of the left arm by raising the elbow to shoulder height. With left arm and shoulder muscles providing the snap, the windup was released by shifting weight quickly back to the right foot. The torso swung to the right in follow-through and *POW*! All the one-punch knockouts I ever scored (inside the ring and out) have come from Marty's windup.

I became Marty's assistant coach and continued to fight as a semipro outside the college circuit in the Midwest. One memorable match my freshman year took place at Jackson's Tournament of

Champions. I was pitted against Mike Papeck, a Michigan state champion several years running. In the first few seconds of the first round, I got off my new left hook on Papeck's chin and floored him. I dropped him two more times in the first round and won a technical knockout.

In December of my junior year, disaster struck at Pearl Harbor. The response on campus was shock that turned quickly to outrage. That week, my entire fraternity enlisted for duty. I chose the Marine Corps because I didn't want a job on the periphery, and I had always heard that the Marines were the toughest outfit. The Marine Corps gave me an eighteen-month deferment to finish my bachelor's degree, which I accepted with mixed feelings. It was hard seeing some of my buddies leave before I did.

Marty, a reserve officer in the Coast Guard, was told to expect a summons to active duty for North Atlantic antisubmarine patrol. When Marty heard that I would be sticking around through my senior year, he suggested I think about taking over his coaching job. I was surprised and flattered; Michigan had never had an undergraduate as head boxing coach. We both knew I would have to work hard to become equal to the task in the eyes of our stern and rigid athletic director, Fritz Crisler. I needed to turn pro, Marty said, and I needed to do it quickly and decisively.

Marty's plan to put me in the head coach position hinged on my turning pro in Mexico, helped by a promoter friend of his in Juarez. In a country noted for its abundant lighter-weight fighters, I could easily get four or five professional bouts under my belt during a summer trip, Marty said. I would then return to Ann Arbor with valid international pro experience that would appear at the top of my résumé to dazzle our athletic director.

In retrospect, I question the wisdom of my boxing coach's plan to send me south of the border with no handler, no Spanish, and no backup. But at the time, I found Marty's idea ingenious. We were dealing with long odds in trying to maneuver me, an undergraduate boxer, into the position of head boxing coach at the University of Michigan, and I was willing to go the distance to overcome them.

On a hazy day in June, I crossed the El Paso-Juarez international bridge carrying a small suitcase of clothes and a large duffle bag with my boxing gear. The local promoter, Marty's friend and probable relative of Don King, assured me that my first opponent would be a "poosh ober." By the time I climbed into the undersized ring in that dingy Juarez warehouse, the crowd was already worked up, chanting passionately in unison:

"*Mata al gringo! Mata al gringo! Mataloooo!*"

The bad news was that I was the gringo. The good news was that I had not yet become familiar with the Spanish verb "to kill." Standing in my corner listening to this ominous chant, I reviewed the unsettling facts: I was a pale, skinny Midwestern kid within minutes of making my professional boxing debut in Mexico. (Although in this seedy border town, "debut" was probably too elegant a term for what was about to transpire.) Here boxers wore four-ounce gloves, half the US regulation size and only slightly thicker than dress socks.

In urgent need of reassurance, I asked my second, a teenager from El Paso, what the crowd was so excited about. He replied, deadpan, "I sink zey saying you welcome to Juarez, meester."

Against the hail of heckling, the announcer barked out his introductions: "Four rounds! First preliminary bout! Fifty-five kilos!" (Neither contestant had been weighed.) "Between Baby Salinas of Reynosa" (a small town across the border from McAllen, Texas) "and Johnny Hood of Ann Arbor, Michigan." In the announcer's Spanish, my ring name came out as Yony Ooth de Analba, Michoacán (a large state in Western Mexico).

As the referee gave us the litany of rules, it became clear to me that "Baby" was an ironic misnomer. Lines of scar tissue crisscrossed Salinas's puffy eyebrows under enough Vaseline to grease a large pig. Salinas was tightly coiled and clearly no stranger to brawling. It appeared that my one advantage was towering a ridiculous ten inches over him.

We met in the center of the ring, and, after warning us in fractured English not to hit on the break, the referee slapped us both on our protective cups with the backs of his hands and wished us a "pretty battle." As I jogged to my corner to await the bell, the crowd broke into its chant, "*Mata al gringo!*"

By the middle of the first round, my nose was bleeding profusely from a head butt. The welcome sight of gringo blood seemed to energize both Salinas and his noisy supporters. Things got worse when Salinas almost broke me in two with a left hook to the liver just before the bell ended round one. I doubt there has ever been a Mexican boxer not possessing a good left hook to the liver. From Ruben Olivares to Julio César Chavez, the Mexicans seem born to deliver this devastating punch. When I returned to my corner, the ring spinning, my second told me the round had lasted just over five minutes.

Spoiling the minute of recovery time in my corner was the surprise that my second had no astringent or collodion—just a crusty jar of Vick's VapoRub and a Coke bottle half-filled with murky water. To add insult to injury, the referee walked over to my corner and shouted, "No hold! No hold!" In response, I just tapped my right side where my liver had been before round one.

Deciding that my survival depended on not getting caught with another one of those left hooks, I made a couple of adjustments in round two. I began to circle to the left. When Salinas charged in, I moved back and to the left. I carried my right elbow in a little tighter to neutralize his relentless left.

During a wild exchange at mid range, Salinas caught me on the jaw with a roundhouse right. I landed on the seat of my pants. This was only the second time I had been floored, but instinctively I knew what to do. I quickly got to one knee, drew a deep breath and faced Salinas. My opponent was shadowboxing and snorting in a neutral corner. The referee was counting rapidly in Spanish with his fingers in my face, the crowd counting with him.

I arose at *ocho*, feeling preternaturally clearheaded and functional. Salinas charged forward for the kill. I bounced backward a couple of feet and set myself. He fell short with a miscalculated overhand right, and I lunged in, catching him with a right uppercut to the pit of his stomach. My adversary suddenly stopped; his whole body sagged. I pounced on the opening to wrap things up. Pinning Salinas on the ropes, I dug heavy rights and lefts to his body with no return, flooring him in his own corner at the bell.

Returning to my corner, I noted a dramatically quieted audience. Salinas was unable to come out for the third round. My reward: six dollars, minus a dollar kickback to the promoter and fifty cents to my second.

The following morning I met with the promoter to see what else he had in store. He recommended my next fight be a six-round main preliminary in Veracruz, and he threw out the figure of twelve dollars. I agreed, silently reminding myself I had not come to Mexico to turn a profit. I let him know that I planned to change my fighting name from the hard-to-pronounce Johnny Hood to Kid Montana, in honor of my birthplace.

Veracruz was a lovely, southern coastal city where my name appeared on the marquee as "Kid Montaña de Analba, Michoacán." I caught a break with two easy knockout wins and a clean, inexpensive rooming house close to the gym. The charge was thirty cents a night for room, breakfast, and all the tortillas I could eat.

With lots of downtime between fights and eager to immerse myself in my first foreign experience, I decided to try my luck at dating. My first couple of outings were with the pretty and charming Maria Eugenia. Despite my struggles to pronounce her double-barreled name, things between us were pleasant, if dull. We went to the movies—no talking required—and then out to dinner.

Our third date proved more lively. We went to the birthday party of a friend of hers with loads of people, dancing, and friendly mixing. One of the señoritas laughed sympathetically at my Spanish infinitives and spoke a little English. I asked her out for the following night.

Admittedly, I should have handled the unceremonious dropping of Maria Eugenia for one of her friends with more diplomacy. That night in the wee hours, I was awoken as Maria Eugenia appeared at my second-story rooming house window, squirmed over the sill, and landed with a thud on the floor. She brandished a knife so large it almost qualified as a sword. She was ranting furiously; I understood only a few words, one of which I had learned recently—liver.

Befitting a rooming house in my price range, my pillow was nearly four feet long and tightly packed with sawdust. I leapt out of bed and employed the sausage-shaped pillow as a lance in the best Errol Flynn tradition to evade Maria's wild swings as I retreated to the door.

Making it downstairs in three jumps, I left an impressive trail of sawdust through the lobby. I found a hole-in-the-wall bar in which to wait out my attacker until daybreak, when I felt safe returning to my room, limp pillow in hand. I found that Maria had made off with my duffle bag and shoes. I should have taken this as a sign that my luck in Mexico was beginning to run out.

Cashing my next-to-last traveler's check, I headed up the eastern coast to Tampico. Tough, hot, dusty, and full of bars, Tampico reminded me of a Western movie set. Now, without a promoter but with rapidly improving Spanish, I went down to the boxing hall and arranged for a six-round preliminary against a young local fighter who had recently turned pro. The regulars at the Tampico gym spoke reverently of his spectacular amateur career. They described him as very *guapo*, clever in the ring.

The fight was a bigger event than I expected. As I arrived, a big mariachi band serenaded a boisterous and growing crowd. As I had in my other Mexican bouts, I looked and felt like an oddity. Being redheaded and sunburned was part of it; I also wore a black mouthpiece that drew a lot of comments. But I was feeling confident, having watched my opponent work out in the gym; I worried more about the decision of the Mexican judges.

During the feeling-out phase of the first round, we tentatively stalked, feinted, and showed off just out of range. After a half-minute or so came our first real exchange, a flailing spectacle common with preliminary fighters. Following a second or third flurry, we ended up in a clinch in my corner. The referee was willing to let us wrestle, urging us to fight our way out of the clinch. While backing out of our embrace, I caught my foe flush on the temple with a beautiful Levandowski left hook. It knocked him out cold. I stood tall in the neutral corner, endorphins flowing and feeling like the king of all I surveyed.

The only semblance of audience enthusiasm I could spot came from my second, Nicanor Alvarez. A bright and amiable Tampico amateur boxer who had been my sparring partner, Nico clapped nervously while the rest of the crowd fell silent. When my opponent revived, the announcer gave the time of the knockout, proclaiming Kid Montaña the victor.

In the prize rings of Mexico, custom mandates a sequence for acknowledging victory. Hands held high, palms facing each other, the victorious Mexican boxer walks along the ropes. A brief stop and a stiff bow are in order on all four sides of the ring. The ritual is performed just after the boxing gloves have been removed, but with sweaty hand-wrappings still in place.

As I began my tour of triumph around the ring to dead silence and angry stares, it came to me that rather than circling the ring, Nico and I might want to circle the wagons. As soon as the mariachi band struck up, we ducked out over the lowest rope and low-profiled our way toward the distant dressing room. We had gone about twenty yards when two portly young men began to curse me loudly in English. As we reached their row, both let fly with beer bottles. Nico was struck in the face; he dropped to his knees, bleeding from the nose and mouth. The second bottle struck me hard on the right shoulder.

Enraged, I picked up one of the bottles and brandished it at our two laughing assailants. For good measure, I unleashed all my recently mastered Spanish expletives. Instantly, they rushed me. I met the first with a beautifully timed, bottle-breaking crack on the head. As he hit the floor, I took care of his charging friend with a very low left hook to the body. After all these years, I am convinced this was the most productive one-two punch I ever threw—not to mention the most ill-advised.

No sooner had I knelt to check on Nico than we were set upon by five or six policemen. They swung their batons wildly. One swing broke my collarbone. They kicked and pummeled us and ripped off my robe and trunks. After a few minutes of lively police brutality and a few shouts of *Bravo!* from the bleachers, the mauling came to an end. We were dragged out of the arena and taken to the prehistoric Tampico auxiliary jail.

It was a minimum security facility housing mainly drunks and prostitutes and offering little in the way of facilities. As I slouched down onto the urine-soaked sawdust covering the floor, the sum total of my outfit was a purple leather athletic supporter and one sock. My hands were still taped. The jail welcoming committee, ten aging prostitutes, made a fuss over my purple cup. Nico and I languished there overnight and were offered lunch the next day, the only meal served. It featured two courses: tripe soup served in half a gourd and two marijuana cigarettes. I finessed the intestines and exchanged my pot for oranges through the fence with some street vendors.

When Nico and I were finally allowed a meeting with the warden/ chief of police/magistrate to plead our case, we had been in jail for three days. The warden let me know I could not communicate with the US consulate and that my purse would be split: half would go toward the rehabilitation of the prison's statue of the Virgin of Guadalupe, and the remainder would support a fund for destitute boxers. I could agree to these conditions, or I could protest and wait for the Tampico judge to come back from a two-week vacation.

With gracious acceptance of the terms, our stay at the auxiliary jail was over. Nico was turned over to his father. The warden said that if I was interested in reconnecting with any of my missing gear, both city pawn shops were across the street from the bus station, where a squad car was waiting to take me north as a gesture of US-Mexico friendship.

At the border the next day, dressed like a Tampico gardener, I caught sight of myself passing in front of a full-length mirror at customs. I looked neither like a French major from Ann Arbor nor a professional boxer. The US vice consul who interviewed me summed it up nicely: "You draft dodgers are a bunch of bums."

On paper, I managed to make my sordid Mexican boxing experience appear quite respectable, and I did become head boxing coach my senior year. It was an honor and great fun to work with the talented Wolverine athletes, but campus life had changed considerably since my junior year. Many classmates had left for parts unknown to fight in the war. I kept myself busier than ever by working nights at a defense machine shop. Just a skeleton crew remained at my fraternity. The first one downstairs in the morning shouted up, "Anybody going to college today?" A reply rarely echoed back.

Though the war stayed constantly on my mind, the demanding romance language program at Michigan required my concentration. In spite of the hard-knock way I was introduced to Spanish over the summer, I was drawn to it. The language struck me as more modern and much richer than French. I squeezed in as many Spanish courses as I could my senior year, but I had too many credits to change majors. I ended up earning my Bachelor of Arts in French with a strong affinity for Spanish.

In many ways, I felt well prepared for boot camp that summer. I had finished two years of CMTC as a cadet captain and had been serving as a marine reservist. I also considered myself a lifelong student of the military, starting with my days following funeral processions as a young boy in Columbus, Montana. At Michigan, I was captivated by the hours-long weekend lectures of military historian Slam Marshall and had followed the events in the Pacific closely, reading every detail I could. With excitement, purpose, and youthful patriotism, I left for Parris Island on June 30, 1943.

•••

Boot camp began poorly, with an all-night ride from Detroit in nonreclining, sardine-style seating. A thick and durable layer of grit covered all the visible surfaces of our under-lubricated vintage train. As we crawled into the Beaufort, South Carolina, station on that steamy July day, nothing stirred. No mayor, drum majorettes, or Marine honor guard graced the station's weathered platform.

Our quiet arrival had all the feel of a missed appointment. Expecting trumpets, we six hundred Midwestern Marine officer candidates had to settle for crickets. Cold drink vendors, who could have cleaned up, were nowhere to be found. I had read that in certain ways South Carolina was still antebellum. On the day of our inauspicious arrival in Beaufort, it felt anti-Marine.

Since no authority figure came forth to command our detraining, we were at the call of a one-man Greek chorus occupying the station's only bench. He was a drunkenly assertive AWOL or off-duty Marine corporal. He ambushed each arriving recruit with his insistent message as we filed past the makeshift command post that he shared with Jack Daniels.

The unsteady corporal promised the certainty of our regret should we not turn back now. "'Cuz if yawl don't, yawl be sorry. Or daid." What prevented any of us from taking the corporal's prescient warning seriously was the timing. We were still bursting with the idea of our future Marine-hero selves. What we didn't know was that this moment, our depressing arrival in Beaufort, would be the apex of our morale.

I knew that Marine Corps boot camp had the reputation of being the toughest basic training program in the military; it was part of the reason I chose the Marines. Even so, I was unprepared for the grueling and relentless drive toward personality demolition. Our individuality was obscured immediately by the issuance of one-size-bags-all clothing; I remember the trousers being particularly sack-like, especially on my skinny frame. Then came fumigation and the infamous boot camp haircut.

After an electrifying afternoon of head shaving, the drill instructor (DI) took over. He marched all of us, the hundred boots in Platoon A, about a mile to our new barracks. The march would not have seemed so bad had we not each been toting—and alternately dragging and kicking—a seabag containing everything we owned, including a helmet. By the time we reached our destination, there was a silent consensus that the only two words our DI knew were "shit bird."

Being bald for the first time since birth seemed like the least of our problems that night. We were beat, dehydrated, and under considerable stress after the introduction to our DI, our own personal tormentor. The next morning, when we shuffled our way into the cavernous community head to shower and shave, our hairless reality hit us. Dumbstruck before those battalion-size mirrors, silence fell over the bald boots. It was followed by assorted curses and gasps, then insincere chuckles, and, finally, hysterical laughter.

One of the Marine Corps' boot camp tenets is standardization through humiliation—and vice versa. Most of the destruction of the young male ego and identity occurs during the first week. The sole enforcer of this psychological and behavioral degradation is the DI. After hitting bottom, the boots (the ones who will make it) begin their courageous climb out of the snake pit. Despite all the harassment, vituperation, and scorn, there is no Marine of my acquaintance who does not believe at the end that his own DI was more God than devil.

My DI, Joseph Julian, was perfect for his job. Decorated for heroism on Guadalcanal, he was well over six feet tall, handsome, athletic, and possessed a great booming voice and a gift for acting (indispensable for making it as a DI). Julian's commanding presence was chilling: a mixture of charisma, menace, intolerance, and wisdom. He had a way of strutting, saluting, and holding his swagger stick that would have made John Wayne drool.

We heard gossip about Julian's heroism on Guadalcanal, but he never talked about it. He was a master of weapons and small-infantry tactics. Blindfolded, he could disassemble and reassemble the classic Marine assault rifle of World War II, the Browning Automatic Rifle (BAR), in a matter of seconds. He never told us to do anything that he couldn't do to perfection. At the core, his only game was winning.

Julian never smiled. As a substitute for smiling, he had perfected several types of snarls. Some came with sound; others worked better silent. His curses dripped with disdain. Julian's Boston accent somehow made his obscenities, with their broader a's, a bit more elegant. His creativity in blending expletives could be riveting. Though we strived to follow his example in all things, he made it clear that he would never countenance profanity from his boots.

At mid-morning there was a thirty-minute break in field drilling known as "grabass." Sessions were replete with fascinating lectures and old gunny sergeants showing off their wares from World War I. Grabass topics ranged from venereal disease (with slides) to cleaning field stoves without water. We learned about manufacturing homemade fragmentation hand grenades: "You take a large handful of black powder together with ten or twelve feet of barbed wire..." Once we were instructed in ways to quietly and bloodlessly kill an enemy using bare-handed strangulation techniques.

Grabass also featured serious daily combat between randomly selected boots (usually those who were spotted falling asleep). We were forced into wild boxing and freestyle wrestling matches, some in deep sand, others on hot tarmac. As usual, the objective was more intimidation than instruction, and it gave the DIs a break from doling out the physical punishment themselves. At least we were allowed the brief luxury of sitting for the lectures and matches, which we did in a large semicircle of several rows.

At one of the very first sessions, Julian announced there would be three one-round boxing matches: "I want three knockouts before lunch! Give me two whiteheads, two redheads, and two blackheads!" It was a hard choice to make since we had been virtually scalped just two days earlier. We were all wrinkleheads with a speckling of five o'clock shadows. I was seated in the front row next to a varsity halfback from the University of Illinois, a husky 190 pounds and, like me, a redhead. We were selected as bout-one entertainment and equipped with large training gloves.

I weighed a scant 130. At such a weight and strength disadvantage, and with an aggressive and wild-swinging opponent, wisdom suggested limiting my participation to one punch. Goliath wound up with a huge round-house swing, allowing me to step inside and knock him cold with a left hook to the temple. As I eased him forward to break his fall on the tarmac, I was instantly joined by Julian. I could tell that my new DI was impressed because he called me by my first name.

It became clear from Julian's questions about my background that he was an avid boxing fan. He invited me to join him after dinner to talk boxing at his quarters. It was just the beginning of what would become regular late-hour talks. Boxing was the usual theme, but inevitably we moved on to combat techniques, where Julian was a wizard. He was convinced that Asians felt an inherent advantage over Westerners in the area of night fighting. "The Japanese will never counterattack, except at night. You must," he endlessly insisted, "*must* train your Marines and yourself to be every bit as effective after dark as you are in daytime operations.

"As hot and boring as it is out there on the islands, train for everything blindfolded—daily. All maneuvers—repairing weapons and equipment, digging foxholes, eating, retreating, ambushing, swimming, first aid—everything blindfolded! Don't make night operations and night combat second nature. Make them *first* nature." I can't imagine any new second lieutenant heading into warfare against the Japanese with a clearer advantage than I after so many hours of counseling from Julian.

After that first grabass match, Julian submitted my name to represent our platoon at the monthly all-Navy boxing program at the base amphitheater. These Parris Island boxing matches were big time. The entire camp turned out by order, highlighted by officers in whites and their ladies in hats and gloves. Present, too, was an enormous marching band, which on these occasions sat and played Sousa.

My opponent was Tony Vero of Rome, New York. He was the base lightweight champion. It was a typical messy Johnny Hood production: nose bloodied in the first round, cut over the left eye in the second, curtains for Tony in the third.

Julian, who had sat in my corner, said under his breath as we exited the ring, "Liked the left hook." It was the only thing I ever heard Julian say to anyone that might have been construed as a compliment. Just then, the band broke into my favorite march, "Under the Double Eagle." It took all my self-control not to break into a Mexican victory strut as I puffed with pride.

Hot, pressure-filled August days blurred into weeks. Though each day could feel absolutely unending, the end snuck up on us. Before we knew it, forty-seven out of our original group of one hundred boots in Platoon A had made it through basic training. In recognition of this, we were summarily promoted to privates first class and paid twelve dollars more each month. Joe Julian's last words to me as we shook hands were, "Don't give the Nips the night. If you do, they'll kill you."

•••

My next stop was Officer Candidate School (OCS) in Quantico, Virginia. As much as I had basked in Julian's attention and soaked up his wise counsel, I heaved a sigh of relief to arrive at Quantico, where no DIs greeted us with notebooks and nonstop hazing. I spent twelve weeks in Company B, 39th Reserve Officers' Class, which focused mainly on small-unit infantry combat. In practical terms, OCS gave new lieutenants the edge they would need to lead more experienced and battle-hardened enlisted men.

As the end of my training period loomed, I kept my mind off the war by boxing on the side. With no regular matches scheduled at Quantico, I snuck off one weekend to box a ten-rounder in Norfolk, Virginia. For this I was paid $225, my biggest purse yet, and equal to three months of Marine salary!

About 80 percent of my class graduated from OCS. We celebrated our elevation to second lieutenants on a bitterly cold December day with a sparkling parade for Quantico townsfolk and proud relatives, including my parents. Also in the reviewing stand were two notable guests, the Duke and Duchess of Windsor. We passed before the stands in our crisp dress uniforms, show-stopping with our synchronized, seemingly mechanized cadence. Then we reformed our ranks opposite the reviewing stand and stood at parade rest to hear the duke's remarks.

Emotionally, and with his halting royal articulation, the duke concluded his remarks: "You Marines are known as the very best of America. From your oldest and closest ally, we think we are frightfully fortunate to have you leading the way." We let out a great "Hurrah!" when the duke finished, a moment of considerable euphoria all around. And then, with even smoother synchronization than before, the new second lieutenants fairly floated off the parade ground to the battalion commander's cadence call "Oy lao" ("And your left").

Departing Quantico, my thoughts returned to what I had absorbed in boot camp—those intensive, formative, branding weeks with Joe Julian. Sorted out and sanitized a bit, his credo, his advice, and his tactical teachings seemed like parables to me. I was convinced his was the advice I was going to be pounding into *my* troops (I just wished I could replace a BAR firing pin as artistically as he).

Julian and I exchanged a couple of letters over the next year, until he went overseas again. Then we lost touch, and I never saw him again or heard anything about his second tour in the Pacific. Forty-five years later, while browsing in a small bookstore in Old Town Alexandria, I found a book featuring World War II heroes. I learned that Julian had earned the Congressional Medal of Honor after falling in action against the Japanese on Iwo Jima in March 1945. I was amazed to learn that he was only two years older than I.

3

1944–1949

I doubt if I will ever get the mud off, but I don't care in the least. I am pretty sold on the average Marine. My men really took care of me. Will write again when my eyes come back out of my head.

—Letter home from Guam, 1944

From Quantico, my first westward stop was California. After a couple of days at Camp Elliott in San Diego, I boarded an unescorted Dutch freighter headed for New Caledonia, an archipelago 750 miles east of Australia. The capital city, Noumea, lay twenty-three zigzagging days away on the lumbering *Sommelsdijk*. En route, our opposition was limited to one inept Japanese submarine that attacked mid-morning about twenty days out of San Diego. Although two of the sub's torpedoes were aimed correctly, both were duds.

There were some thirty lieutenants aboard the *Sommelsdijk*, all of us green, and not just from seasickness. Complementing this commissioned bunch of beginners billeted topside were about three hundred enlisted Marines crowded below deck. Most of them were newly released brig rats. The naval prisons on the west coast periodically emptied their cells in a burst of calculated forgiveness. Such acts of liberation always coincided with urgent calls to replace overseas casualties.

I shared one of the nicer cabins with a lieutenant of memorable grace, talent, and antecedents. A two-time All-American end from the University of Wisconsin, Dave Shreiner was as genial and bright a pal as I have ever had. Although assigned to different regiments, we managed to continue our shipboard dialogue every few weeks throughout the Pacific War. Shreiner's regiment, the 4th (Shanghai) Marines, together with mine—the 22nd—formed the 1st Marine Brigade under General Lemuel Shepherd.

The Marine replacement depot was located some distance up-country from Noumea, within a short walk of a lovely village named Saint Louis. The centerpiece of the village was a large French Catholic mission. It was home to five extremely well-nourished priests and the largest ecclesiastical casks I have ever thumped (and they never thumped empty). As the only French-speaking Marine, I was hustled into complicated community disputes fit for a lawyer. Thankfully, these negotiations were always followed by a congenial happy hour.

I was assigned to replacement depot quarters with two outstanding fellows: Marine Lt. Quentin Saracino of Philadelphia and Navy Lt. (JG) Robert Becker, a physician from Los Angeles. Although we would not have guessed it then, we three were destined to live and fight the war together and to become tent mates for most of our overseas tours.

Quentin had been a successful IBM electric typewriter salesman in south Philly. He had a fine voice and taught everyone within earshot his entire repertoire of Italian arias. He could have given Pavarotti and Domingo a run for their money on sheer number of arias known by heart. Dr. Becker, a handsome and athletic man in his late thirties, was a hematologist and champion swimmer. Becker had an incredible knack for diagnosing what others could not.

In Quentin and me, Becker found an attentive audience for his medical stories and diagnostic theories. Becker tried his best to train us as physician's assistants, as he was forever running short of corpsmen, but Quent and I lacked a natural proclivity for handling gore. We advanced very little beyond the endless dipping of large swabs in calamine lotion. Given the way we slathered that useless liquid around, it is surprising we had not turned the Pacific pink by war's end. Becker finally did teach me how to suture, a skill that often came in handy.

With Dr. Becker on Guadalcanal

I was initially a rifle platoon leader of Charles company, a formidable and seasoned bunch in the 22nd regiment. Saracino commanded the 1st Battalion's heavy (water-cooled) machine gun platoon. Becker started out as the first assistant battalion surgeon. The only difference between a battalion surgeon and his assistant was simple and ironclad: the assistant battalion surgeon worked in the forward aid station, the battalion surgeon worked in the rear station.

Together in the same small tent under the palm trees, no more than twenty feet from the high-tide mark on a sandy beach, the three of us lived together for more than eight months on Guadalcanal between the invasions of Eniwetok, Guam, and Okinawa. Because of the intense heat and humidity, our units trained from 7:00 a.m. until about one in the afternoon. To cope with the muggy heat, we went shirtless virtually all the time, ensuring dermatologists job security for years to come.

My afternoons were largely dedicated to learning Japanese. There was a Japanese POW stockade nearby, which made it easy for me to corner an unsuspecting prisoner with my phrase book and dictionary for a few hours. Payment was made in cigarettes—the only legal cross-cultural tender at that time on Guadalcanal. The Japanese preferred Camels.

We trained six days a week to kill and survive, nothing more. There was never a change of pace. Yellow from Atabrine (an antimalarial drug) and skinny from bad food, we were finally reduced to three continuing preoccupations: getting mail from home (three to five weeks delayed), theorizing and agonizing about how to surmount the next Japanese stronghold, and finding a way to get rid of fungus in all its endless variations.

I wrote my family and college sweetheart as often as I had anything interesting to say. The mail was stringently censored; we weren't even allowed to write where we were stationed. But I found ways around that. In one letter from Guadalcanal, I wrote, "This is a really interesting place. I could write a book about it, but Richard Tregaskis beat me to it." Later, my family told me they got my not-so-veiled reference to the war memoir *Guadalcanal Diary* and were thrilled to know where I was, at least for the moment.

The monotony of our routine on Guadalcanal stopped abruptly with the ominous appearance of troop transports off shore. The food would improve for two days, and then off we would sail to kill or be killed. For Marine rifle platoon leaders, the odds of getting through two or three assault landings unscathed were fairly poor. Certain blessed or lucky ones would survive the slaughter to be recycled into training mode again, wiser, sadder, and much more fatalistic. Lucky Lager beer was the only drug administered for depression and anxiety.

In the heroic history of the 22nd Regiment, from Eniwetok to Guam to Okinawa, and finally to China, our first real test came in Guam. Our relatively simple two-day assault on Eniwetok didn't do us any favors in preparing us for the type of combat we would encounter later. Once ashore on the island of Engebi in the Eniwetok atoll, we quickly established overwhelming small-arms fire. The machine gunners, bandoleers of ammo draped heavily over their shoulders in Mexican bandit style, led the charge, shooting nonstop from the hip. They held their light (air-cooled) machine guns with asbestos gloves.

Instead of the standard alternating fire and movement by individual advancing troops, we found that building an overwhelming fire base on the flat island allowed for a steamroller approach. The attacking skirmish line of the 22nd infantry stood as one and lunged forward. It worked on Eniwetok, where resistance was relatively light, but it was a naïve and ill-advised assault technique that couldn't and wouldn't work in other combat venues.

We arrived on the shores of Guam in late June of 1944. The beauty of that island eluded us warring island-hoppers, who thought of beaches as killing fields and jungles as ambush sites. The initial task of the 1st Brigade was to secure the heavily defended beach in front of the town of Agat. We lost twenty of our amphibious vehicles and many men just trying to land. We secured the beach by the end of that long first day. From our toe-hold, we were to attack to the northeast across the neck of the Orote Peninsula, the location of the old Marine barracks and air strip. If successful (or, as we say in the Marines, *when* successful), we would seal off the peninsula and trap the large numbers of Japanese troops defending Orote.

For six days we battled northward across the neck of the peninsula, the combat relentless and the losses heavy. On the morning of the fourth day, I caught a tiny shard in my wrist from a Japanese hand grenade. It had apparently cut a vein and my company corpsman and I were unable to get the bleeding stopped. He escorted me to our nearby forward battalion aid station for a quick stitch or two.

Even though our daybreak assault had just begun, the aid station was full to overflowing with at least fifteen wounded Marines crowded into a small, crudely camouflaged area in a rocky ravine, just a hundred yards behind the front line. A few casualties lay on stretchers. Others were sitting slumped over with eyes closed. All were silent.

Men were awaiting attention or triage from the assistant battalion surgeon or from the capable and compassionate pair of Navy corpsmen helping him. Several of the most seriously wounded had a yellow, waxy pallor that made them look like refugees from a death camp (which, in a sense, they were). The worst off were hooked up to plasma bottles taped to a little picket fence of tent poles and rifle stocks.

None of the wounded appeared so moribund as the figure carried into the aid station shortly after I arrived. His face and hair were smeared with gore. He wore a large, lumpy, dark red bandage over one eye and ear. One of his arms dangled limply along the stretcher. His entire dungaree jacket was caked with chocolate-colored blood.

As the two Marines who had carried their leader in departed, they suddenly turned back and saluted. One of them saluted three times, in tears. A corpsman approached the newly arrived casualty to check his vital signs. Then, after kneeling over him a moment and removing a portion of his facial bandage, the corpsman turned to the battalion surgeon, "Lt. Meyer is not going to make it, Doc."

Instantly, the condemned lieutenant sat grotesquely upright on his stretcher. Haltingly, in a strangely guttural voice, Cord Meyer rasped out, "You sonsabitches, I *am* going to make it! But for Christ's sake, get me some plasma and morphine!"

Though I would never have recognized him at the aid station that day, I knew Meyer well. I had met him on our ship en route to Eniwetok. He was one of the best and bravest among the junior officer corps of my regiment. Intense, brilliant, articulate, and virtually worshiped by the men of his platoon, he usually favored a contrarian and more daring strategy than our colonels.

Having uttered possibly his final mortal command, Meyer collapsed. He sagged back onto his bloody stretcher, apparently unconscious. A Japanese hand grenade had exploded by him at very close range. In addition to having lost an eye, he seemed to be missing much of the flesh from one side of his face and neck. I could not shake that image as I went back into the fray with my sutured wrist.

After two more days of bloody and nonstop action, we managed to isolate the peninsula. Fresh intelligence estimated that we had trapped over four thousand Japanese on Orote. Fortunately for them, the doomed enemy was not without comfort. In our push for Orote, we had stumbled upon the location of the Japanese storehouse for hard liquor to sustain the emperor's troops throughout the central Pacific.

We Marines wondered, when the reality of their predicament dawned on the Orote-based troops, how would they react? Would they try to stall and slow our advance to have a few extra days to draw down their inventory? Or would they choose to tank right up and have it out with the hated Marines in one gloriously boozy banzai charge? Within hours of closing off the peninsula, it became obvious from the steady escalation of drunken cries and clinking sounds that the Japanese had chosen option two.

The first drunken wave came forward at around eleven o'clock that night. There was no moonlight, and it was raining heavily. Their raucous assault was off to our regimental left, generally in front of the 4th Marines. In the distance, their attack sounded like a high school football game in overtime. Since the Japanese had been telegraphing their rum punches for several hours, our supporting heavy weapons were targeted, waiting, and primed when the enemy staggered to the attack. In a matter of just a few minutes, perhaps two thousand Japanese troops were blown away by mortars, naval gunfire, and artillery. Then silence.

An hour later, a second alcoholic wave surged forward. This time the target was the defensive position of my regiment. What we saw coming toward us—under the glare of the star shells—was a formation so wobbly it seemed blurred. Several Japanese soldiers somehow managed to reach our perimeter but were easily cut down by small-arms fire. The third wave, presumably even more exalted than the first two, actually overran the platoon to my right. They killed several of my friends, including the lieutenant in charge.

At daybreak the next morning, we witnessed the gory sight of a sea of fallen enemy troops. For once my Marines seemed quite disinterested in collecting Samurai swords, pistols, flags, bugles, and gold teeth. This round of carnage yielded something far more valuable: scattered as far as the eye could see were bottles of synthetic scotch and authentic sake.

The light-headed Japanese brigade had been repulsed with 100 percent enemy casualties. Were there any Japanese still alive? Yes, some, according to our intelligence. They were well sheltered in bunkers and pill boxes positioned between the brigade's former stronghold and the old Marine barracks. Most of them were Imperial Marines.

During our push the next day, closing in on the barracks, my regiment encountered less resistance than did the 4th, which had the bad luck of swampy terrain to our left. As a result, by nightfall my regiment held ground about a hundred yards ahead of the 4th. This left an uncomfortable and potentially dangerous gap between regimental fronts. Belatedly, General Shepherd decided it should be closed. Since my half-strength platoon was at the moment in battalion reserve, I was anointed to take my Marines after dark to plug "that Goddamn gap."

I quietly collected my men to assign them positions and get our night signals and jungle telegraph sounds straight. We were about twenty strong and very tired. To reach the gap, we had to skirt several still-occupied Japanese pill boxes. Flamethrower teams aggressively tried to neutralize them before we passed by.

As we moved behind the first bunker, which was aflame, we could hear the muffled commotion of the doomed Imperial Japanese Marines. They were screaming, singing, and blowing bugles. At the moment my runner and I passed behind the lieutenant in charge of the flamethrowing operation, a bulky Imperial Marine—two hundred pounds at least—burst out of a side entrance of the bunker.

Holding high his huge Samurai sword, his hair and clothing afire, he spotted my lieutenant friend. With a maniacal scream and a mighty dying lunge, he struck the lieutenant at an angle between the neck and shoulder, almost cutting him in half. They fell together in a smoldering tangle.

I strung out my exhausted men across the one-hundred-yard regimental gap. We hadn't had any real sleep for the six previous nights. Or was it seven? Beneath us were layers of coral rock. Unable to dig in, we made good use of the abundant coconuts all around us. Each two-man team of my vulnerable mini-platoon fashioned a coconut rectangle on the coral and settled in warily for the longest night ever. We of Charlie Company's Third Platoon were lying on our backs or sides, two to a coconut rectangle, head to toe.

Almost immediately we became aware that our superficial position intruded into a still largely unneutralized semicircle of Japanese bunkers. As the black and rainy night wore on, we began to hear ominous sounds from nearby enemy pill boxes. The Japanese were drinking to boost their courage for the final assault. They were yelling, breaking bottles, and in general seeming to prepare for their moment of banzai. All of their random noisemaking was interspersed with shrieks of "Maline die!"

Then, out of their bunkers, they started to crawl, making distinctive, low, and prolonged scratching noises. It was the sound of boxes of hand grenades being dragged over coral rock. Like unseen ants, the enemy came on hands and knees. They babbled and mumbled as they fanned out in all directions, both in front of our line of coconut squares and behind it. We heard them or sensed them at times just feet away. At one point I was hit on the butt by a fast-rolling coconut, which almost scared me to death.

This became the sequence for the rest of the night: the click of a Japanese hand grenade being struck against a helmet or box. Four seconds later, a grenade explosion. The cracking wham of a BAR or M-1 rifle. Next a scream or a groan, and then the gurgle of approaching death. Unfortunately, I could not distinguish between Asian and American death rattles.

My men and I had agreed on a number of code words beforehand, but the background cacophony made our signals useless. Were we being wiped out? Were some of my brave men bleeding to death? How long would those hand grenades last? Drunk as they were, could the enemy find their way back to the bunkers for resupply? We asked ourselves many rhetorical and practical questions during that endless night. But none so fervently as: *can we possibly survive this?*

The worst part for me was my inability to communicate or keep score. The only confirmed casualty I knew about had been secured by my sharpshooting coconut square mate. He had killed an Imperial Marine at point-blank range. When hit, the portly soldier lunged toward the rifle flash and landed right on top of me. It was an absolute horror for about two minutes as I alternately tried to stab and disengage from the bleeding monster atop me. The upside was that the corpse provided us with much better protection than the coconuts.

At dawn they lay in random and distorted postures: over one hundred Marine bodies strewn around and between our coconut defenses. None wore US Marine dungaree green. Those remarkable corporals of mine prevailed in an overwhelming fashion; we had killed all comers. Our most lasting souvenirs from that night were minute black shards from hand grenades exploding around us all night long, now embedded under our skin.

•••

After our first hot breakfast in a week, the other shoe was dropped on us. Another frontal assault, said the rumors. We were approaching the old Marine barracks, the historic spot where a woefully undergunned contingent of 153 Marines had surrendered to more than five thousand Japanese troops on December 10, 1941. It was my company, decimated as we were, that had been chosen to lead the assault on the airstrip serving the old barracks.

When my company commander, Captain Warren Lloyd, advised me that my half-platoon would lead the glorious attack on that landing strip, I began to understand the Japanese banzai mentality a little better. Looking hard at the strip through my binoculars, I perceived no cover, concealment, or even undulation. It was a moonscape—nothing but exposure. I asked my machine gun consultant, Quentin Saracino, if he could guarantee full machine gun flanking fire for at least ninety seconds. Quent explained that his thirties were nearly burned out after eight days and nights of heavy firing, so he'd have to fire in shorter bursts—not ideal.

The traditional, terrifying Marine act of frontal assault—even when leading fresh troops—always feels like slow motion. The assault by our thin and shaky skirmish line over the naked, flat expanse seemed to last forever. Halfway across the strip, with ricochets skipping and zinging all around us, we had no clue who was firing at us. Are Saracino's heavies trying to stay just yards ahead of our advance to lead us to safety? Or are those Nip guns trying just as hard to mow us down?

I fell several times from sheer nerves and adrenaline, which probably made me harder to hit. By luck, and with the help of Saracino's barrel-burning base of heavy machine gun fire, we took the airstrip late that morning. Our trophies were two: an unusable, pock-marked, rutted airstrip, and a twisted pile of sheet metal once known as the Marine barracks.

Later at lunch, I had an opportunity I'd long hoped for to tell a *New York Times* reporter that at the peak of our attack "the issue was never in doubt." Captain Lloyd received a personal "well done" from our regimental commander Colonel Merlin F. Schneider. Late that afternoon, Old Glory was raised at the center of all the tangled beams at the barracks. And then, release. I slept fourteen hours straight through, watched over by a pair of Chamorro guides, Guam's indigenous people.

A few days after the Marine barracks ceremony, the 1st Brigade began a new phase of conquest. We traded the relentless onslaught of organized combat for the intermittent panic known as jungle patrol. One of the worst parts of a "mopping up" operation is that nobody wants that telegram from Marine Corps headquarters telling his parents, "Your son was killed mopping up."

By all available means we had been warning Guamanians for a week to head for the coast until further notice. After that warning, we shot anything that moved in the bush. In venturing out on those patrols, one had to assume that thousands of defeated and dispersed Japanese troops were lurking in the wilds of southern Guam, hankering for revenge. One could also assume that the hunted held almost every advantage over the hunter in this arrangement.

We went after them with reinforced platoons of about fifty men each. But these were suddenly sloppy units, remnants of several platoons randomly thrown together. Beyond being dispirited and dead-tired, they would need weeks of training to become a team. The saving grace was a large handful of my original corporals whom I fielded to bolster each platoon.

I respected those with the lowly rank of corporal more than all other noncom grades combined. By the time I had survived my first assault landing, Marine corporals had become my only yardstick for taking the measure of fighting men. Anyone who would choose to drink Aqua Velva instead of bourbon *has* to be tough (and twitchy). Gun-shyness becomes especially pronounced among first, master, and gunny sergeants—those who have begun to develop a tummy, or a family, or a better understanding of the law of averages. Corporals are the men who win land wars, and they are rifle platoon leaders' secret weapons.

My support team during my jungle patrols on Guam consisted of three gifted Chamorro guides together with three stalwart corporals: Bernard Booker, George Campbell, and Vic Goslin. Confusion reigned at first as I tried to deal with the fact that all my local guides had the first name "Jesus." All three of them lived up to that name. At times their intense loyalty struck me as almost embarrassing, given how little the US had done for them before and during the war.

Relying on the eyes and ears of my corporals, the loyalty and instincts of my Jesuses, and the dead-eye shooting of Maine native Bernard Booker, I survived two weeks of dense jungle patrolling. The six of them charmed my life throughout an exercise that was in every sense suicidal. Instructors from Marine Corps Schools could have found 4 or 5 perfect ambush settings over every mile we trudged. The

Japanese always selected the best sites for maximum slaughter and easiest escape.

A Chamorro scout accompanied the two-man point of our patrol. One of the Marines on the point was a sharpshooter. The second carried a BAR. Some six to ten paces behind the point followed another Chamorro scout. He served as a key link. His role was to maintain visual contact between the point and advance party. The latter consisted of me, another BAR man, and another Jesus. My peerless BAR man, Corporal Booker, insisted on walking two or three paces behind me at all times on patrol.

Two days of patrolling south to Inarajan on the coast netted very little beyond mud, mosquitoes, and—to our gastronomic joy—the occasional suckling pig. We had seen signs everywhere of enemy troops but had encountered none. Our tense boredom was soon brushed away by the beautiful people of Inarajan.

We came to their village in single file, looking grubby and quite unmilitary. From a distance we could see the townsfolk lining both sides of the trail leading into town. Finally we were close enough to hear the lyrics of their enthusiastic song: "Sam, dear Uncle Sam, won't you please come back to Guam!" Our attitudes adjusted instantly. Never before had I felt heroic and a brother and member of another culture at the same gleeful time.

Villagers of all ages were overjoyed to see us, and even more so when they learned my name was Vaughn. Years before, a Navy lieutenant based near Inarajan had the same last name. From his friendship and good works, the earlier Vaughn had become something of a legend and regular sender of Christmas presents. I did not deny being one of the lieutenant's closest relatives.

On our third day, after reluctantly abandoning the jubilant citizens of Inarajan and heading back into the jungle, Booker suddenly came up on my left side on the narrow trail. As he moved past me, the corporal whispered out the corner of his mouth, "Flash of metal at eleven o'clock." As he said "o'clock" he stepped in front of me and crouched. Snap shooting from the hip, he emptied the twenty rounds from his BAR in about three seconds. Booker had converted his semi-automatic to full automatic by filing down the seer. Three Japanese manning a Nambu light machine gun had been unable to get off even one burst before Booker blew them away.

An hour or so later, a similar drama was repeated as our patrol came into a small abandoned village. Booker and two of our Jesuses instantly saw or sensed danger. Something signaled them that one of those eight or nine huts was occupied. This time my star corporal's bag was five Imperial Marines. He killed them all before they could activate either of their two machine guns. He achieved this feat even though his BAR jammed after firing twelve rounds.

Probably leaving several thousand Japanese still roaming the jungle, the bloodied, depleted, and partly bowed 1st Marine Brigade, now labeled 1st Provisional Marine Brigade, sailed back to Guadalcanal. The task before us was to prepare for the invasion of Okinawa. When my opera-singing pal Quentin Saracino was diagnosed with serious kidney damage, Dr. Becker and I sadly saw him off on a transport home. It would come down to the two of us dishing out calamine lotion all the way to the East China Sea.

•••

Prepping for the invasion of Okinawa, scheduled for April Fool's Day, 1945, seemed like déjà vu. The replacements for the many good men lost on Guam seemed too young to become anything but cannon fodder. Our older battalion commander, Lt. Col. Walfried H. Fromhold, was also replaced by a much younger man, Major Thomas Jerome Meyers. Hailing from Buies Creek, North Carolina, Meyers had all the qualities of a military superstar and was a protégé of the divisional commander, Major General Shepherd.

We added over five thousand men to the brigade and joined with the new 29th Regiment to become the 6th Marine Division. When Tokyo Rose got the word, her broadcasts referred to us as "the last dregs of so-called American manpower." Being Marines, of course, we elected to hype the launch. What better modifier for Japanese and US consumption than "striking"?

With the christening of the Striking 6th Division came bundles of red and gold shoulder patches—free for enlisted, ten cents for officers. The new emblem featured a neo-Samurai sword rising through the number six. "Raise high the rod!" we bellowed. The patch modestly proclaimed "Micronesia-Melanesia-The Orient." Dr. Becker argued that The Orient should be replaced with "Amnesia," a fitting end to our Pacific tour.

The merging of the 29th Regiment into the brigade went over badly. There was no mood for it and no apparent benefit. To surrender one of the most prestigious names in Marine Corps history—1st Provisional Marine Brigade (there had been several)—was pain enough. To be forced to accept a no-famer "6th," with zero image and track record, left us all cold. My men just left their 1st Brigade patches in place, and for a while we referred to the new division as "1st Brigade Reinforced."

The old hand brigade guys also smarted under the unconventional style of their new regimental commander. A veteran colonel with experience in France during World War I, the 29th Regimental Commander had obviously lost it. He was the Marine Corps' foremost authority on bush warfare and heavy machine guns, but his peculiar mannerisms and wild comments turned him into a division-wide joke and led to a great deal of mimicking. General Shepherd mercifully relieved him of his shaky command just before his new regiment hit the beaches of Okinawa.

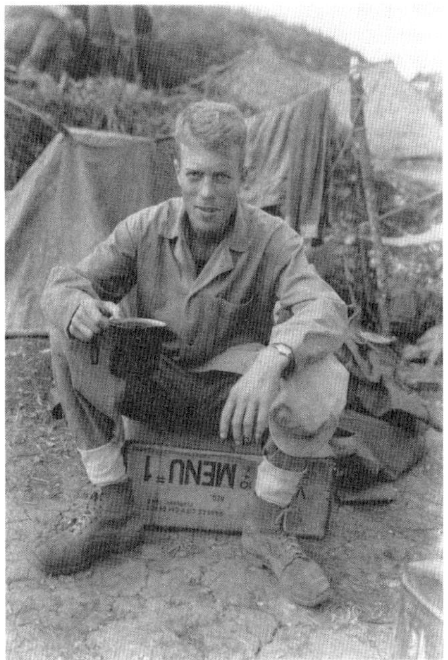

Another great day in the US Marine Corps

My own (22nd) regimental colonel was a very appealing hulk of a guy, florid, squinty, and about sixty years old. Although his name was Merlin Schneider, he was affectionately known to all as "Red Dog." He loved to invite junior officers over to his big tent and hold court, drinking manhattans that he mixed in a pail and reminisce about his days at the Naval Academy.

After five months on Guadalcanal training to blend our expanded team, we arrived on the western shores of Okinawa on April 1, which happened to be Easter that year. We made land easily with cover from the seasoned group of battleships parked off the beach. Arriving with barely a whimper from the opposition felt ominous, as though the Japanese must have something bigger planned.

Our mission was a familiar one: seal off the peninsula. This time it was Motobu Peninsula to the northwest. Once we secured the neck, some Marines from the 6th Division stayed to do battle at the center of the peninsula where the Japanese stronghold sat in a craggy complex of ridges and valleys.

My regiment headed over rough terrain to the northern tip of Okinawa, encountering spotty and unpredictable Japanese fire from dense forest hideouts. We made our way through the wilderness much the way we had on Guam jungle patrols, with an advance party, a point man, and a scout between us. We really could have used the lifesaving premonitions of our Jesuses on Guam; there was virtually no way to anticipate the enemy in this hilly and wooded terrain.

On one occasion, I was creeping through the tangled underbrush, hearing just our footsteps and jungle noises. Then I heard the whizzing sound of air being cut by a bullet, followed immediately by a thud to my right. I swiveled to find my scout, just four feet from me, flat on his stomach, shot between the eyes by a sniper. We weren't able to effectively return fire; we never caught a glimpse of the shooter or even saw a bush rustle.

When we reached the northernmost part of the island, nerve-racked and exhausted, we dared to hope that our work was done. Okinawa would not be the epic confrontation that many had predicted, and perhaps the Japanese were more depleted than we knew. Then we got word from the southwest coast, where the 27th Army was bogged down in a relentless battle along the Naha-Shuri-Yonabaru line, a belt of defense along the island's midsection. "Send in the Marines!" came the call from Fleet Admiral Chester Nimitz.

Stretching from coast to coast, the iron-clad Naha-Shuri-Yonabaru line traced the high ground. Its deeply imbedded strong points and clusters of interlocking defenses were anchored by Shuri Castle in the center and Sugar Loaf Hill to the west. Demonstrating its practical survivor wisdom, 10th Army headquarters assigned the 1st Marine Division the nasty task of frontally assaulting Shuri Castle, a veritable mountain of stone. Less fortunate still, the 6th Division was ordered to take Sugar Loaf Hill.

We began our trek through the mountains southward to meet our fate. I was looking at a map with our battalion commander, Tom Meyers, in a draw just north of Naha when he was shot in the chest by a Japanese sniper.

A week later, seven senior 1st Battalion officers were conferring in a small shack near our forward observation post when a large-caliber artillery shell scored a direct hit. All hands inside were killed or wounded. Included in this group were battalion company commanders and liaison officers handling air, artillery, and naval gun support. That one devastating bull's-eye pushed the burden of battalion command right down to the platoon level. I wasn't at the ill-fated briefing because I was interrogating the very first Japanese officer we had captured during the campaign. Unfortunately, he only wanted to talk about his emperor and the Geneva Conventions.

With Sugar Loaf Hill looming, we faced our hour of truth with virtually no officer corps. Our one surviving senior officer was Major Earl Cook. Like Meyers and the others who had just been wiped out, Cook was a rock and oblivious to danger. Since officer replacements were apparently out of the question, Major Cook faced the necessity of commanding a large contingent of non-coms—mostly sergeants and corporals—without even knowing their names.

The battles during that endless May took place on a series of hills connected, we would discover bitterly, by an extensive and sophisticated system of tunnels and underground infrastructure. The enemy could quickly shift their resources from hill to hill, unseen and in unknown numbers, making the attacks endless as the Japanese continuously replenished troops and supplies underground.

Our regiment started at Charlie Hill, named for my company, most of whom were killed on its rocky slopes. Six-wheel drive trucks hauled us and our ammo into the assembly area surrounding Machinato airfield to prepare for battle. Just as we came within

Japanese artillery range, it began to rain in torrents. We looked on the bright side: it made digging into our defensive positions a bit easier.

By midnight, under increasingly heavy and accurate fire, we were fully dug in along a ridge line outside the capital city of Naha. Overnight our foxholes filled with surprisingly cold water. Still the rains came and intensified. Before long the water in which we floated—or sank, if you kept your cartridge belt on—began to stink. Everything shriveled, foremost our morale. Eerily, the only frontline sounds for days were the splashing of bombs and shells among soggy Marines.

One of my musically inclined men attempted a little levity to counter the process of Japanese water torture. He thrashed and splashed wildly in his Jacuzzi-sized foxhole to the tune of a popular back-home radio commercial: "Super Suds, Super Suds. It's more suds with Super Suh-uh-uds. Rich and thick and lasting, too…"

The appearance of the sun, finally, did little to boost anyone's spirits; it only provided a better view of what lay before us. The flies were thick and aggressive. Our muddy battleground had turned into a dump and a graveyard. Those of us who weren't killed or wounded suffered through malaria, fever, and all manner of stomach problems. The smell was atrocious. There was no corner or hole into which you could crouch to escape the horror for a minute, and there was no getting dry—ever.

We spent three bloody days advancing and retreating over an agonizingly short distance up and down Charlie Hill. Finally we brought enough power to the crest of that hill to ensure our position could not be repulsed. Without missing a beat, we moved into position at Sugar Loaf. It took us ten days to conquer that bitter little mound, which really looked more like a landfill. In the demoralizing process, we would repeatedly take the crest of the hill only to be battled back by an influx of fresh Japanese from neighboring hills. The Striking 6th captured and then lost Sugar Loaf eight or nine times before securing it for good.

The Japanese Commanding General Mitsura Ushijima ultimately had 110,000 troops at his disposal for the defense of his Shuri and Sugar Loaf complexes. The 6th had two Marine regiments totaling possibly nine thousand men, but we could not be denied. We routed Ushijima and his Manchurian veterans to hell. In the 22nd and 29th Marine regiments, two out of every three men fell, including all of my closest friends. "The most critical local battle of the war," was how *Newsweek* defined the gunfight at Sugar Loaf.

One of my most stoically fabulous corporals, Vic Goslin of Missouri, won a Navy Cross there for his feats of daring achievement on both Charlie and Sugar Loaf. Okinawa was the final confirmation of my theory that it is those corporals like Booker, Campbell, and Goslin who win battles, with or without commissioned officers to spur them on or take the credit.

Sugar Loaf exacted a toll on our beloved and eccentric Col. Red Dog. If he was hard on liquor, Red Dog was one of the few Marine colonels soft on pushing his men beyond their limits. On one especially bloody evening, the colonel informed his general that for the time being he would not push his shattered troops farther. Red Dog was replaced in a flash by a fierce-looking and elegantly mustachioed colonel who was killed the following week.

After dismantling the Naha-Shuri-Yonabaru line, the Striking 6th was ordered south through the capital, Naha. With major combat done, I became an intelligence officer, patrolling former Japanese encampments and strongholds to gather information, neutralize any remaining explosives, and ferret out recalcitrant enemy soldiers.

On one patrol outside Naha with Sgt. John Kimlin of Poughkeepsie, we found an astounding underground system. Completely hidden in one nondescript hill were enough sleeping quarters, services, and supplies to sustain roughly six hundred troops. Long corridors, about six feet wide and three hundred yards long, were lighted and had space for sleeping mats and personal belongings. Officers had private alcoves with covered entryways and wall hangings; one even had easy chairs and a desk. There were supply rooms, radio and gun repair shops, a galley, and roosts for carrier pigeons.

On the opposite side of the hill from the main entrance were forty holes that could be used to enter and exit the corridors. It was easy to see how the enemy had kept us off balance, and it made me even prouder of our ultimate victory.

The Japanese had fled the complex quickly and most of their personal belongings remained—postcards, good luck charms, and photos. Kimlin and I encountered only one hill dweller in our investigation of the underground maze. He stepped out from an alcove, shouted at us, and reached into his pocket. Kimlin fired three shots, taking him down still grasping his grenade.

On another occasion during that period, I was asked to guide *New York Herald* correspondent Homer Bigart through the actions taken by the 22nd Regiment the day before. Assuring Bigart of the complete safety of our foray into an open field, I was suddenly contradicted by two silent enemy rounds. One ninety-millimeter mortar round fell within five feet of Bigart, the other a few feet beyond me. Both were duds, as was the suddenly silent interview. Bigart fled to genuine safety. Despite that misstep, I received a Navy Commendation Ribbon for intelligence gathering on Okinawa.

When we finally reached the southern tip of the island, Okinawa was declared secure. It was June 21, eighty-two days after the arrival of the Striking 6th. Sadly, even that day of triumph brought heartbreak. My cabinmate and friend, Dave Shreiner, a company commander on Okinawa, was shot and killed by a sniper. I dropped everything and scrambled over a mile of battle-scarred landscape to find the spot where he lay beside a chalky path. On the other side of the path was piled the garbage of death and suffering—what remains when a busy field hospital is moved.

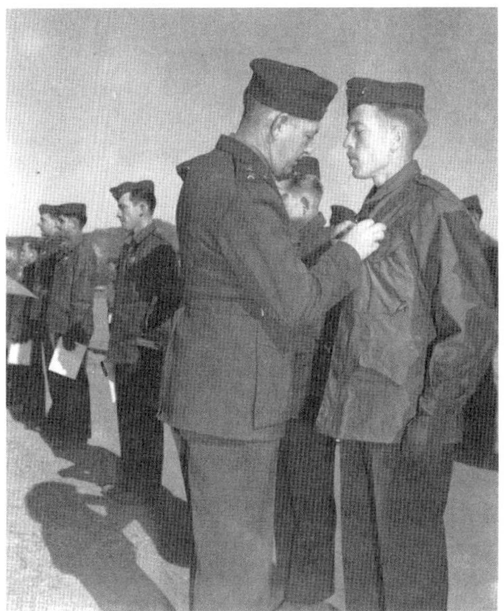

Receiving the Navy Commendation Ribbon from Gen. Lemuel Shepherd

A poncho had been pulled over Dave's head. He seemed much too big for his stretcher. And although he had been dead for at least an hour and a half when I arrived, a dozen of his men still stood or kneeled around him in silence and obvious devastation. The loss could neither be rationalized nor recouped. Of the large number of superstar athletes and all-around good guys I have known, Dave was the standout. He was twenty-four.

The next day, the 6th Division had the well-deserved honor of raising the Stars and Stripes on Okinawa. Despite the declaration of victory, we all knew there had to be thousands of dejected Japanese troops still hiding out; they had dug more than sixty miles of tunnels in preparation for our arrival. Their ruthless and intricately planned defense of the island took an incredible toll. In all, 8,300 members of the 6th Division were killed or wounded on Okinawa, the bloodiest conflict in the Pacific. We received the Presidential Unit Citation for our actions.

With our dead buried and their crosses erected, the division sailed away in early July 1945. The parting image of Okinawa on all our minds was the sobering expanse of the 6th Division's cemetery. There were acres and acres of crosses. If there is any joy or pride to be derived from surviving, it cannot be sustained after saying goodbye to those wonderful men who were not as lucky. I have never recovered.

•••

We went back to Guam to begin the process once again, and the rumor mill started up in earnest. Lacking any authentic sources at our junior officer level, we tended to believe Tokyo Rose. She announced that the entire Marine Corps—all six divisions—would be landing around Tokyo Bay "for their final destruction." We figured Rosie had it about right.

Masses of fresh replacements joined the division, looking more like junior high school students than soldiers. At first intimidated by our tales of the South Pacific, new arrivals were soon almost indistinguishable in gait and monosyllabic speech patterns from the oldest salts, those of the long-distance stare.

The historic Enola Gay A-bomb scrubbed all plans. Instead of a suicidal attack around Tokyo Bay, it was off to the coast of China. We were ordered posthaste to occupy Chefoo, well up the Shantung peninsula. Beleaguered General Chiang Kai Shek lacked the forces to retake his country from the Japanese, so we were sent to secure the city and facilitate the repatriation of tens of thousands of Japanese troops. But we were really stumbling into the birth of another conflict: the Cold War.

Ten days outside the coastal city of Chefoo came the news that it had just been overpowered by Communist troops. A mid-course correction through a typhoon brought the Marines to Tsingtao, a much larger city farther down the peninsula. We heard that Tsingtao had been the preferred liberty port for the British Navy between the world wars. What we found went well beyond our dreams. Before moving into luxurious villas once occupied by foreign missionaries, we junior officers took over the plush Edgewater Beach Hotel. The war ended for me the minute I stepped onto that five-star beach.

After a brief encounter with resort-style luxury, reality set in. It was October: winter and the Chinese Communists were not far off. The city was surrounded by Chicom troops, and my men were not looking for a fight. I was now a company commander with a whole new set of problems: troop morale and behavior, starving and looting Chinese civilians, and Communist infiltration. Chiang's Nationalist forces, corrupt and unhelpful, seemed interested only in making it to Taiwan.

Looking around for a saving grace, we found the Tsingtao Brewery. It was fabulous beer. A huge Shantung slurping sound came as twenty-two thousand Marines switched from Lucky Lager to Tsingtao after one taste. Every day became Oktoberfest, even as we staggered into November. The beer ultimately did little to ease the frustration and unruliness among my men, who had won the war and wanted to go home while there were still a few single girls left.

As the liaison officer between my regiment and a Chinese Nationalist division, I quickly saw the writing on the wall: Chiang Kai-shek's troops had been defeated by the Communists. They had done everything but lay down their arms on the beach and start swimming southeast. As far as our relationship with them, they wanted only the protection of the 6th Marine Division and access to our post exchange for cigarettes. That we could handle.

I left China on December 12, 1945. When I reached California, I went directly into Treasure Island Hospital off the coast of San Francisco to deal with the effects of grenade fragments and Japanese white phosphorous burns. My shoulders, which suffered the worst burns, never fully healed. In 1970, I finally had plastic surgery in Colombia that stopped the continuous peeling of burnt skin.

I felt lonely, gloomy, and still consumed by what had happened on Okinawa; I certainly didn't feel heroic. In any case, it was too late for that. The victory days, parade days, and hero welcomes were long gone. The confetti had biodegraded. Talk was all about the GI Bill of Rights and getting on with our lives. Every evening I found myself still trying to get off Sugar Loaf Hill.

It was January 1946, two and a half years after I had set off on the slow train to Parris Island. During the discharge process from Treasure Island Hospital, I had been offered lifetime disability benefits, but the siren call of the boxing ring made accepting disability payments seem ludicrous. My only serious side effect from the war was chronic and lifelong insomnia. Not willing to completely let go of my military career ambitions, I enrolled in the active reserves. Then I boarded an eastbound bus to return to my former life.

My parents and sisters met me at the bus stop in Albion, Michigan. My college sweetheart, Joanne Smith, had been wedding planning since my boat left China, so everything was ready for our nuptials on a frigid day in February at The Little Church Around the Corner in Manhattan. Our Mexican honeymoon renewed my love of the Spanish language and Latin culture. After two years' immersion in Japanese and Chinese, the romance of Spanish and French was stirring.

When we came home, I decided to fall back on my adolescent ambition of pursuing my PhD and becoming a professor of romance languages. I could think of no better place to do it than my alma mater, the University of Michigan. Veterans flooded back to the U of M to take advantage of the GI Bill. I fell right into the familiar confusion of language overload, taking classes in Spanish, French, and Italian. I even dabbled in Russian, thinking it might come in handy. As a graduate student, I was a teaching fellow for French and Spanish, which I enjoyed tremendously; it was a heck of a lot more fun than studying.

Marty Levandowski returned from the war to bigger things, working as athletic director at several prestigious colleges. I once again took the helm of the boxing department at the U of M. The program came back better than ever, with more young men interested in boxing after serving in the military. I continued to fight professional bouts every couple of months. I collected my master of arts in romance languages in June 1947, my first milestone toward a career in academia.

As I began my PhD program that fall, a feeling of claustrophobia set in. Not only did I have to specialize in one area of French or Spanish literature, but I also had to pick an obscure topic for my dissertation. I had thought that a PhD would open up the world to me, but it was just the opposite. I found myself overcome with boredom at the idea of existing in a niche.

I shared my theory of the shrinking world with a close friend, Ray Chambers, who was also a teaching assistant and PhD candidate in the romance language department. Ray had the same sinking feeling I did about his doctorate: we both wanted out. A friend of his at the University of Pennsylvania told him there were several assistant professor positions open in their romance language department. This was hardly a radical departure, we conceded, but a feasible first foray out of our PhD ruts. Equally important to me, the pay would be $2,000 more per year. My first child, Kathryn, was born in March, and, in addition to the pride of new parenthood, I felt the pressure to provide for my family. Ray and I were both hired to teach at Penn beginning in the fall of 1948.

•••

A HIGHLIGHT OF MOVING to Philadelphia was reuniting with my buddy Quentin Saracino, who had returned to his career as a prosperous typewriter salesman. We spent every Sunday with Quentin and his wife, Gloria, who taught me how to make her authentic, old-world spaghetti sauce. The recipe was never written down, but I learned by watching her drop mountains of fresh tomatoes into an astonishing amount of olive oil and simmer the mixture all day. While the sauce cooked, Quentin and I bellowed out the great tenor arias he had taught me during the war. That summer I boxed as much as I could to earn extra money. I sparred with some of the greats, like Jake LaMotta, Sugar Ray Robinson, and Willy Pep, as they prepped for big fights.

Though I had taught Spanish and French at Michigan, at Penn I taught only Spanish at the women's college. I had an introductory class at eight in the morning composed of freshmen who were there for a basic language credit. Many of them arrived late, and most of them knitted or crocheted during class. They sat there transfixed by their knitting, occasionally looking up as I struggled to get their attention and lead them into the process of learning Spanish, which they did not.

About two months into the semester, I came in on a Monday feeling out of sorts and tired from a tough fight in Scranton over the weekend. When I looked out at the women trailing in late, sitting down, and making a commotion as they took out their knitting supplies, I reached the end of my rope. I stopped my lesson and made an announcement: "If you memorize and recite the poem *Cobardía* ("*Cowardice*") by my favorite poet, Amado Nervo, and knit me a pair of argyle socks, I will guarantee you at least a C in the course and you will never have to come to class again." At first, the women weren't sure I was serious, but I repeated my offer as they filed out that morning.

Soon my students stopped coming to class and I started getting argyles. The young women came during my office hours to recite Amado Nervo, so horribly pronounced as to make that lovely poem nearly unrecognizable. Then they deposited the argyles and left. Those slightly uneven but sturdy socks lasted twenty years, much longer than my academic career.

I flew under the radar quite successfully until just before the end of the semester, when I was called in by the dean of the romance language department. He repeated the rumors he had heard about my deal with the freshman coeds and asked if any of the claims were true. I told him they were. The dean expressed considerable shock and informed me that Penn was an Ivy League school with the highest academic standards, integrity, and faculty commitment. I didn't exhibit any of these, he said. Not open to discussion on the topic, he closed his remarks with an emphatic, "*Adiós*."

My friend Ray thought it was hilarious—the funniest thing he'd ever heard. For me the episode hit harder and with less humor. The dean had given me until the end of the month to collect my last paycheck and leave. I was making $3,500 a year teaching at Penn, and I hadn't even made it through the year. I had no savings and a wife and baby to support.

My first thought was of an FBI ad I had seen in the newspaper seeking Russian interpreters. Though I had taken only a few courses of intensive Russian at Michigan, I could read proficiently and knew the words to several Russian folk songs. I thought I could get that FBI job at least on an interim basis. I took their exam and was turned off by the meanness and arrogance of the people I met. Moreover, they said my background check would take two or three months. I couldn't wait that long without having to write home for money, which I had no inclination to do.

Then I saw on the bulletin board at Penn that the United States Information Service (USIS) was expanding its binational center program in Latin America. They were looking for people who had done graduate work and spoke Spanish, French, or Portuguese to work as teachers and administrators in the roughly thirty centers throughout Latin America. The binational centers offered information, education, and American cultural events, with an emphasis on English language classes.

I applied and was hired effective immediately. I went to Washington to attend a six-month orientation program with the understanding that I would be sent to Tegucigalpa, Honduras, as a teacher of English. I liked my fellow trainees and the USIS staff very much. They were a special breed: they were sharp but easygoing, had a sense of humor, and possessed a genuine interest in and appreciation for Latin culture.

At the end of the training period, I was told that instead of working as a teacher in Honduras I would be going to La Paz, Bolivia, as director of their new binational center. My salary was $3,000 a year, slightly less than Penn, but entirely worth the sacrifice.

4

1949–1961

The only thing I learned from all the meetings is a new definition of an underdeveloped country: a country where women in streambeds try to break rocks with their clothes.

—Letter to my wife, Leftie, circa 1969

I ARRIVED IN LA PAZ in the late summer of 1949 on a two-year contract to direct the Centro Boliviano Americano de Cultura. The city of Nuestra Señora de La Paz sits at a breathtaking 11,975 feet in western Bolivia in the shadow of the Andes. I immediately felt at home; the clear, brisk air and snow-capped peaks reminded me of Montana, where I lived as a boy. More than half the population of Bolivia is indigenous, primarily Quechua and Aymara, and they speak almost forty different dialects. I found the people friendly and bright.

Shortly after I arrived, I was asked to escort a USIS bigwig who was flying down from Washington to inspect our fledging program. I picked him up at the airport, aptly named El Alto, and led him to my car. Then I ran back to the terminal to collect his suitcase. When I returned, my passenger was nowhere to be found. I searched the parking lot and airport and then alerted the police. With a cast of dozens searching, we finally found him passed out beneath my car, a victim of the altitude.

Student enrollment at the binational center, which primarily offered English classes, approached two thousand. We ran the only lending library in Bolivia, hosted an annual seminar for all English teachers in the country, handed out scholarships, and showed educational films. The staff were mostly American women married to Bolivians; they were wonderful and very in tune with the locals.

The best part of my job was teaching English classes, which attracted a diverse group of housewives, diplomatic wives, and students of all ages. Numerous among them were Jewish refugees who had escaped the Nazis. One refugee from Europe, Eva, made an impression on me as the brightest in the class. I ran into Eva forty years later and found that she had married Intel CEO Andy Grove.

I taught one particularly lively class composed of street urchins—the children, six to eight years old, of women street vendors. We literally took them off the street and taught them English. One of these girls was named Aida Choquetaxi, whose last name translates to "taxi wreck." An Aymara Indian and brilliant student, she picked up English quickly. She later became president of the Higher University of San Andrés in La Paz.

Part of our mandate at the binational center was training Bolivian English teachers across the country. For our first training effort, we invited sixty teachers to our center for a month during the summer. They were very uneven in background and ability; some could barely speak English, and others had no training. When I asked to see their teaching materials, several said they had none; others presented me with a British textbook written late in the last century. The book gave unusual attention to use of the word "hark." Practice sentences included, "Hark, my postilion has been struck by lightning!" and "Hark, what is the noise I hear from beyond yon wall?"

I sat down with our director of courses, Irving Lewis, and together we wrote a book called *Practical English: An Elementary Text*, with basic drill exercises using common, modern vocabulary. We printed the book locally and sold it for the bargain price of twenty-five cents. The textbook was a hit and went on to sell in Chile, Peru, Paraguay, and Argentina. A couple of years later, in Costa Rica, my staff and I created an intermediate-level textbook in the same style.

As we developed our programs in La Paz, the binational center earned a positive reputation across Bolivia, and we received interest from the University of Cochabamba to create a branch of the center on their campus. Cochabamba was then the second-largest city in Bolivia, located in the middle of the country about four hundred miles from La Paz. Called the City of Eternal Spring, Cochabamba has a milder climate than La Paz, perfect for growing coffee, sugarcane, and cocoa beans.

Bolivian universities in the 1950s bubbled with enthusiasm for socialism, communism, Marxism, and Leninism. There were few defenders of capitalism. The Communist training program, the Common Turn, had concentrated its efforts on colleges in Bolivia and elsewhere in Latin America with great success. It seemed clear to me that an unstated purpose of the USIS binational cultural centers was to counter this Communist influence by explaining and demonstrating American democratic values.

Despite the Communist bent on campus, the English faculty at Cochabamba spearheaded the effort to bring a binational center to the university. My initial trip to Cochabamba was very encouraging, and when I talked the idea over with the US ambassador and my boss, the public affairs officer, they were intrigued. My boss told me to return to the university, negotiate the details, and find an office and classrooms. The Cochabamba business owners I met with showed great interest, and I felt sure we could establish the center at little cost and attract a large number of students.

As I walked across the university campus toward the end of my week of scouting and negotiations, I noticed an unusually large group of about thirty students and a few older men. They brazenly approached me, and two of them grabbed me by the arms as they announced their intention to hang me as an enemy of the people, a spy, and an imperialist agent. They had come prepared with a noose that they threw over my head, then hustled me to a huge tree on a grassy square in the middle of campus. They tossed the end of the rope up over a branch and pulled it so that my head was jerked up from the tension.

The group's leader said they had gotten wind of plans to set up a binational center and do what "Yankee imperialists" usually do: brainwash the people with their message of capitalism. I struggled to look for someone to help, but it became impossible to move my head as my captors teased the rope around my neck. Eventually, I had to stand on tiptoe to keep from being choked.

I recalled from USIS orientation that if we ever got into a bind (although Communist lynching was not specifically covered), we should get the ringleader talking or arguing as a delay tactic. So I began to ask questions, speaking the best Spanish of my life. The men completely ignored me and began a discussion among themselves about my impending death: whether they would just leave me there or drag me away, and if they should get a photographer.

It seemed to me that they debated endlessly about the formalities of my hanging. One of the men occasionally jerked on the rope, and I would instinctively jump up. Just as things were beginning to seem hopeless, a military patrol jeep came speeding toward us across the grass. The uniformed officers jumped out and chased the mob with clubs. My attackers scattered, and I collapsed on the ground, the rope still around my neck, and my body exhausted from standing on tiptoe.

The military police told me my assailants were local leaders of the Trotsky Party, which was at its peak in the late forties and early fifties in Bolivia. I later saw a mug shot of the group's leader in the embassy, so he was known by the CIA and embassy officials. For reasons too classified to be shared with someone at my pay grade, he was never charged with anything; he had only intimidated a gringo.

When I got back to La Paz, I told my story to the ambassador, the colorful Irving Florman. An inventor and Broadway lyricist, Florman designed an ergonomic pipe mouthpiece that doubled as a toothpick for removing tobacco bits from between the teeth. Perhaps to impress him, I started smoking a pipe, a habit I maintained for the next three decades. Florman agreed with me that the hostility in Cochabamba was too great; we couldn't ensure the safety of our office and staff. USIS eventually did start a center in Cochabamba, but it was long after both Florman and I had left Bolivia and the bloom was off the Trotsky rose.

I credited my boxing workouts with helping me survive the attempted lynching. No longer boxing professionally since I had embarked on what I hoped would be my legitimate career, I still shadowboxed and jogged every morning.

I always looked for other ways I could supplement my income, so I was intrigued when one of my students, a Russian émigré, told me he had devised a method of smelting lead using a local flowering plant called *yareta*. He said that in the absence of coal, which was nonexistent in Bolivia, smelting lead using steam from burning *yareta* was much cheaper than using electricity. He claimed that if we went into business we could make quite a bit of money.

We named our company Plomo Boliviano S.A. (Bolivian Lead, Inc.). We bought basic lead ore from the mineral bank and then sold the smelted lead back to the bank at a guaranteed fixed price. In the beginning, we did make some money. The president of the mineral bank took a ten percent cut of our profits, which was an expected cost of doing business in Bolivia. When he left, his replacement wanted ten percent, and so did the vice presidents, and the next thing we knew we were paying almost everyone at the mineral bank ten percent. My partner and I were eventually left with zero percent, and the company went under.

My next adventure in Bolivian heavy metals came when I heard that much of South America's gold could be found in Tipuani, a village in the mountains northeast of La Paz. They said you could still see the earthen benches worked by the Incas four hundred years ago. One weekend I drove up into the clouds on a cliff-side dirt road to a campground for gold prospectors. The locals directed me to a spot along the Tipuani River bank where they promised I couldn't miss. In my third scoop of gravel, I was stunned to find a gold nugget in my pan. I went berserk; my panning velocity increased by 300 percent.

I stayed in a squatting position digging and sloshing with my pan in the ice-cold water all day. My energy renewed with each nugget I found, and there were many. I was getting rich! When it became too dark to see those flecks of gold and I was forced to go back to camp, I found I had a problem. I couldn't return to my original upright position—I was frozen in a squat. The local guides had to haul me back to camp face down, hooked sideways over a burro.

For several years, I kept my nuggets in glass bottles tucked away in the back of my sock drawer. As I let the nuggets appreciate I fantasized about my golden nest egg. But before I could melt or cash in my haul, my daughter tossed the nuggets over the balcony of our apartment during a bout of toddler mischief. Thus Bolivia's natural resources were returned to its people, painfully but rightfully so.

As I settled into my new life below the equator, things were beginning to heat up on the 38th parallel. Having witnessed the

Communist aftermath of World War II in China, I followed the reports out of South Korea with special interest and uneasy feelings. When the US started sending troops to South Korea, I tried to volunteer for active duty, but the Marines denied my request because I was working overseas. I finally left the Marine Corps Reserve in 1956 and never looked back, happy with my gentler niche in foreign relations.

After a year in Bolivia I was eligible to take home leave, a paid trip back to the States. We decided to spend a month at my family's cabin on Duck Lake in Michigan. I sublet our La Paz apartment to a recently arrived CIA agent who hadn't found permanent housing. Shortly after the agent moved in, a burglar broke into the apartment, and the agent fatally shot him.

The Bolivian police threw the young CIA agent into the notorious downtown jail called El Panóptico. An architectural marvel completed in 1897, El Panóptico is a round building in which all parts of the interior are visible from a single central point. Like most of Bolivia's jails and hospitals in those days, El Panóptico had few survivors. As a thoughtful convenience, a narrow, one-way road led directly from the jail to the city's principal cemetery. Somewhere between a threat and a promise, a large wooden sign over the cemetery entrance read, "*Moriras y Aquí Vendras*" ("You Will Die and Here is Where You Will Come").

When I returned to La Paz, I found the CIA had done nothing to help its agent. Since he had been my tenant, and I knew something about Latin American jails, I took a personal interest in his case. He was kept in a large room, like a bull pen, with another dozen or so alleged murderers. I visited him frequently with hot soup and miniature bottles of vodka artfully implanted in half loaves of French bread. By the time the CIA finally decided to pay the Bolivian government to release him, I had left the country.

•••

In the spring of 1951, several months before my two-year tour ended, I was transferred from Bolivia to fill a director vacancy at the cultural center in Costa Rica. It would be hard to find two Latin American countries as different as Bolivia and Costa Rica. The latter has no significant indigenous population and is mostly white. Only about ten degrees north of the equator and mostly sea-level, the climate is tropical. The country is more democratic than any other Central American nation and had recently abolished its army, a move that kept the government from going bankrupt and allowed them to invest in more productive pursuits.

Costa Rican society impressed me, as did the leadership of President Pepe Figueras, whose son would also serve as president. Figueras Sr. was president three times and made a profound impact on the future of his country. When he decided to eliminate the army, he funneled that money into education, mandating that compulsory education be raised from the sixth to the ninth grade. Figueras also gave women and blacks the right to vote.

I was assigned to a well-established cultural center in downtown San José on Central Avenue. The Centro Cultural Costarricense Norte Americano had a fine reputation and a student body of around 5,500. People of all walks of life attended classes there. We had highly trained teachers of English and a great library. The center showed movies seven nights a week and offered lectures and all sorts of cultural and artistic activities. It was an effective and smooth operation; I just maintained what my predecessors had created.

I found the embassy staff in San José first-rate and got to know them well. One of them, Bill Stedman, went on to become our ambassador to Bolivia. Through social contacts, I received an invitation to go fishing on the yacht of a prominent local businessman.

Along on the trip was my boss, Public Affairs Officer Al Harkness, Stedman, and Winnie Went, a Foreign Service officer. The four of us and the Costa Rican businessman met on a Friday afternoon to board his very elegant yacht, planning to catch fish and drink beer for two days on the Pacific Ocean.

As we stood on the dock at Puntarenas waiting for our gear to be loaded, the weather looked rather ominous: the water was murky, the sky a troubled gray-black. We were slightly concerned, but our businessman host said that he had weather reports from up and down the coast saying this wasn't going to be much of a blow. He thought we could expect clear weather by the next day as we headed west to the fishing grounds. We gamely climbed aboard and enjoyed a delicious supper of grilled *dorado* (mahi-mahi) with fried plantains.

By nightfall the weather had closed in, and we were pummeled and tossed by strong winds, high waves, and heavy rain. We dropped our sea anchor to keep from drifting too fast, and when that didn't work, used the engine to fight the current. Against increasing wind and rain, the engine overheated, and the drive shaft snapped. With no power, the boat began to pitch and spin and almost capsize.

Our debilitating sea sickness was somewhat dulled by the panic of seeing huge waves of water crash on board the ship. We spent most of the night hunkered down against the sides of the yacht, holding on with one hand and bailing with the other, getting enormous blisters on our palms. Heavy trunks of equipment were tossed overboard.

The next morning, as promised by our skipper, the sky was clear and the sea calm. Everything was completely saturated, including our radio equipment. It didn't make much difference, since we couldn't tell anyone where we were. The sea anchor line had broken at some point during the night and the yacht had been pushed way off course. We were thoroughly exhausted, sore, and lost. Given the local prominence of our host, we thought that the air search and rescue would be out in force. Yet no one came.

We bobbed along all day under the blistering sun in our storm-ravaged boat that felt more like a life raft than a luxury yacht. Bedraggled in our droopy, wet clothes and improvised sun hats, we were hungry. A couple of wrinkled packages of peanuts and crackers was all the food we had. Sunset came with no signs of life in our lonely patch of the Pacific. Finally, just before dark, we spotted a tramp Panamanian freighter coming up the coast from Panama City. We flagged the ship down, and they threw us a line to tow us back into port at Puntarenas.

Shortly after I was delivered from the Pacific Ocean, I went to New York for the birth of my second daughter, Carol. I took a side trip to Washington with career advancement on my mind. Despite my promotion to a bigger program in Costa Rica, I had been denied a raise by USIS when I moved from Bolivia. Now with a family of four to support, I needed something that paid better.

Through the grapevine I had heard that the International Cooperation Administration (ICA), a precursor to USAID, needed to fill positions in agricultural development, work that appealed to me both in salary range and subject matter. I thought if I knocked on doors something interesting might bubble up. It turned out that I didn't even have to knock. As I crossed Fourteenth Street in downtown DC, I ran into an old acquaintance from USIS orientation. He had since moved over to ICA, and when I told him my intentions, he assured me he would put in a good word for me.

It must have been a magic word, because a couple of phone calls and interviews later, I was offered a job as a program officer with ICA in Panama. I never did go back to Costa Rica. After a two-month orientation in Washington, our family moved to Panama City in March 1952.

•••

When I arrived in Panama, I became the newest member of the Institute of Inter-American Affairs (IIAA), Nelson Rockefeller's World War II initiative created to counter German and Italian propaganda in Latin America. IIAA was soon merged with a program called Point Four, inspired by the fourth point of President Truman's 1949 inaugural address: "I believe we should make available to peace-loving peoples the benefits of our store of technical knowledge in order to help them realize their aspirations for a better life."

The program set out to provide not just temporary economic support but practical knowledge and technical training on a permanent basis. Instead of combatting the Nazi influence, we were now presenting an attractive alternative to communism.

Panama, the isthmus connecting Central and South America, is Costa Rica's neighbor to the southeast. The US Army Corps of Engineers completed the forty-eight-mile-long Panama Canal between the Caribbean Sea and the Pacific Ocean in 1914. Until 1979, the US occupied not only the Canal but the five miles on either side of it called the Canal Zone. Panama is the most urban of all the Central American countries, and its cities are bustling and comparatively sophisticated. The indigenous population has for the most part mixed with the white population, and virtually everyone speaks Spanish.

My boss in Panama was Vance Rogers, the director of Point Four. An Atlanta native and graduate of the London School of Economics, Rogers was a great economist and strategist who appreciated and understood Latin Americans. Rogers had been in Costa Rica during the war, in charge of providing fresh produce for US troops in the Canal Zone. Rogers gave me big, interesting projects and supported me as I encountered bureaucratic roadblocks at IIAA and political shenanigans in Panama City. I had the utmost respect for Rogers and considered him a mentor.

Vance Rogers

My closest friend among the Point Four staff was Bob Avery, a former public administration professor from the University of Tennessee. Bob created the civil service system in Panama and designed the Colon Free Trade Zone at the Atlantic gateway to the Panama Canal, the largest port in the Americas. Bob's large-scale accomplishments in Panama demonstrate just how much flexibility, range, and power we had in those days. Well funded, respected, and given long reins, we young Point Four officers ran with our ideas and, more often than not, achieved our outsize goals.

The Point Four offices were located in the Colpan building near the heart of downtown. Bob and I had offices with adjoining balconies overlooking the street. Almost every day at around three in the afternoon, someone across the street would play an album by

Los Churumbeles de España, a very popular band out of Mexico with hits like "*No Te Puedo Querer*" and "*El Beso*." The music played loud enough to wake the dead, so there was no escaping it; we'd hang up our phones and submit to the Latin beat. I would usually dance across the balcony to Bob's office for a Churumbeles break.

I managed a group called the Joint Fund Service for Economic Development. We significantly increased the inventory of decent, low-cost housing in Panama City, created credit co-ops in the poorest rural areas, improved rural access to water, and helped industrial companies boost their productivity. I was also in charge of selecting talented Point Four technicians for advanced training. The agricultural staff, who trained at the University of Arkansas, was a particularly impressive group.

Given Panama's abundance of ranches, farms, and arable land, the ag staff and I wondered why the country didn't have its own agricultural college. We decided that we'd help them build one. The University of Panama in Panama City agreed to host the venture. We identified sixty Panamanian agriculture experts to become the faculty and sent them for training all over the world, but mostly to the University of Arkansas, where we had trained our own staff with such success.

Using grants and contributions from universities and foundations, we started a program within the University of Panama's School of Natural Sciences and Pharmacy. We set up a scholarship fund to attract talented Panamanian students regardless of age or income. I was in charge of interviewing and selecting the many scholarship recipients. Quite a few of those students became Panamanian statesmen and my good friends.

In virtually every project I managed, I worked closely with Panamanians. They were my kind of people: fun-loving gamblers, smart, and slightly cynical. Perhaps because of the long-term US presence in the Canal Zone, Panamanians understood Americans better than any other Latin Americans did, and they could use that knowledge to play us off against each other. I found myself quickly picking up local expressions, socializing with as many Panamanians as Americans, and enjoying the activities for which the Panamanians are famous: boxing, cock fights, lotteries, and horse racing. I was in my element.

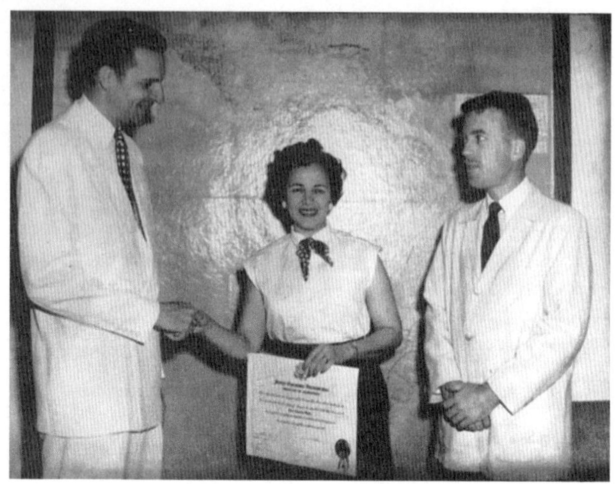

Bob Avery and me presenting an award

The racetrack, Hipódromo Juan Franco, was right in town on the edge of a neighborhood called Paitilla, just a couple of blocks from where I lived. Being so close, it seemed a shame not to go there frequently. I went virtually every weekend and holiday with my buddy Bob Avery. The two of us were a memorable sight—Bob was as lean as I but almost a foot taller.

Bob kept a log of horse and jockey performance and used his data to pick winners with astounding accuracy. My approach was less scientific; I usually went with my gut and was a sucker for hot tips, which were abundant and questionably sourced. Despite our different techniques, Bob and I always claimed to come out ahead at Juan Franco.

In classic Panamanian style, the atmosphere at the track was raucous, with lots of screaming, shouting, and showing off. The racetrack itself presented a unique challenge for horses and jockeys: it wasn't level. The back stretch dipped down in an area referred to as "*la bajada de Paitilla.*" The dip made things interesting; we could usually count on a new leader when the horses galloped back up. Despite its quirks, Juan Franco was a training ground for some world-class jockeys, including the great Panamanian Laffit Pincay Jr., the winningest jockey in history when he retired in 2003.

Horse racing was the national pastime in Panama, and I got swept up in the drama and financial possibilities of the sport. I learned that one could actually buy a racehorse, or an interest in one, on credit. After consulting with my sources at the track, I purchased a half interest in a beautiful mare named Discovery II. She died a week later of diarrhea. Lucky for me, I had made only a modest down payment. That early setback turned me off of horse ownership, but not horse racing, which became a lifelong passion.

Bob and I found that anyone who was anyone in Panama went to the track. We became friends with Juan Franco regular Panamanian President José Antonio Remón Cantera, affectionately known as Chichi (Babyface) Remón. A career military man and Panama's former head of police, he was in his mid forties and well liked. An avid horseman and gambler, he owned a stable of racehorses and surrounded himself with people who shared that interest. American Ambassador Selden Chapin disliked horse racing, so Bob and I happily filled in for him as part of Chichi's racetrack entourage.

President Remón was known for his *cojones.* In one story circulating in Panama City, a couple of Honduran crooks tried to finagle a government contract by blackmailing the president. Knowing Remón's weaknesses, they lured him into a compromising position with a pretty Costa Rican girl and photographed the pair at their moment of maximum friendliness. When presented with the incriminating pictures, Chichi sorted through the piles enthusiastically. "I'll take half a dozen of this shot, maybe four of that slightly blurred action shot, and give me three of this close-up that shows my tattoos!"

Though his salary had been $225 a month as chief of police, Remón had accumulated a significant fortune. The source of Chichi's wealth and that of his brother, Toto, could be summed up in two words: army surplus. In the Canal Zone, arms and equipment could be purchased for a song from the US Army. The well connected and shrewd could turn those goods around with astronomical margins. I had a Panamanian friend who became wealthy buying new DC-3 airplane engines at zone surplus centers for $100 each and slowly unloading them in overseas markets as if they were gold-plated.

The Remón brothers made a killing from Panama's neighbor to the east, Colombia, which was embroiled in a decade-long civil war called *La Violencia*. The Remóns answered requests for arms from both sides. They bought Colt .45s from US Army surplus for $25 apiece and sold the pistols to the Colombians for as much as $350 each. The guns and ammunition flew out of Panama regularly, completely filling up a DC-3 or Curtiss C-46.

Though the Colombian fighters had a huge appetite for the guns, I wondered how effective they really were. In Marine Corps boot camp we used to say, "Shooting a Colt forty-five pistol in combat is like trying to hit a bull in the ass with a banjo."

On New Year's Day, 1955, Remón greeted Bob and me warmly as we entered the Juan Franco clubhouse. We headed to the second floor where we had been invited to sit at the table of Everardo Duque, the Colon Free Zone manager and member of the wealthy family that ran the national lottery. Also with us was Clay Schroeder, a range management expert whose knowledge of tropical grasses had made him a local hero. We drank red vermouth on ice and kept our ears open for tips that might float up from the first floor, where the president sat.

I overheard Remón boast that his mare, Valley Star, was a sure thing on Sunday's race card, so the next day I returned to the track. Once again I sat in the president's section of the clubhouse on the second floor with Bob. We stayed until dusk and the last race of the day to put money on the president's horse. As predicted, Valley Star won by a head. Amid the usual cheers and commotion, Bob and I hustled down to the cashier's window to collect: six dollars and forty cents to win.

As I turned from the window, I heard an explosion of noise: gun shots, screams, and shattering glass. We ran out to the now darkened grandstand and saw that the mayhem was coming from the clubhouse, where fluorescent lights illuminated a chaotic scene of bodies, overturned tables, and people scrambling for cover.

An assassin with a submachine gun had launched an attack on Remón from the bushes at the edge of the track. When Remón's bodyguards returned fire, the gunman fled as invisibly as he had approached. The president was shot. Two friends seated at Remón's table were killed, and three others in the clubhouse were wounded. When Bob and I got close enough to survey the scene, we saw that two of the legs on the table where we had been sitting minutes before had been shot off. National Guard troops rushed the president to the hospital, where he died later that night.

The police quickly arrested about twenty people, including Panama's former president, Arnulfo Arias, whom Remón's police force had overthrown four years earlier. Arias and the other suspects were released when a young Panamanian lawyer confessed to the assassination. He too was released when he claimed that Remón's vice president, José Ramón Guizado, had been the mastermind behind the shooting. Guizado served only a couple of years. The racetrack was appropriately renamed Hipódromo Presidente Remón and has since become a much classier operation.

Panama could feel like the Wild West, and not just at the track. Rioting was fairly routine as tensions over the US presence in the Canal Zone struck a dissonant cord with many Panamanians, especially students. US government employees were instructed to stay home, doors locked, during anti-US demonstrations. To me, riot days were vacation days, and I always headed out for some fun. My behavior drew disapproving comments from the American community, but it raised my profile and reputation among my Panamanian friends. They began to talk about me as though I were more Panamanian than American, which I took as a great compliment.

Along with growing Canal Zone discontent, the mid fifties were a lively time of Communist infiltration in Panama. The Soviets were making a concerted effort in Central America to overthrow less stable governments, and Panama became a focal point for revolutionaries. The first one I got to know was Che Guevara, Fidel Castro's comrade who helped overthrow Batista in Cuba and tried to foment revolution throughout Latin America. Though he became a folk hero and iconic figure, I met him when he was a penniless drifter going by his real name, Ernesto.

Friends of mine at the University of Panama had taken a shine to Guevara and were helping support him by giving him research assignments. I saw him fairly regularly at social gatherings during his time in Panama. He was thin, scruffy, and pale, and showed no evidence that he bathed or brushed his teeth. I gave him a University of Michigan T-shirt, which he wore backward.

Born in Argentina, Guevara had serious asthma. Because he went to medical school there at government expense, he was required to serve three years in the army. He told me that before his military physical, he got into an ice cube-filled bathtub, knowing this would trigger an asthma attack. The asthmatic episode he suffered during his physical nearly killed him, but he considered it sweet revenge because it exempted him from serving the government of Argentina, which he despised.

Guevara made it clear to me that he hated Americans, too, and not just because of our capitalist ways. He held a personal grudge against us ever since he was attacked by three drunken American sailors at the port of Valparaíso, Chile. He claimed they beat him savagely, kicked him in the ribs, and left him for dead. As an asthmatic, the pain of having his rib cage bruised was indescribable. Someone took him to a charity clinic, where he hovered between life and death for days. He said he never fully regained his strength.

At that time Guevara seemed to have no network of Communist contacts, and he obviously wasn't being funded. He left Panama and made his way north to Guatemala, because he admired the initiatives of leftist President Jacobo Árbenz Guzmán. The US overthrew Árbenz in 1954, and Guevara moved to Mexico City, where he met Fidel and Raul Castro, and the rest is history.

I'm convinced I would never have thought about Guevara again had he not become so famous in the years after we met. I've known a lot of impressive Communists, mostly in academia, who were interesting, intelligent, and passionate. Guevara was not in that category; he spouted slogans but seemed to have few thoughts of his own.

I later crossed paths with another notorious Argentinian, the recently deposed dictator Juan Perón, who was visiting Panama during a period of exile. Perón's powerful and popular wife, Evita, had died in 1952, and while in Panama Perón lived with two young women he claimed were a nurse and a masseuse. They lived in an apartment just a block from mine.

A very elegant man of about sixty, Perón walked with a cane that he didn't need. An inveterate walker myself, I saw him regularly. Eventually, I couldn't resist introducing myself. We subsequently had several conversations, and I found him personable, articulate, and engaging. Perón was a regular at Panama's famous nightclubs. He met his future wife, Isabel, at a taxi dance establishment called Happyland, one of many "ten cents a dance" places. He invited her to move in. His apartment must have been too crowded with the four of them, so they moved to a bigger place at the Roosevelt Apartments, right across a large patio from the American embassy.

Shortly after they moved in, the CIA erected a telescope on the embassy roof, and the quartet became a hot topic of conversation among the embassy staff. Perón wised up and left with Isabel for Venezuela, and later Madrid, where they married. Isabel succeeded her husband as president of Argentina after his death in 1974. She was overthrown in a military coup two years later.

•••

I WAS APPROACHING THE end of my second two-year tour in Panama. It was also near the end of the 1955 fiscal year, prime spending time for all late planners in the federal government. Out of the blue, the National Security Council decided to subsidize doubling the size of the Panamanian National Guard, the country's army. Since end-of-year surplus foreign aid funds were to be used to finance this troop expansion, it fell to me to prepare the appropriate program justification and documentation in Panama.

The document I produced was a fiery denunciation of the entire outrageous scheme. Given the tensions already at play in the country, I knew that an American-financed army expansion would arouse the greatest suspicion, fear, and resentment among the Panamanians. I charged that of all the activities being considered for Panama, more troops should rank either last or not at all. Better police training?

Fine. But, please, no more underemployed garrison officers on either side to muddle Panamanian-US relations.

It was unclear if the audacity of my memo got me transferred back to Bolivia, or if I would have been sent there anyway. I left Panama peacefully, if reluctantly, clutching the Vasco Nuñez de Balboa medal for distinguished diplomatic service given to me by Panamanian Foreign Minister Enrique Obarrio. The medal held special meaning for me, because I had attended a ceremony at the Panamanian embassy in Washington some years before where Ambassador Roberto Huertematte awarded the Balboa medal to Eleanor Roosevelt.

Bolivia in the spring of 1956 felt like a homecoming. The bracing air and mountain vistas were familiar, as were many faces, both American and Bolivian. The ICA program in Bolivia had been expanded as a gesture of support for the democratically elected government of Víctor Paz Estenssoro. When I arrived as a program economist, Bolivia had the largest aid mission in Latin America.

President Estenssoro, the founder of Bolivia's Movimiento Nacionalista Revolucionario (MNR), was elected in 1952, shortly after I left USIS in Bolivia. His greatest accomplishments were granting Bolivians the right to vote, nationalizing tin mining, and instituting agrarian reform—that's where I came in. My job with ICA was to monitor and advance the country's huge and political agrarian reform initiatives. The thrust of the programs was to preserve land for the peasants who lived on it, rather than ceding it to huge conglomerates. My staff and I negotiated land deals and trained locals to make their plots sustainable and profitable, all while navigating messy Bolivian politics.

As I got to know the players in La Paz, it became clear that I had two problems. The first was the minister of agriculture, who was in charge of the national agrarian reform program. The minister's name was Sandoval Morón, which concealed the fact that he was a genius in double bookkeeping. He never met with me personally, but the officials he sent to our meetings sensed I was suspicious because of my pointed questions about the habitual shortchanging of local farmers in land deals.

Second, the US ambassador, my ultimate boss, was a stiff: politically, socially, and sartorially correct but lacking even a trace of humor, humility, or cultural sensitivity. Ambassador Phil Bonsal and I immediately disliked each other.

After I had been in my post several months, Bonsal requested a brief from me on the progress of the agrarian reform program. I had been to remote outposts talking to ICA technicians and local farmers. I found that some farmers were unable to transport their produce to market because of substandard roads, and many were being denied credit by Bolivian banks. In addition, Morón's corrupt management of the program was getting in the way of progress.

I sent Bonsal my findings and didn't hear back from him. At a social gathering a couple of weeks later, I asked him what he thought of my brief. "I have never read such lighthearted froth," he said coldly.

I said something like, "You must not be very well-read, Mr. Ambassador." When he didn't respond, I walked away.

Bonsal and I were spared additional hostilities by the arrival of my new boss, Warren Wiggins, the deputy ICA director. Wiggins was a Harvard-trained economist who impressed Bonsal immediately. Wiggins served as a buffer between me and Bonsal; he did the same for ICA Mission Director Ross "Dinty" Moore. Moore was a rugged agricultural extension agent from the southwest who also had a difficult time with the refined, Boston-bred ambassador.

Warren Wiggins was a decorated pilot who "flew the hump" from India to China early in the war and served with distinction in the Marshall Plan. We worked easily together: he didn't know much about Latin America and didn't speak Spanish; I knew Bolivia well and was fluent.

Warren Wiggins

He and I were in effect the chief operating officers of the agrarian program: we implemented, encouraged, and troubleshot. In the field, we worked to get rural farmers the equipment, technical training, and transportation they needed to make a living. Despite our very different backgrounds and strengths, Wiggins and I became great friends.

Every three months or so, the two of us would set off from La Paz to visit our outlying rural posts and the five to fifteen ICA technicians stationed there. On our first trip, Wiggins and I flew to Santa Cruz, at that time a small town in the plains area of the southeast where people grew sugarcane and raised cattle. Pigs and dogs meandered the unpaved roads, and the locals, Cruceños, walked donkeys loaded down with sugarcane. Santa Cruz was also the hometown of Agricultural Minister Morón. As a Movimiento Nacionalista Revolucionario (MNR) party leader, Morón essentially ran the town.

After a day of meetings and farm visits, we threw a party for our technicians and their counterpart Bolivian workers and their families. It was crucial to us that the locals felt they belonged to the mission and could trust us, so we held a social gathering like this at every outpost we visited. Santa Cruz had a large staff, and all of us crowded onto the property of the ICA guest house, which was basically a mobile home with a small swimming pool. To circumvent the restrictive ICA regulations on swimming pools, our records listed it as a cattle dip.

The party was in full swing with about sixty people, some swimming and others in line for barbeque or eating at small tables. Suddenly an open military jeep skidded to a stop at the fence around the pool. The driver stood and lifted up a .45-caliber submachine gun, the old-fashioned kind with a circular drum. With each eruption of gunfire, bullets sprayed into the air above us. Our guests scattered, running into the house or jumping into the pool. As the gunman continued to fire haphazardly, several of us, including Warren, ran toward the jeep. Seeing us coming, the man threw down his gun and sped off.

The shooter was immediately identified by our party guests as the minister of agriculture. One of the Cruceños called the police but said that since Morón was such a powerful figure, chances were our emergency call would rate a *mañana* response. Sure enough, the police never showed. Wiggins and I disassembled the gun and passed out parts to the guests as souvenir paper weights.

Given the dramatic turn of our Santa Cruz trip, I was glad Wiggins hadn't come with me on my jaunt to Oruro, south of La Paz. The principal money-making industry there was mining: tin, tungsten, silver, and copper. But I went to Oruro to learn how ICA technicians were combatting the serious problem of soil erosion on local farms; I heard they were having some success with mulching. I flew in for the day and caught the last plane that evening for the short trip back to La Paz.

It was an old Lloyd Aéreo Boliviano DC-3, just three seats across, every seat occupied and the overhead compartments stuffed. As I looked out my window, I was impressed to see dozens of large crates marked "*plata*," (silver) being loaded along with our baggage. The plane shuddered violently as we gained speed on the runway. Before the nose even left the ground, the landing gear sheared off, and we hit the tarmac with a crash. The plane skidded and twisted at great speed; bags careened out of the overhead bins, and babies flew out of their mothers' laps. A heavy bag fell on the man sitting next to me, knocking him out.

When we finally came to a stop in the brush beyond the runway, the entire contents of the cabin had shifted—dramatically. Thanks to my window seat, I had been relatively insulated from flying objects, but many others were not as lucky. Those of us who were able lifted the injured passengers off the plane. As we waited for help to arrive, I managed to locate my badly damaged bag on the debris-strewn runway. Grateful to be alive, I caught the next plane back to La Paz.

My two years in Bolivia were lively and challenging and, like Panama, quite heady for a young aid officer. In early 1958, at the completion of my two-year assignment in Bolivia, I was transferred to Washington, DC, to participate in a new mid-career training initiative for ICA program officers at the Johns Hopkins School of International Studies.

Though I would have been considered a mid-career officer myself, my experience with important, large-scale projects in Panama and Bolivia had boosted my standing, and I was selected as a faculty member for the program. I found these students much more eager than my Penn undergrads and had great fun teaching what I had learned about economic development.

While I was at Johns Hopkins, new management arrived at ICA headquarters in DC. Their assessment of ICA Latin America found that it was too much a program apart: distinct from ICA worldwide, and even clannish in its culture. To combat this phenomenon, ICA brass decided that any aid officers who had been stationed in Latin America would not be going back.

After six months of teaching, I was assigned to the office of Jim Grant, the ICA deputy director for program and planning in Washington. Grant seemed to me the sharpest knife in ICA's drawer. He later became the head of the United Nations International Children's Fund. In Grant's office, I was reunited with my Bolivian traveling buddy, Warren Wiggins, who worked as one of Grant's deputies. I was Wiggins' assistant in charge of ICA in Europe and Africa.

Europe at that time was declining in importance; the Marshall Plan was winding down, and our presence there had become less critical. Africa, on the other hand, was growing rapidly as a site for ICA programs. France had begun to rethink its African colonialism after a long and costly revolutionary war in Algeria. Charles de Gaulle came back into office in 1958 and created a new constitution giving all of France's African territories the right to claim independence.

When it was put to a vote, Guinea was the only territory to take the plunge and immediately sever its French ties. Guinea was run by a tyrant and murderer named Ahmed Sékou Touré, who turned to the United States for foreign aid. When we didn't respond, the Communists flooded in. Grant decided that someone should go to Guinea to stem the red tide. I packed my bags and left for Conakry just after Christmas of 1958.

•••

The Republic of Guinea, commonly known as Guinea-Conakry to distinguish it from Guinea-Bissau, was the first country in French West Africa to declare its total independence from France. Fed up with colonialism, the new nation became independent on October 2, 1958, spurning membership in the French community and abandoning French as the official language.

Ahmed Sékou Touré, Guinea's first president, was a Muslim with no formal education who rose through the ranks of labor unions. Fiercely nationalistic and anti-imperialist, he was outraged that despite his country's wealth of bauxite, iron, gold, and diamonds, most Guineans were subsistence farmers.

Guinea's bold move offended the patriotic senses of French President Charles de Gaulle. France cut off all aid to the former colony, froze Guinea's assets, instated a media embargo, tightened visa requirements, and tried to recruit allies to turn against the new nation. President Eisenhower initially appeased de Gaulle by postponing official US recognition of independent Guinea. Meanwhile, politicians, diplomats, and spies from the Soviet Union, Hungary, and East Germany descended on Conakry.

When reports to the State Department from our embassy in Guinea gave proof that the Cold War had arrived in Africa, US strategy shifted. The State Department wanted an aid program that would ingratiate the US with the Guineans and put the squeeze on the Communists. Washington had received few useful details from the new and understaffed embassy in Conakry.

My predeparture due diligence calls on diplomats in Washington had been discouraging. Staff in both the British and Israeli embassies urged me to postpone my trip until the Soviet flurry was over. The French ambassador praised the US decision to send such a minimal response (i.e., me)—a classic French put-down.

I arrived in Conakry from Paris on a Friday morning in December 1958. Throughout the city was evidence of destruction by the French from their hasty and vengeful exit. Several of the major paved streets had been rendered impassable by deep fissures from zigzag plowing.

I quickly got to work meeting with cabinet members and ministers of government to find out what the country really needed—or what they would be willing to accept—from the US. I stood out among foreign representatives in that I spoke French. Virtually none of the Soviets did, even when they were sober enough to enunciate clearly.

Though I established a friendly rapport with the officials I met, I couldn't get them interested in my offers of training scholarships; they preferred to train their young people in China or the Soviet Union. Of the material aid I offered, rice had the greatest appeal. Under a program referred to as Public Law 480, the US government purchased surplus crops from American farmers for distribution to developing nations. Our opening gambit for Guinea was six thousand tons of Louisiana rice, delivered in three shipments of two thousand tons over the course of a year. The rice would be sold cheaply on the local market, and we would use the proceeds for economic development programs, a typical ICA technique.

While I waited for the rice to arrive, I decided to venture out of Conakry to meet with tribal leaders and get a feel for the less populated areas. I went by train to Kankan, Guinea's second largest city about four hundred miles east and a full day's travel by rail from the capital. The train was packed full of lively revelers wearing magnificent *grand boubous*, embroidered white kaftans. I was told that these were hajjis on their way home from Mecca; there were several hundreds of them.

Not knowing the town at all and thinking I would be able to find reasonable lodging near the train station, I hadn't made a hotel reservation in Kankan. Everywhere I went, the hajjis had been there first. I walked around town with my suitcase for hours, eventually begging people to take me in and offering a highly inflated price for any type of lodging. By 1:00 a.m., I still didn't have a room.

As a last ditch effort, I went back to a pension run by a French woman who had already turned me away. I asked if she would allow me to sleep on her front porch. She said no, but she did explain (with considerable exasperation at having been woken) that I could try a house just down the block. It belonged to a teacher who had gone back to France for summer vacation. She said the house was locked, but if I could get onto the roof, there was a skylight I could pry open.

The small house was one story with vaulted ceilings and, as promised, a skylight. Leaving my suitcase by the front door, I shimmied up the drain pipe to the roof and crawled up the steeply pitched shingles to the skylight, which opened easily. Looking down, I was greeted by a black abyss. After pausing briefly to review my options, I decided to go for it. Lowering myself down until I hung from my fingertips, I dropped, landing with a crash. My right foot plunged into the toilet and my head slammed into the tile wall, knocking me out.

When I regained consciousness, my trapped foot was throbbing. One of the least romantic things I have felt is my heart beating in the bottom of a toilet bowl. Realizing I was really stuck and would probably never see my suitcase again (I didn't), I began shouting. I fainted a few times in the early hours of the morning but continued to shout periodically in French. Finally someone heard me and called the police, who broke down the door and smashed open the toilet bowl to extract my swollen foot. I was taken to a French clinic with a large lump on my forehead, bruised legs, and a broken foot.

I thought carefully about the wording of my telegram to the ambassador in Conakry explaining my extended stay. Embassy staff would surely have taken my plight more seriously had I not plunged into the can in Kankan. The tale made the rounds in Washington and followed me for years. Even more unfair, I was denied reimbursement for my unusual Kankan expenses: door replacement and toilet repairs.

Things began to look up when I got word, after an endless wait, that our first shipment of two thousand tons of rice had arrived. I went down to the wharf with the minister of agriculture to receive the delivery with fanfare, speeches, and photo ops. The minister was an odd fellow, and when we climbed onto the bags of rice for our photo, he maneuvered so as to appear a few inches taller than I. After the ceremony, he said to me with a playful look, "Have you heard about the Chinese rice?"

"What Chinese rice?"

"Well, it happens that I was here yesterday welcoming the Chinese rice."

"How much was it?"

"Twenty thousand tons."

My heart sank. I asked the agricultural minister if I could see the rice, which he said was stored in a nearby warehouse. The rice was loose, not bagged, and it made for an awesome spectacle—a great, golden pyramid. The whole unfortunate incident called to mind my favorite comedian Henny Youngman's description of Confucius's last words: "I hate rice."

The answer to our PR problems came in the form of the first material Soviet aid, which arrived the following week. I went to the wharf to witness the Soviet attempt at what was beginning to feel like Guinea's new national sport: material aid.

The rusty Soviet freighter sitting at the dock held twenty snowplows. They were massive, primitive machines with exhaust pipes that encircled the driver's cabin to provide warmth during long, Siberian winters. By the time the Guinean drivers got the engines warmed up to drive the plows off the dock, they were sweating buckets from the exhaust heat. By the time they delivered the plows to the parking lot, the drivers were almost incinerated. A couple of them bailed out prematurely, diving into the Atlantic for relief.

I assume the Soviets intended the plows for clearing debris, because it has never snowed in Guinea. Whatever the plan, it never came to fruition. When I went back to Guinea years later, the snow plows were still parked bumper to bumper where they had been left by their scorched Guinean drivers.

Beginning with these first overtures of material aid, President Touré was quite effective in playing the US and Soviet Union off each other. In truth, he was more interested in communism than democracy. Though the US viewed Touré as a moderate, he ruled Guinea with an iron fist, eliminated his opposition, murdered many of his cabinet members, and drove his country into the ground.

I spent only a few months in Guinea before returning to Washington with recommendations for a long-term aid program there. I felt no sense of accomplishment leaving Guinea—quite the opposite. I wasn't sure if I would be sent back, or if I wanted to be. ICA decided that I would be going next to Dakar, Senegal, as its first mission director for Senegal, the Sudanese Republic (Mali), and Mauritania.

•••

All three countries, like Guinea before them, were poised to declare independence. I hoped that with the hard knocks of Guinea under my belt I would come to Dakar with more insight, better strategies, and, God willing, some staff. Headed for a post with more legitimacy and permanence, I brought my family with me as I headed back to West Africa in late 1959.

Senegal is on the African west coast just north of Guinea and bordered by Mauritania to the north and Mali to the east. The capital, Dakar, sits on a small peninsula that is the westernmost point on the African continent. Its economy at that time depended strongly on peanut farming. The president of Senegal, Léopold Senghor, was different from Guinea's Touré in almost every way. A well-educated Christian, Democrat bordering on socialist, and overall smart leader, Senghor was also a poet who wrote Senegal's national anthem.

Senegal had recently joined with the Sudanese Republic to form the Mali Federation. They were to officially declare their independence the following year. The US government assumed that

Senegalese Prime Minister Mamadou Dia, a leftist Muslim with broad tribal support, would become president of the Mali Federation. The Francophile Senghor was given no chance to survive in the "new Africa." The initial goal of our aid program was to try to understand Dia, what he wanted to achieve, and how we could help.

Dakar was a city of about one hundred thousand with a relaxed, colonial atmosphere. The largest foreign community was the French, who populated the posh horse and tennis clubs. As was the case in Guinea, I started alone and from scratch. Thankfully, ICA shortly sent a handful of program officers. There were two American oil companies with a few employees, one American missionary (well known and liked because he owned a plane), and an American consulate and ICA office comprising not more than twenty people.

Mostly flat and arid, Mauritania and Mali give the impression of never-ending expanses of land. While Mauritania has a coastline, Mali is landlocked and extends into the Sahara Desert. The weather can be extremely hot—up to 120 degrees in the summer. Each country is more than three times the size of Senegal and much more sparsely populated. The mostly nomadic people sustain themselves by raising sheep, goats, and cattle. Like Senegal, Mali and Mauritania are overwhelmingly Muslim.

The Mauritanians chose a tiny coastal fishing village named Nouakchott as their capital when they became independent in 1960. I met with new President Moktar Ould Daddah in Nouakchott regularly. These visits were excruciating, and not just because Daddah was clearly in over his head. I was invited every month to the president's home for a lunch of roasted sheep. Custom required that the honored guest be given the eyes of the sheep. From a quick glance at these slimy orbs, it was obvious they were too big to swallow whole. Chewing proved unproductive—too tough and rubbery—so I surreptitiously made a cavity in my couscous big enough to bury them.

Very little happened at my visits with Daddah, who came from a distinguished background and was the first Mauritanian to graduate from a university and become a lawyer. Despite his credentials, Daddah didn't have the experience or the vision to construct a brand new capital in a newly independent nation. His challenges included a population almost completely isolated from the modern world. Nomads and herders flocked into the new capital to camp in the sand with their camels and sheep; as a result, the city grew haphazardly.

Daddah's wife was a French woman he met during college. Always present at our lunches, she demonstrated a clear resistance to US aid, a stance that seemed to influence her husband. This attitude was endemic among the French remaining in West Africa. In all three of my ICA countries, the ministers of budget and planning were French, and it was a huge setback to our progress. They would say "*non*," and things didn't get done.

Among my ICA colleagues in West Africa, our frustration was enormous at being invited in with great enthusiasm by these African nations and then being thwarted at every turn by French officials. Unfortunately, we Americans had few talented French speakers able to work around the French and beat them at their own game. I felt that our presence in the former colonies was in many ways futile for the Africans and for us; the environment was not ripe for progress or improvement. Our greatest contribution to Senegal, Mali, and especially Mauritania during that difficult time was training their future leaders in agriculture and administration.

•••

The tedium of banging my head against French West African walls was broken up considerably by the US presidential campaign of 1960. In October, I watched the third Nixon-Kennedy debate at the residence of our ambassador, Henry Villard. I thought Kennedy's performance was electric. Later that night, the future president flew to Ann Arbor to deliver a speech at my old alma mater, the University of Michigan. It was 2:00 a.m. when he finally arrived on the steps of the student union, where a crowd of about ten thousand students and faculty had waited hours to see him in person. Kennedy spoke about volunteer service abroad, his first reference to what would become the Peace Corps.

"How many of you, who are going to be doctors, are willing to spend your days in Ghana? Technicians or engineers, how many of you are willing to work in the Foreign Service and spend your lives traveling around the world? On your willingness to contribute part of your life to this country, I think, will depend the answer whether we as a free society can compete. I think we can! And I think Americans are willing to contribute, but the effort must be far greater than we have ever made in the past."

Kennedy's words were heartening to me. In addition to his vibrant, youthful personality on the union steps, the magic and the appeal of Kennedy in that moment seemed to flow from his blending of service, sacrifice, urgency, reward, and patriotism. It ignited that group of bright, liberal, socially conscious students at Michigan, and across the country. Kennedy wasn't the first politician to talk about volunteer service abroad. Senator Hubert Humphrey and Congressman Henry S. Reuss proposed a similar idea, with Humphrey even calling his "Peace Corps." But neither of those men had the platform or charisma of John F. Kennedy.

In the spring of '61, I had my first encounter with the Kennedy administration when Vice President Lyndon Johnson came to Senegal on a four-day visit. It was Johnson's first overseas trip as vice president. He came with his wife, Lady Bird, and a retinue of staff to celebrate Senegal's first year of independence and bolster our efforts to fend off the Communists.

The Mali Federation had gone belly up in August, with Senegal seceding in a coup we all suspected was orchestrated by the French. The Sudanese Republic became its own independent country called Mali. It was still presumed that Mamadou Dia would play a major role in independent Senegal once Senghor was voted out. Johnson's top priority during the trip was to meet with Dia.

I was one of the few embassy staff who spoke proficient French and knew what was going on outside the capital, so I became Johnson's escort and interpreter as he went to call on Mamadou Dia and tour the countryside. Johnson and I met with Dia at his office. The Muslim politician was dressed in his tribal *grand boubou* and maroon fez. Johnson wore a dark suit and cowboy boots. As the two sat in chairs next to each other and the cameras starting clicking, Johnson moved closer and closer to Dia, eventually resting his hand on Dia's knee.

Johnson leaned in and his voice lowered to a hoarse whisper, as though he were bringing Dia into his confidence. Johnson spoke eloquently about his passion for civil rights and his plans to improve the lives of black people in the United States. Dia reacted to Johnson's approach with surprise at first but soon became hypnotized. His only response was an occasional, quiet "*tiens,*" French for "wow." It was a virtuoso political performance; in fifteen minutes, Johnson had Dia in his pocket.

Unfortunately, Johnson's efforts would be for naught. Several months later, Dia was imprisoned for plotting to overthrow President Senghor, and he never again rose to a level of influence in Senegal. Senghor's presidency lasted until 1981, despite the State Department's predictions.

The next day, the vice president, a few of his staff, Ambassador Villard, a reporter for *TIME* magazine, and I set out in the ambassador's limousine along the north coast to visit a fishing village. As we drove through the countryside, Johnson compared everything he saw to Texas. The village was picturesque, with rows of brightly painted fishing boats along the shore. They were hand-carved, pirogue-style boats with curved bows that came to a point. They made a wonderful backdrop for photos.

We stopped at the village's medical clinic, used primarily to treat injured fishermen. It was an absolutely ghastly place that looked and smelled like a slaughterhouse. Villard couldn't bring himself to go inside, but Johnson handled it gamely. When we left the clinic, Johnson struck up a conversation with the village chief. He said in mock dismay, "I'm very disturbed to find that all of your outboard motors are Evinrude. I don't understand why you don't have Johnson motors!"

The chief explained that Senegal's Evinrude dealer was a close relative of the president. As we left, Johnson said, "I'm going to send you a Johnson outboard motor when I get back to Washington."

When Johnson was approached by an old lady or young kid asking for something, he would assure them that when he got back to Washington, he'd look into it. He also handed out hundreds of old campaign pens. They were cheap, faded, and read, "Vote for LBJ—the most for the greatest number." The Senegalese were thrilled with them. But the pens came back to haunt me when people discovered they were dried out. An endless trail of shepherds and fisherman lined up outside my office requesting ink refills. Johnson did remember the outboard motor, though, which arrived a month later, and it worked beautifully.

After the fishing village, we headed to the interior to visit the sites of ICA programs dealing with cattle and rice. Our driver got lost on the way, giving us a wonderful opportunity to listen to Johnson. Stories of his rise in politics and his relationship with Kennedy were facilitated by the *TIME* magazine reporter and frequently interrupted by Johnson, who had acquired a bad case of diarrhea. Periodically he would shout for the driver to stop, bolt from car and disappear behind a date palm. Between pit stops, Johnson diplomatically described his relationship with the president as "respectful, but at arm's length."

Eventually, Johnson asked about my background. He was especially interested in Panama, because he sensed there was growing disenchantment among Panamanians over the US Army presence in the Canal Zone. He felt the Army and the Pentagon got their own way in Panama regardless of State Department or White House policy, and he sensed the situation was coming to a head. I told him he was 100 percent right. I said I thought we were behaving like colonial occupiers in the Canal Zone, and our policy was foolish and shortsighted. "Eventually, we will be shooting each other."

During Johnson's trip I had the chance to meet Bill Moyers, clearly the stand-out among the staff and a favorite of Johnson, who treated him like a son. Moyers, only twenty-six, had sophistication far beyond his age and a marvelous sense of humor. The Texas native started most of his stories and one-liners with, "As my daddy used to say…" I liked all of Johnson's staff and thought the trip had gone well, with the possible exception of the Dia visit. Misreading Dia's political future in Senegal was just one of many bad calls that the US State Department made in newly independent Africa.

Not long after the vice president's visit to Senegal, another VIP arrived: Sargent Shriver. Although it had launched in March with great fanfare in the US, the Peace Corps was virtually unheard of abroad. With applications pouring in from college graduates wanting to become volunteers, Shriver urgently needed to find jobs overseas. He toured the world to drum up interest in the program and generate formal requests for volunteers, hoping that the global popularity of his brother-in-law, President Kennedy, would help his case.

I had done some legwork for Shriver before he arrived in Dakar. My contacts in Senegal, Mali, and Mauritania were quite interested, especially the ministers of education and agriculture. They said they would be delighted to speak with a Kennedy relation. My estimate was that the three countries combined could use about seven hundred volunteers at first. That number seemed to horrify US diplomats in Senegal as far too many, but Shriver was pleased: "That's about the number I would have guessed."

Shriver and I hit it off immediately. He was a somewhat aloof Maryland aristocrat and a smooth, immaculately groomed lawyer from Yale, more in the style of the sophisticated Cole Porter era than of the present day. A rich Kennedy in-law, movie-star handsome, and socially effervescent, he was also a man of all people and all classes of people. He was a devout Catholic who liked to quote Catholic philosophers but just as easily quoted Third World dictators.

After a full day together covering a great range of topics and working on his French, Shriver broached the possibility of my heading up the Peace Corps in Latin America. Warren Wiggins, my old ICA buddy, had become the director of worldwide operations for the Peace Corps and suggested I would be a good fit for the job. Many of Wiggins' regional operations staff were the cream of the ICA crop: seasoned, adventurous, and bright. Most importantly, they brought an understanding of Third World reality. These experienced ICA retreads stood in sharp contrast to the more kinetic people Shriver brought aboard to run the Peace Corps in its start-up phase.

Shriver was skittish about bringing on too many "foreign aid types" (as he put it). He was adamantly opposed to bureaucracy; he wanted to grow the Peace Corps quickly and felt that career people would slow down and gum up the works. Despite his misgivings, Shriver promised to send me a formal offer when he returned to Washington.

I was ecstatic. Like so many others, I was inspired by the philosophy and style of the Peace Corps. Also, I didn't see the foreign aid program in French West Africa making progress. I had been unable to get qualified staff and was frustrated by the petty but significant opposition of the French. The prospect of returning to Latin America thrilled me. I shared the news with our new ambassador, Phil Kaiser, and other embassy staff. Kaiser said the Peace Corps would be laughed out of its host countries in six months. "You'd be a fool do to it."

Most embassy officers viewed this new volunteer program as a threat or folly. Some called it a potential nuisance: the presence of large numbers of volunteers would place additional burdens on medical, administrative, and security staff at US embassies. Amazingly, nobody offered ideas about the need for and placement of volunteers. Crusading is a concept bureaucrats approach very gingerly.

In a week or so, I received a cordial handwritten note from my new friend Shriver—it was a Dear John letter. He was reluctant at that early stage to burden his new agency, he wrote, with any more foreign aid officers. Crushed, I was revived the very next day by a phone message assuring me that Shriver had definitely decided to offer me the position, with one minor caveat: I would have to accept a one-grade decrease in salary. That final twist was classic Shriver—testing the mettle. In Panamanian Spanish it's also known as being a *pichicuma* (tightwad).

When I arrived in Washington in October 1961 as the Peace Corps' first regional director for Latin America, Wiggins explained what had happened to change Shriver's mind. Upon hearing about the decision not to hire me, Wiggins had casually asked Shriver if he was aware that I used to be Michigan's head boxing coach and had been in the ring with Sugar Ray Robinson. "Good grief! Why didn't someone tell me?" Shriver had exclaimed. "He's a natural for the job!"

5

1961–1964

The Peace Corps is a unique government agency in many ways, and one is that it has made the cheapest way of doing things the most effective way.

—Speech at the Harvard Business School, 1968

When I became regional director in October 1961, Latin America had by far the fewest volunteers of the Peace Corps' four geographic regions—Africa, Far East, North Africa-Near East-South Asia, and Latin America. Sargent Shriver's special interest was English-speaking Africa; the State Department's priority was South Asia. When the first volunteers left for their assignments in September, hundreds went to Kenya, Tanzania, the Philippines, Indonesia, and Malaysia. My program had sent small groups to Chile,

Colombia, and the Caribbean island of Saint Lucia. I was instructed to play catch-up.

Two weeks after I moved into the Peace Corps' Washington headquarters in the Miatico building on Connecticut Avenue, I left with Shriver, his special assistant, William Haddad, and the director of the Puerto Rican field training center, Raphael Sancho-Bonet, on a barnstorming trip through South America. Six countries were on our agenda: Colombia, Chile, Ecuador, Peru, Brazil, and Venezuela.

We met with presidents and ministers of health, agriculture, and education in each country to solidify relationships and build new ones. Across the board, we were well received. It seemed that the more politically savvy the president, the more he understood the role of the Peace Corps in stimulating creativity, initiative, and social change. Presidents Alberto Lleras Camargo of Colombia and Rómulo Ernesto Betancourt of Venezuela were standouts.

When we visited him, President Betancourt was recovering from a Fidel Castro-backed assassination attempt. Badly burned, with his hands and forearms still heavily bandaged, Betancourt was a diminutive, rotund, pipe-smoking figure who looked like a puppet behind his huge presidential desk. "Do you know what the Castro terrorists are doing to us? They are killing five or six of our policemen every day in Caracas." Venezuela had become Castro's number-one target. If he could capture the natural resources of Venezuela—oil, steel, and iron ore—he would position himself to take over the whole region.

Betancourt impressed us as inspired, tough, democratic, and bright, and he obviously thought highly of Sargent Shriver. The feeling was mutual—Shriver always liked a fighter. We tried to do as much as we could through the Peace Corps to help Betancourt, and he was always very supportive of our initiatives. By the end of our swing through South America, we understood that Betancourt was a beacon of freedom for his countrymen and his neighbors as the Castro pressure increased.

Our three-week tour gave me an opportunity to see how Sargent Shriver operated and also to convince him that I was up to my job. I thought Shriver was superb. Whether he was with President João Goulart of Brazil or the mayor of Arequipa, Peru, he immediately set the right tone or asked the right question, and his great enthusiasm was contagious. He crackled with happy electricity. Even lacking foreign language skills, Shriver established instant rapport with everyone we met.

In each country, a formal banquet was held in our honor, hosted by either the president or foreign minister, and Shriver would be called upon to give a toast. Starting with our second country, without fail he would raise his glass, exclaiming "Viva ___!" and name the country we had just left. He carried it off well, and everyone took it in good humor.

When we weren't meeting with dignitaries, we were out in the wilds of South America visiting volunteers and future volunteer sites. On one trip from Lima to Machu Picchu, Shriver and I traveled by rail with Peru Country Director Frank Mankiewicz on a hand car powered by two Peruvian Indians. Gradually we rolled to a stop, and our technician informed us that there was trouble with the equipment. Darkness descended on the Altiplano, and sounds of wildlife echoed around us. After a long while, Shriver asked anxiously, "Jack, do you suppose there are any other trains coming through on this track?"

"Just the express, Sarge."

Shriver prided himself on his energy; he could work anyone under the table. It became my goal to keep up with him, and even outlast him. We got along well, and Shriver seemed impressed by my Spanish and my rapport with the people we met. We came away with requests for thousands of volunteers.

Just a few weeks later, President Kennedy made his first trip to Colombia and Venezuela to promote the Alliance for Progress, a program he initiated to fight communism in general, and Castro in particular, in Latin America. The Alliance was an expansion of the old Institute of Inter-American Affairs (IIAA), the development program I had worked for in Panama.

Kennedy's charisma, comforting Catholicism, and solemn commitment to making the Alliance for Progress succeed won over his audiences. He returned to Washington with his relationship to President Lleras Camargo of Colombia and Venezuela's Betancourt cemented—mutually respectful, close, and warm. President Betancourt told me later that his meeting with Kennedy in 1961 had been the high point of his life.

Back in Washington myself, I found the scale of the work before me sobering. I had to develop programs, create jobs for volunteers, and establish overseas offices across the continent. Most importantly, I needed to quickly recruit large numbers of volunteers and staff.

My most immediate task was finding qualified staff for the headquarters. Unlike Shriver, who shied away from "career types," my instinct was to mine USIS and ICA (now called USAID) for the best talent. These were professionals with overseas experience who knew the language, the culture, and the quirks of the host countries. Not long after I joined the Peace Corps, Shriver relaxed his anti-Foreign Service stance to offer junior officers in the State Department two-year assignments in the Peace Corps. He thought this would give the officers a chance to work outside the normal career pattern, and their expertise would be a boon to the Peace Corps. I jumped at the chance to hire them.

My second critical priority was installing a management system for overseas staff. The poets, aging jocks, bored lawyers, and unfulfilled professors we attracted to staff overseas offices needed serious instruction in management and accounting—more than the brief training in Washington provided. Happily we found the answer before anyone went to jail: his name was Darwin Bell. A longtime USAID administrative officer in Latin America, Bell had the ability to simplify government regulations, streamline accounting, and explain procedures clearly to neophyte staff members.

As new countries suddenly opened up, Bell flew down to negotiate leases, equip offices, procure vehicles, and co-opt embassy administrative officers. He installed an accounting system and trained local staff to run it. Although theoretically based in Lima, Bell was on constant call to salvage a wide variety of fiscal snarls in neighboring countries.

Virtually all of my staff came to the Peace Corps for the same reasons that volunteers did: they were inspired, energized, and driven by the organization's mission and methods. I recall only a small handful of missteps in staff selection during that start-up period. The most memorable was Liddy Hanford, later known as Elizabeth Dole, Senator Bob Dole's wife. A graduate of the prestigious White House Fellows Program, she was assigned to be my special assistant during her summer off from Harvard Law School.

She wanted to go with me to all my high-level meetings (of which I had virtually none), travel with me, and meet with foreign ministers and presidents. Our department was still understaffed and we were working our tails off. I didn't need a special assistant, especially one with no overseas experience and no Spanish, so I told her she would be my secretary. As talented and ambitious as she was, we were mismatched. I missed her potential, I think, because I was so put off by her arrogance. She went on to run the Red Cross and serve as a US senator.

While I had no patience for playing politics as I staffed my department and developed programs, Shriver was working the politicians in Washington like a virtuoso. When you've learned politics in Daley's and Rostenkowski's Chicago, like Shriver did, Washington becomes little more than a finishing school.

There were many doubters and naysayers in Congress on the subject of the Peace Corps, and Shriver visited every one of them. He made politicians feel like part of the program. When traveling abroad, he wrote as many notes and postcards to legislators as he did to volunteers' parents. Shriver desperately needed Congress's support: the Peace Corps was born by executive order, but Congress had to approve its funding.

In those early days, Shriver couldn't wait for tangible proof of the Peace Corps' impact, so he instructed his staff to permanently weld the words "Peace Corps" to "success." Peace Corps: a success. The successful Peace Corps. The New Frontier's first success. It stuck. Even before the first volunteers could speak their host country's language, the Peace Corps was being widely heralded as a success.

One of Shriver's smartest moves was hiring Bill Moyers as his deputy. Shriver had the energy; Moyers was a better manager. They were both men of strong character and commitment. Their great senses of humor and timing accompanied an unerring political instinct. Volunteers loved them, and so did the staff. Peace Corps' opponents in Congress wondered how we could unleash thousands of young Americans on the world and keep them out of trouble and youthful indiscretions. Shriver and Moyers, so upbeat about our prospects, won over enough skeptics on the Hill to secure funding from Congress.

Moyers had already been a superstar in Vice President Johnson's office. He was a Baptist pastor, a graduate of Southwestern Baptist Theological Seminary in Fort Worth. I had gotten to know him in Senegal as wise beyond his years and extremely funny. In his press statement after being hired by the Peace Corps, Moyers said, "George Custer received such an appointment when he was only twenty-six. He headed west for an early scalping. At twenty-eight, and being a bit less aggressive than George, I will settle for a slowing receding hairline for my efforts."

Though Shriver was brilliant in many of his staffing choices, he suffered from quirks in matters of personnel. He micromanaged, to the point of wanting to interview my overseas staff secretaries; he never hired women for management positions; and he couldn't fire anyone. When he realized that a staffer was not living up to expectations, he put him in a corner and ignored him. Then he hired a replacement. Sometimes he had three or four people in the same position, which was the case with his director(s) of administration; he never could find just the right one.

Shriver had a deep passion for athletics that spilled over into his hiring practices. The Peace Corps was crawling with athletes and former athletes, including me. His particular weakness seemed to be mountain climbers. Bob Bates, president of the American Alpine Club and conqueror of K-2, was appointed country director in Nepal. Willi Unsoeld, on his way to climb Mt. Everest, was brought on to be Bates's deputy. Distinguished cardiologist Charles Houston, MD, who had climbed K-2 with Bates, became the first Peace Corps representative in India. An ace pitcher from Cornell, brilliant polyglot Glen Ferguson, served as Shriver's associate director.

Often when I returned from a trip, I found the names of old professional boxers on the list of people to see me. They had been assured by Shriver that I could give them a great job in Venezuela or Brazil. I couldn't hire any of them—they were too punch-drunk and over the hill—and I was sorry about it. There were some greats on that list, including a couple of world champions.

When sticky issues arose that Shriver didn't want to touch, he gave them to Moyers. Shriver handed him the baton during the Peace Corps' dust-up with the Christian community. When Dr. Lowell Kelly, the Peace Corps director of selection, wrote a letter saying that Peace Corps volunteers could not teach Sunday school, a religious uproar ensued. Dr. Bob Jones, president of Bible college Bob Jones University in Greenville, South Carolina, was the most fervent critic of the policy. His frequent references to Moyers as "genius boy", though, show that he was correct on at least one count.

The Peace Corps depended on many religiously affiliated schools to train volunteers, but it couldn't be associated with religion. After much debate, the Peace Corps decided in 1963 to end its training programs at religious institutions. Our biggest loss was Notre Dame, which had started the Peace Corps off on the right foot in Chile. University management, especially Father Theodore Hesburgh, took the news very hard. He wrote Moyers, "It is time some of you arrogant, high-handed, and radical bullies got it through your thick heads that you are the servants of the people..."

I was not exempt from doing work Shriver preferred to avoid. In early 1962, Attorney General Robert Kennedy had his sights firmly set on assassinating Fidel Castro. Bobby was operating all over town, convening meetings on short notice with a short temper. Nobody turned down his meeting requests except Shriver, who knew better than to play second fiddle to his much younger brother-in-law at an official meeting. Shriver sent me instead, which clearly irritated Bobby.

On one occasion, Bobby set up a large meeting in the conference room of Under Secretary of State George Ball. Ball, like many other senior US diplomats at the time, couldn't stand Bobby. In his memoir, *The Past Has Another Pattern*, Ball described Bobby as "always the better hater." After a very rancorous session, I made my way to the door, where Ball and Bobby were talking. As I squeezed my way past Bobby, I touched his elbow and interrupted, "Mr. Kennedy, why do you keep referring to Sargent Shriver as 'the boy scout'?"

"None of your fucking business. You Peace Corps people need to grow up," Bobby snarled. Ball rolled his eyes at me and returned to his office.

I saw Bobby's animosity toward Shriver as jealousy. Almost overnight, Shriver had become the prince of Washington. Our headquarters attracted people from all over the country willing to give up high-paying jobs in the private sector to gain entrée into our exciting, joyful sanctum. The US press was good to the Peace Corps, and the reception of host governments overseas was most enthusiastic. That Bobby was envious made perfect sense to me.

Several months later, I had the misfortune of being invited to another meeting led by Bobby about his latest effort to quash Castro. The attorney general was rallying support for regional police academies—the first one planned for the Canal Zone in Panama—that would provide Latin American police with training, weapons, and equipment to better defend against Communist infiltration. I had no reason to be involved in such a project, but several people in the State Department knew that I had served in Panama and understood the country well. They brought me in fairly late in the process.

About forty people attended the meeting, half of them from the Pentagon, several from the FBI, and several senior police officers, security people, and State Department officials. Foreign aid officers attended as well, because the project would be funded by aid money taken from development projects. Bobby energetically described the eight or nine academies planned for Latin America, assuming the pilot program in the Canal Zone went well.

When the presentation concluded, Bobby asked for opinions or suggestions. Having listened to all of this in horror, I stood up. "I think this is the wrong approach. The one thing police forces in Latin America don't need is more and better weapons." I went on to say that the program would lead to further militarization of Latin America and would exacerbate the conflict in many countries between the police and the army.

Bobby gave me a hostile dressing down. He said I had no business being there, that I didn't know what I was talking about and didn't understand the dangers the program addressed. I countered on several points, but he didn't give an inch. Ultimately, I am happy to say, the police academy idea never materialized.

•••

When Shriver was deciding how to structure the Peace Corps, he read a paper prepared by my old friend Warren Wiggins. In early 1961, from his desk at ICA-Far East in Washington, Wiggins had written a treatise called "The Towering Task," in which he defined the practical application of the Peace Corps and recommended a system for deploying volunteers.

When Shriver read it, he immediately saw the wisdom of Wiggins' plan and brought him on board to help shape the agency. The paper's major thrust was to start big, sending large numbers of volunteers to maximize impact and give the agency a better chance of producing results in the short term. Wiggins also recommended that the agency be separate and independent from the State Department and ICA/USAID. As a reward for his inspired design, Warren Wiggins got the best and toughest job of all: director of Peace Corps overseas operations.

Shriver stuck firmly to the precepts laid out in Wiggins' treatise. He committed large numbers of volunteers to each country whenever he could, and he insisted that the Peace Corps be an independent agency, apart from US foreign aid bureaucracy. The greatest fear of Shriver and his staff was that the Peace Corps would be subsumed by USAID. Once devoured, it would quietly suffocate.

In fact, such a nightmare scenario was actively being pursued by White House staff. The leader of the effort was Kennedy's special assistant and enforcer, Ralph Dungan. A profane and belligerent man, Dungan claimed that Kennedy wanted the Peace Corps to become part of USAID. History would show that Kennedy, hardly an organization man, had no vested interest in the Peace Corps' bureaucratic home. No one else close to Kennedy cared much about the Peace Corps; our biggest supporter was Lyndon Johnson, hardly a White House insider.

When news reached Shriver's little staff that Dungan was planning to dump the Peace Corps into USAID, panic set in. Shriver turned to Moyers, who turned to Johnson. Frozen out by White House staff, the vice president made the most of his position as chairman of the Peace Corps' National Advisory Council. He advised Mr. Dungan in no uncertain terms that the Peace Corps would remain bureaucratically independent. For reasons nobody could fathom, Johnson prevailed. After that, the vice president became more closely identified with and personally committed to the Peace Corps' success. The rigid separation of the Peace Corps from USAID and the Alliance for Progress remained in place indefinitely.

Unfettered by cumbersome bureaucracy, I managed my region the way I wanted, and things ran remarkably smoothly for a start-up. I had the advantage of a staff who spoke Spanish or Portuguese and had lived and worked in Latin America. By comparison, few staffers in Africa and the Far East had experience in those countries; they were starting from scratch. Also, volunteers in Latin America weren't faced with much hostility from their host countries. Less fortunate were volunteers in Pakistan and Guinea, who were roundly disliked and asked to leave.

The most significant difference between Peace Corps Latin America and the rest of the world was our focus on community development (CD) projects. Well over half of Latin America volunteers worked in CD, in which the volunteer was assigned alone or in a pair to help villagers do whatever they wanted done. Often this was an agricultural or construction project, and sometimes it was related to public health or education. Whatever the project, it improved living conditions in the community.

Community development was the core thrust of the Latin America program throughout the sixties; it was also the major bone of contention among Peace Corps staff. There were many who thought the CD model was not viable. They didn't like unskilled volunteers being shotgunned into rural communities unsupported, with no specific job and no specific leadership. They compared it to being dropped on Mars with no manual. I agreed that volunteers badly needed better language and skills training, but I loved the CD model. I had seen the futility of narrowly defined development projects imposed on disinterested villagers.

My commitment to CD wasn't shared by many on my staff, but it was supported by a research project undertaken by Cornell University in Peru. The study set out to determine what difference it made to have a CD volunteer in a village for two years, measured by the number of new institutions in that village. It defined an institution the same way the Peace Corps did: anything, from a public shower to a co-op, library, PTA, sports league, or basketball court, that improved the quality of life. The researchers found that over a two-year period, the rate of institution-building was three times greater in the CD volunteer's village than in a nearby village with no volunteer. This was the case even though not all of the volunteers spoke proficient Spanish or had a skill.

The study convinced me that we were arguing about the wrong thing. We knew that CD was an effective program. The issue was: can we provide sufficient foreign language and skills training in three months so that volunteers go armed to succeed from day one? I was one of the very few at the beginning of the Peace Corps to argue about training, which was being conducted by top-tier US universities. I felt many of those schools poorly prepared our volunteers for success in the Third World.

Meeting volunteers in Panama

Initially, volunteers received only fifty hours of language training over two months. By protesting loudly, I got the number of language hours up to 150—better, but it really should have been three hundred. I remembered during that first trip to South America with Shriver, government officials invariably asked, "Will they speak enough Spanish when they arrive?" My idea of enough was seriously at variance with the Peace Corps trainers'.

The university professors at our training sites didn't know how to teach languages quickly; they used the old grammar translation method. Training at these venues bore the unmistakable imprint of the romantic junior year abroad. In addition to unrealistic language training, no effort was made to give volunteers practical skills, like how to grow crops indigenous to their host countries, complete basic construction projects, or do bookkeeping. Even more frustrating, there seemed to be almost as many staff psychologists roaming the campus as trainees.

I thought this arrangement did a disservice to the Peace Corps and that training should take place overseas in the real world, not at Berkeley (one of our most used centers) or other elite college campuses. However, since the Peace Corps depended on good relationships with those universities to recruit new volunteers, no one wanted to rock the boat.

Wonderful exceptions to our normal training venues were two Outward Bound camps in Puerto Rico. They provided language immersion, rural living, and useful skills like water safety, wilderness survival, and mountain climbing. Shriver felt, rightly, that it was important to give people a taste of what they were getting into: the fungus, the diarrhea, and the mosquitoes. Unfortunately, this highly practical training was a mere postscript, lasting only about five days after eight weeks at a comfortable US university.

•••

I SPENT COUNTLESS DAYS traveling during my time as regional director, especially during the first two years. I oversaw the start-up of new programs, toured training sites, and visited volunteers. I worked fifteen hours a day and traveled fifteen days a month, and I loved every minute. The travel wasn't just a matter of getting to the country; once there, it was tossing around all day in a dusty or soggy jeep and eating food that more likely than not would require a large dose of streptomagma to recover from.

In early 1963, I flew out of Washington National Airport to visit several sites in Central America with Shriver, his aide Mike Edwards, and one of my good friends, Leveo Sanchez. Shriver left no margin for error in his schedule and typically ran about fifteen minutes behind. His staff was accustomed to running interference for him as he arrived progressively later throughout the day. On this trip, Shriver had not appeared by the boarding call, and I stayed back to ensure the plane didn't leave without him. I had coaxed the steward at the plane door to give us five minutes, and then another five, but finally he said,

"I'm sorry. I can't hold this plane any longer. I don't care if it's the president's brother-in-law, I'm not going to hold this plane!"

"As a matter of fact…" Just then Shriver came running down the ramp at full speed, giving the steward the shock of his career.

Because of his last-minute boarding, Shriver's luggage didn't arrive with us, and he reminded Leveo repeatedly about his need for a clean shirt as we visited projects that afternoon in Guatemala City. Leveo sent our Guatemala rep, Dave Fledderjohn, over to the Arrow shirt plant to buy a white shirt for Shriver. After we checked into our hotel—always the cheapest possible place—Leveo and I set out to explore and have dinner. On our way home, we ran into Shriver walking along Quinta Avenida looking for a toothbrush. He was in a particularly bad mood, and when we offered our assistance he grumbled, "Once you two leave the States, you become Latins!"

Fledderjohn arrived at our hotel that morning with a crisp new Arrow shirt. Shriver asked him how much it cost; when he heard the answer, he handed the shirt right back, saying it was too expensive. I had to intercede with Shriver's secretary, Maryann Orlando, to get Fledderjohn reimbursed for the overpriced Guatemalan shirt. For the rest of the trip, Shriver resorted to a technique I have used many times myself: washing out the day's clothes in the hotel sink with a miniature bar of soap.

Shriver prided himself on being non-bureaucratic but democratic. When he proposed an idea that drew objections, he would listen patiently to his critics and then say, "Let's do it anyway." One of the most daring examples of this was in Venezuela, where Castro had gained a foothold and was pushing for total domination. It was thought at the time that Venezuela's Universidad Central de Caracas was the most Marxist-dominated university in the world.

We decided to send volunteers to teach there: American Literature, American History, English, and, the door-opener, basketball. We recruited volunteers and started training. Soon I heard from the US ambassador in Caracas, officials at the State Department, and other intelligent people saying that our plan was misguided and foolish. They said we absolutely shouldn't go through with it; if we did, it would endanger the volunteers and create enormous problems for the United States.

Shriver was fond of pithy sayings. One of his favorites he learned from President Sukarno of Indonesia: "Show 'em your teeth, not your tail." That's what he told me when I reported to him the reaction to our University of Caracas plan. We sent the volunteers anyway, with the full support of Venezuelan President Betancourt. For months, the volunteers were harassed, threatened, and obstructed from doing their jobs, but they hung in there and won in a big way. It ended up being one of the most successful programs we had.

Not long after our success in Caracas, Shriver received a two-page letter from President Betancourt sent via the governor of Puerto Rico, Luis Muñoz Marín, a mutual friend of Betancourt's and Shriver's. Marín wrote "Bravo!" across the top before delivering the letter to Shriver. I was called in to translate. Betancourt's letter revealed itself to be as brutal as any missive I'd read in a diplomatic setting.

"Not since the first Texas and Oklahoma roustabouts landed in this country to steal our oil have the people of Venezuela encountered the degree of arrogance and insensitivity displayed by your State Department economists, whose latest mission is to instruct us on how we must manage our society, and, most pointedly, reform our sovereign institutions to mirror Anglo-Saxon models."

The letter called into question both the competence and ethics of the US State Department. According to Betancourt, nothing had been achieved under the Alliance for Progress. Castro was steadily gaining ground as the US continued to send economists. Betancourt was not an enemy or a skeptic; he was an ally. He was a democrat who wanted to reform and to defeat Castro, but he was completely disenchanted with the Alliance for Progress, the US effort to help him fight communism.

Shriver said we had to visit the president with this news. He called the White House and was given the standard, "President can't see you; maybe tomorrow or the next day." Shriver responded, "This is a national emergency; the president will want to know about it immediately. I'm coming over now."

Ten minutes later we walked into the Oval Office. President Kennedy sat in his rocking chair and half stood to shake our hands. Compared to his appearance when I had seen him at a Rose Garden ceremony two or three months earlier, he was changed. Pale, with redder-looking hair, the president seemed brittle and dispirited. I soaked up every detail; this was my first personal meeting with the founder of the Peace Corps.

Kennedy tapped his eyetooth with a forefinger, and then his pencil, as he rapidly skimmed my translation of Betancourt's letter. Slowly shaking his head, the president reread the letter more deliberately. Finally, looking up and out the window, he said, "Christ, Sarge. Can't we do anything right? We do have Peace Corps down there, right? How are they doing?"

Shriver told the president about our daring and successful program in Caracas, and Kennedy concurred with our assessment of Betancourt's significance to the region. He noted that Colombia's President Lleras Camargo was the other Latin anchor. Those two presidents represented the kind of leadership our South American friends richly deserved and so seldom got. Kennedy, maybe because of his ill health and mood at the moment, didn't offer any suggestions. He roundly criticized the State Department, which he called "the Goddamn fudge factory."

It was a depressing meeting. We needed Betancourt and Lleras Camargo in our fight against Castro. We had President Frey in Chile, but he was untested, and most of the others were not very distinguished or very democratic. It was undeniable that the Alliance for Progress wasn't working. From what I had seen, the program was too much cooked up in DC and not based on the realities of Latin America. The thrust of the program was, "You must reform everything to get our aid." But that blast from Betancourt didn't change Kennedy's course, or the program. The same people stayed on with the same US arrogance of "we know best."

As the Alliance fell flat, the Peace Corps shone in Cold War battleground countries. The first group of sixty-two volunteers assigned to Colombia was one of the best. The volunteers overachieved for two or more years in rural Colombia as community development agents. They worked alongside young counterparts within an organization known as Acción Comunal, a group devoted to protecting endangered Indian tribes. Their jobs varied from establishing handicraft cooperatives to building bridges and sanitation systems. Two of them were killed in a plane crash during service: the first Peace Corps fatalities, David Crozier and Lawrence Radley, gave their names to the Outward Bound training camps in Puerto Rico.

The Colombia volunteers were blessed with a well-qualified and distinguished Peace Corps country director, a former ship's captain named Chris Sheldon. Monseñor José Joaquin Salcedo, a famous Colombian priest and head of Acción Cultural Popular, commented in awe that the Colombia I volunteers were the most impressive group of people he had ever encountered. My response: "You should meet Colombia II; they were better trained."

Colombia II had great success using the trappings of that country's recent dictatorship for good. Lieutenant General Gustavo Rojas Pinilla, Colombia's cruel and corrupt dictator during the 1950s, wanted instant communication with every village across the country as part of his authoritarian rule. So he built an extensive network of broadcast towers across hill and mountaintops. The system was rarely used after President Lleras Camargo came into office in 1958 with a democratic government.

In 1962, the Peace Corps decided to use Rojas' system to televise educational programming to schools across the country. The project was led from Washington by Tedson Meyers, who had received well-deserved acclaim for writing Federal Communication Commission Chief Newt Minnow's memorable "Vast Wasteland" speech criticizing US television.

Meyers negotiated with the Colombian ministry of education to create programs at the elementary and middle school levels with a focus on math, science, and English. The project required not only a large number of volunteers experienced in educational TV to work in our studio, but also many volunteers to work in the classrooms as facilitators when the programs were broadcast.

The electronics company RCA donated two hundred giant televisions that volunteers installed in two hundred schools. The program the volunteers created was modern, fun, and different from anything the children had seen before. The students responded very well and especially showed improvement in their mastery of English. It wasn't long before the shows were being duplicated by other Latin American countries. Because of that great program, I had occasion to visit Colombia often, making lasting friendships with the minister of education, the foreign minister, and the presidents, first Lleras Camargo, and then Guillermo León Valencia.

Another stand-out group of volunteers worked in Ecuador. In 1963, twenty-six volunteers began their training; all twenty-six subsequently became Ecuador VI, and all stayed at least two years. They were overwhelmingly successful in instituting accounting and general management practices among Native Ecuadoran credit and marketing co-ops. Many of those volunteers became successful executives in the US. Over forty years later, Ecuador VI volunteers are still returning to Ecuador, accompanied now by their spouses, children, money, and ideas. The payoff continues in ever new and wonderful ways.

In November 1963, I went to visit volunteers in Costa Rica. San José is arguably Central America's most attractive capital, with parks and plazas, charming European architecture, and relatively clean streets. When I visited, the city was quite transformed. A nearby volcano and tourist attraction, Irazú, had been erupting for over a year, depositing a thick layer of powdery gray ash over everything. In the countryside, it destroyed trees and crops; in San José, it covered the rooftops and the streets in a gloomy pall.

On a Friday, the day after I arrived, I was having lunch at a family-style restaurant with a large group of Peace Corps volunteers and staff. Sirens began to wail, people were running in the street, and we heard that it was the American president. I ran to the US embassy, only three blocks away. The big US flag was flying at half-staff. Out front on a bulletin board had been printed large, in Spanish and English, the stunning news of Kennedy's assassination.

Outside the embassy gates were perhaps one hundred people kneeling in the volcanic ash and crossing themselves, crying and repeating, "*Presidente Kennedy, Presidente Kennedy*." Since the embassy was closed, I immediately made my way to the telegraph office to send my condolences to Mrs. Kennedy. As I approached the office, I saw a line of Costa Ricans two blocks long waiting to do the same thing.

Kennedy was the spirit, the soul, and the founder of the Peace Corps. Volunteers in Latin America were called "Kennedy's children." I didn't know if this was the end of the Peace Corps. Would people stop volunteering? As much as Shriver was the man who made it real, Kennedy was always our symbol. As it turned out, of course, the Peace Corps only grew stronger. We were very fortunate to inherit our fiercest political ally, Lyndon Johnson, as our next president.

•••

By 1964, Latin American countries were requesting such large numbers of volunteers that we were having trouble finding enough overseas staff to support them. The young volunteers who had just completed their two years of service came to our rescue. We hired the best of them, and they brought a whole new dimension to the art of helping volunteers succeed. Fluent in Spanish, Portuguese, and assorted Indian dialects, these young staffers excelled in job site selection and negotiation with our overseas hosts.

In late January, I organized a regional conference in Colombia for the dozen or so Peace Corps country directors from Guatemala to Chile. Leveo and I got on a plane bound for Bogotá with an afternoon layover in Panama City, where we took a taxi to lunch at a seafood restaurant on the Malecón. As we sat at our table, we heard what sounded like a thundering herd, at first faint, then growing louder. We walked out to the sidewalk and saw that a crush of rioters was storming through the streets. Cars were being overturned and burned, buildings set on fire, and pedestrians attacked.

Leveo and I immediately started looking for a taxi; we feared Shriver's wrath should we be no-shows at the conference in Colombia. As the stampede of young men and mayhem got closer, we picked up the pace until we were running all out to find a ride on the now-deserted streets. We finally found a cab and got back to the airport and onto our flight. Ours turned out to be the last US airliner to leave Panama before President Roberto Chiari broke diplomatic relations with the US. When we arrived in Bogotá, Shriver was on the phone saying that the Peace Corps had lost contact with its Panama office and that parents of volunteers were frantic.

The American military had been pushing its weight around for decades, and violence had been brewing along the border of the Canal

Zone for years. The conflict began as a teenage game: small groups, mostly students at the *Instituto Nacional*, a high school right across the street from the Canal Zone, hoisted Panamanian flags alongside the Stars and Stripes inside the Zone. The daring forays began in the mid fifties while I was in Panama City with ICA. Confronted by trash-talking and stone-throwing Panamanian youth, Canal Zone Police and Southern Command Army troops always overreacted.

Our ambassador to Panama, until his tour ended in August 1963, was Joseph Farland, who had performed admirably in cooling tensions and avoiding violence. No new ambassador had been installed by January 1964 as the skirmishes with students became more aggressive and the tone in the city turned ominous. On January 9, nearly two hundred Panamanian students—the largest group by far—marched into the Canal Zone carrying their flag.

In the violence that ensued over the next three days, the US embassy was damaged by rioters throwing stones, the US Information Service library went up in flames, and American factories were vandalized. More than twenty Panamanians, mostly young people, and four US soldiers were killed. Americans living in Panama fled to the relative safety of the Canal Zone, and US embassy offices were relocated there after Panama severed diplomatic relations.

While I carried on with the conference of Latin American country directors, Leveo headed back to Panama City on Shriver's orders. Shriver told him to locate every volunteer and get any staff who had fled to the Canal Zone back to work. Anyone who refused to leave the Canal Zone, said Shriver, should be sent home. The climate in Panama right after the break in relations was hostile. There were gangs of men marauding and destroying gringo automobiles and property and roughing up anyone who looked American.

Two women volunteers in Panama were living in a village called Lidice, named after a Yugoslavian town bombed out of existence by the Nazis in WWII. A truckload of Panamanian men pulled into Lidice saying they had come for "*las Americanas*." The villagers surrounded the women's bungalow, pulled out their machetes and told the young men, "You're going to have to take us first." There were other stories like that from around Panama. No volunteers were harmed or had to leave their posts in the chaotic days after the riots. Leveo spent three weeks in Panama with the country director, David Bubion, accounting for volunteers and keeping the Peace Corps running as usual.

After the conference in Bogotá, I went to visit volunteers in Medellín, Colombia's second-largest city. I was there visiting a Peace Corps volunteer in the slum when I was approached by a national guardsman. "*Meester, tiene una llamada de la casa blanca*." I had never had a phone call from the White House, so I thought I'd better take it.

I went to the police station and picked up the phone to hear my friend Bill Moyers, who was now working as President Johnson's special assistant. Moyers said the president wanted to nominate me as ambassador to Panama. He said I had better get back to Washington right away to start the process of clearance and consultations.

I was stunned. I had never coveted an ambassadorship because I was never very diplomatic—I tended to be too blunt. I didn't particularly want it, either, because I thought I already had the best job in the world. I went back to Washington with misgivings and trepidation to interview with senior people in Congress, the White House, the State Department, and the Pentagon.

Shortly before he was killed, President Kennedy had selected Frank Coffin, a former congressman from Maine and deputy director of USAID, as the next ambassador to Panama. Apparently Johnson was not inclined to give Coffin the post. Now, suddenly, there was urgency to fill the vacancy because of the diplomatic crisis in Panama.

I met with Secretary of State Dean Rusk in his imperial-sized, elegantly appointed office, where he sat with my featherweight personnel folder on his hardwood desk. He commented on the paucity of performance evaluations in my file. Both Shriver and my boss in

Panama, Vance Rogers, had wonderfully effective management styles that shunned written reviews. Sadly, Rogers couldn't provide a verbal reference for me; my Point Four mentor had been killed in a helicopter crash in Thailand while working for the World Bank in 1962.

From what he was able to glean from my background check, Rusk believed I was not cut out to be the senior US diplomat in Panama. He mentioned my interest in boxing, horse racing, and traveling to rural villages. He asked if I had ever owned a racehorse. I said yes, I had owned half-interest in a horse with good prospects that had died of diarrhea. Rusk asked me which half I owned. He made a disparaging remark about my moustache before getting down to brass tacks: "We would be reluctant to send out someone as young as you. You would be one of the youngest ambassadors in history." I was forty-three.

After eight or more interviews with Under Secretary of State George Ball, Secretary of Defense Robert McNamara, three-star generals, members of Congress, and White House staff, I felt the consensus about my nomination was wary acceptance. Ball, a big bear of a man with a ready chuckle and relaxed style, thought I was a wild card on policy issues. The top brass at the Pentagon thought we needed an Ellsworth Bunker or Averell Harriman to go in with the weight of reputation and experience.

I'm sure I was nominated because Johnson remembered our long conversation about Panama during our drive in Senegal; Bill Moyers probably seconded him. I wondered if I was being run up the flagpole to see if anyone saluted. Since no one did, would I be run back down again so they could try somebody else?

It was late January 1964, and US diplomatic relations with Panama remained severed while lawyers from both sides hashed out the wording of an agreement between the countries. I resumed my frantic pace at the Peace Corps with the assurance, although not much confidence, that it was only a matter of time before I would be formally nominated. My secretary began answering the phone, "Ambassador's office," after which most callers hung up.

I flew to Chicago that April to visit a Peace Corps training center and deliver a recruiting speech. When I landed at O'Hare, a message over the airport loudspeaker said, "Jack Vaughn, please call the White House." Impressed by the administration's ability to pinpoint my location—and to boost my profile while they were at it—I called and got Moyers. "The president has decided to go ahead, and he wants to send you down right away." I caught the next plane back to Washington.

President Johnson announced my nomination at a press conference immediately upon my return, saying that "few Americans know as many Panamanians personally as Mr. Vaughn does." I wondered if he was counting my racetrack buddies. An agreement between the two countries had been signed the day before, promising to find a "just and fair" solution to the causes of the conflict, known to both sides to be Panama's extreme discontent with the 1903 treaty giving the US total control over the Canal Zone. At the same press conference, Johnson denied reports that he had driven his car at ninety miles an hour on his most recent trip to Texas: "I am unaware that I have ever driven past seventy."

In my private briefing with Johnson later that day, he told me that he worried most about the Communist-led university students, who had become increasingly hostile and well organized. He felt they were capable of anything. "Don't get crosswise with them." Then he said, "Why don't you just sneak in? Don't announce it, and we won't announce it. Just get to your residence and wait for instructions." I agreed, grateful for a low profile going into such a high-pressure environment.

•••

By the time I left the Peace Corps in April 1964, the Latin America region had more than caught up with the Peace Corps worldwide. There were roughly four thousand volunteers working in seventeen nations, from Belize to Uruguay. Nearly half the world's Peace Corps volunteers were either in or headed for Latin America. After all those endless workdays, broken up by the occasional two-martini lunches and long, raucous dinners, my Latin America staff had become family. They were passionate, smart, funny, humble, and dedicated public servants. I am still in touch with many of them.

During the rushed, heady time of my departure from the Peace Corps, Shriver threw an impromptu farewell party for me and a small group of my closest staff at his house in Rockville, MD. It was a warm and casual event, with Shriver serving as bartender. My Latin America team presented me with several props for my new assignment: lots of shiny medals to impress the Panamanian military, a baseball bat to defend myself, and a white flag to wave when things got out of hand.

Working for Sargent Shriver had been the high point in my life. He was my hero, a courageous and inspirational figure. He supported me in absolutely everything I did. He would tell me, "Do it! I'm with you." His daring-do and infectious spirit carried the Peace Corps brilliantly. If there was anything wrong with my experience at the Peace Corps in the early sixties, it was that I didn't have the chance to be a volunteer. When I left my favorite job to join the ranks of the State Department, it was much more bitter than sweet.

I booked a flight on the Panagra milk run to Panama. It was scheduled to arrive in Panama City at 2:30 a.m. I hadn't told anybody about my travel plans, but I assumed that the State Department would notify the chargé d'affaires (who runs the embassy in the absence of the ambassador), Rufus Smith. I also guessed that the governor of the Canal Zone, Robert Fleming, and Southern Command Chief Andrew O'Meara knew I was coming.

It was the beginning of the rainy season in Panama, and my plane bumped and skidded on the runway in sheets of rain. I sat alone in the first-class cabin. As we pulled up to the terminal at Tocumen airport, I looked out my window and saw a group of men, soaking wet and holding a huge sign, streaked but still legible, that said, "Welcome, Jack."

These were men I had known a decade earlier; one was a jockey, one a former foreign minister, and a distinguished assortment in between. My downtrodden spirits soared. I was thrilled to know that my old Panamanian friends had a slightly different perspective from the senior staff in Washington about my arrival as ambassador. For the first time since I got that call from Moyers, I felt upbeat about my prospects in Panama.

6

1964–1965

I know you will love Panama. It's funny and commercial, wild and confused. And what a great thing that I could introduce you two.

—Letter to my wife, Leftie, 1969

DESPITE THE WARM WELCOME from friends and the Panamanian government's willingness to reestablish diplomatic relations, I could hardly miss the mood change in Panama City. The people's traditional ambivalence toward the United States was gone, replaced by hostility in the wake of the bloody riots in January. An angry tone was manifest in the media and academia, among the military, and in the streets lined with anti-American graffiti.

There had been no US ambassador for eight months. Such a vacuum, in my opinion, had been a significant cause of the riots. Panama's President Rodolfo Chiari and the US Chargé d'Affaires

Wallace Stuart had played passive roles in the conflict between US Canal Zone troops and National Institute high school students. It was the Marxist Panamanian minister of education, Solis Palma, who had incited and directed the students' emotional argument over sovereignty, flags, and patriotism. Palma knew that the clash between US soldiers and Latin American teenagers would be the political equivalent of spontaneous combustion. The miracle in January 1964 was that the death toll was so low.

Rage had rippled throughout the country when violence erupted in the Canal Zone that day. One of my dearest Panamanian friends told me how acutely the riots had affected him. He had been educated in the US, employed by an American company, and married to an American woman. "Yet, when I saw our kids on TV being shot and killed, my instincts took hold. I ran up to the attic to get the rifle that I had not touched in ten years. I was armed and out on the street before I knew it." By the time I arrived as ambassador three months later, anger had turned into a simmering national indignation.

Meeting with President Chiari

The diplomatic climate, however, had an entirely different feel. On my first day, I went to meet with President Chiari and his cabinet, most of whom I knew by nickname. When I walked into the presidential suite, the twelve or fourteen ministers and the president stood in a semicircle, applauding. I made my way around the room, shaking hands and slapping backs. I had been told by the legal office of the State Department that it might take several weeks to officially reestablish all channels of diplomacy; it actually took several hours over the course of a day. I also had no trouble picking up where I had left off with many friends and acquaintances from my ICA tour in Panama ten years earlier and my Peace Corps trips since then.

But in the background was rhetoric in newspaper editorials and on the radio and TV denouncing the US and asking for reparation for lives lost. The intellectual community seemed the most hostile. I had no occasion to interact with or confront the opposition; I needed a way to reach them and turn the conversation around.

The answer arrived on my desk in the form of a ninety-minute documentary about John F. Kennedy produced by the United States Information Agency (USIA) and released just a week before I came to Panama. With Bruce Herschensohn as writer-director-composer and Gregory Peck as narrator, USIA had produced a masterpiece called *John F. Kennedy: Years of Lightning, Day of Drums*. Unquestionably the greatest hero in Latin America since Simón Bolívar, Kennedy had been assassinated only five months ago. I knew that I had a powerful tool and needed to use it to maximum effect. After scraping the mold and graffiti off the embassy residence, I was ready to get into the movie business.

My staff and I invited one hundred people to each of five screenings at the residence over the course of a week. The invite list included everyone we could think of who bore a grudge: all the media, the intellectuals, the Communists, the university teachers, labor union leaders, and the military. We asked the CIA to mine their files for the most aggressive anti-US activists. We also included diplomats, senior bureaucrats, and my old friends. They were told it was an informal opportunity to join the new ambassador to remember John F. Kennedy, and asked to bring a friend.

The USIA film showcased Kennedy's courage and sense of humor, his vision and volubility, and his beautiful family. When the lights went up, there were tears and silence. Guests wanted to stay late to drink and reminisce. We talked about how Kennedy felt about Panama and what he had wanted for Latin America. No one mentioned the riots, the canal, or a new treaty.

USIA had given us a gently devastating instrument to address our political challenge of healing. After the private screenings, we broadcast the movie on national television. Within two weeks, we detected a sea-change in Panamanian attitudes; the national conversation became more even-keeled, more conciliatory, and more respectful. One of the wonderful things about Panamanians is their strong preference for love affairs over grudges.

Although we had begun the long trek back into the good graces of Panamanians, the causes of ill will remained: the proliferation of US military bases in Panama and the seriously outdated, one-sided canal treaty. The Canal Zone license plates said it all: "Dividing a country to unite a world."

As the US military had expanded the number and types of bases in the Canal Zone during WWII, there had been no corresponding upward adjustment in the amount of rent paid to Panama. During and immediately after the war, base expansion in the Zone had been dizzying: suddenly there were ten bases, then twelve, and finally, thirteen. Panama's total payment for base rentals remained under $2 million per year at a time when the Pentagon rewarded other countries around the world with rent payments in the tens of millions *per base*.

I had attended one of those rental negotiation farces in 1953 as an observer. After several days of frequently bitter bargaining with the US Secretary of the Army, Panama's chief negotiator, Foreign Minister Galileo Sols, had finally erupted. "Jesus Christ! Don't you understand we are your best friend in all of Latin America? You treat us like panhandlers, throwing us small change."

The antiquated terms of the Panama Canal Treaty were another source of national outrage in Panama. As early as 1959, a US intelligence report from Panama City had noted the damning cocktail party comments of my good friend Fernando Eleta, then the Panamanian minister of finance. After warming up with three martinis, Eleta had argued that Panama didn't receive its fair share of benefits from base rental payments and canal shipping tolls.

He had warned that if no actions were taken by the US to recognize Panama's claim to the canal, students would march on the zone, burn down the governor's house, and maybe even hang the governor for good measure. While the violence never reached that point, Eleta hit the nail on the head in predicting the trajectory of Panamanian discontent five years before the riots broke out.

The calmer mood in Panama City that spring was temporary, contingent upon the US making good on its promise to seriously address Panama's grievances. In the wake of the riots, President Johnson had appointed Special Ambassador Robert Anderson to work on a new agreement for the Canal Zone. In the first months of my ambassadorship, no progress was made on treaty negotiations.

The official US excuse for our delay was the upcoming presidential election in Panama. Set for May 10, the election had boiled down from seven candidates to three main contenders: Marco Robles, Juan de Arco Galindo, and Arnulfo Arias, the two-time former president who had been arrested and held briefly for the 1955 racetrack murder of President Remón. Robles, a former minister of the interior, was the front-runner. Known locally as "Marcos Rifle," he took a hard stance on law and order and had strong connections with the CIA and US military.

The campaign seemed routine to me, with open public debate and propaganda from all sides. The CIA or Army Intelligence apparently saw things differently. Southern Command, the joint military headquarters for all of Latin America, based in the Canal Zone, asked the Pentagon to send the Seventh Fleet from Norfolk to Panama's northern coast. It hovered just off the port of Cristóbal to quell possible Communist troublemaking during the election. At a reception the night before the vote, a marine colonel made a casual comment to me about this massive flotilla standing by; it was the first I'd heard of it.

From my previous tour in Panama, I knew that even though an ambassadorship came with the lofty words "extraordinary and plenipotentiary," the real power and final word in Panama lay with the Pentagon and the CIA. At the top of the chain was the four-star Army general in charge of Southern Command, Andrew O'Meara. Looking a lot like Douglas McArthur, O'Meara was one tough, smart, humorless fellow who scorned the Marines and thought even less of the Peace Corps.

The governor of the Canal Zone, Bob Fleming, also held significant authority. A major general in the Corps of Engineers, Bob became a good friend. Our warm relationship developed partly because Bob hated O'Meara. The balding governor kept a large sign on his desk bearing the warning, "I don't get ulcers. I give 'em." Like all modern Canal Zone governors, though, Bob eventually did suffer from ulcers of his own. I left Panama with a high opinion of both Fleming and O'Meara, who went on to greater things as commanding general of US Army Europe.

The third power player in Panama was the seasoned CIA station chief, Jake Esterline, who had been in charge of operations both at the Bay of Pigs and in Guatemala for the 1954 overthrow of President Árbenz. Esterline was the caricature of a spy: cigar-smoking, hard-drinking, a little overweight, and perpetually perspiring. He was a personal friend of the president. He always wore a slightly lumpy *guayabera*; the lump was clearly a small-caliber pistol.

My relationship with Esterline never got beyond lukewarm. He was probably scornful of my Peace Corps background, and I was suspicious of his clandestine activities. I was tempted never to believe anything he said, and he said very little. To virtually every probing question I asked, his maddening response was, "*That* strikes a familiar chord." Later in my career, when I compared notes with other ambassadors, we were of a common mind on the topic of CIA station chiefs: lucky were the ambassadors who were privy to even half of what their CIA staff were up to. I felt Esterline clued me in to about 25 percent.

Despite knowing basically where I stood in the diplomatic hierarchy—the number-four man at best—the level of obfuscation or oversight in failing to inform me of an entire Navy fleet off the coast of Panama shocked me. Two quick calls revealed that both my military attaché and Esterline were in the loop. It was such a major operation, both men claimed they felt sure the White House had informed me weeks ago.

As a novice ambassador and a political appointee, I was not at all confident about the depth of my White House support; that they hadn't bothered to tell me about a major military action at my post confirmed my worst suspicions. That night my insecurity turned into anger, and I went to the embassy and sent a message to President Johnson.

"Dear Mr. President: It has come to my attention at this late moment that the Seventh Fleet from Virginia is stationed at Cristóbal, Colón. This was a complete surprise to me, and it tells me that I am certainly not chief of mission here. I can't be effective when I'm the last one to know. This is to advise you of my resignation which is herewith submitted. I have booked a flight on Panagra to return to Washington tomorrow afternoon." If nothing else, my telegram got the full attention of the wide-eyed CIA clerk who typed it up.

The National Security Council Secretary at the time was former Harvard Dean McGeorge Bundy. Within twenty minutes of dispatching my resignation, he called my hot line from the White House. I didn't know Bundy well at all, but his was the nicest telephone call of my life—at least from a man. "There has been a dreadful oversight somewhere. I fully appreciate how you must feel. I'll take charge personally of getting to the bottom of this outrage. Your involvement in all aspects is crucial: you are unquestionably the president's top advisor there. He and I have complete confidence in you."

Within seconds of Bundy's call came another. The accent shifted from northeast to southwest, but the tone was reassuringly the same. President Johnson gave his apologies in a soft, husky voice. He punctuated every sentence with "son." "We're all proud of what you are doing for the country down there, son." I wanted to say, "Thanks, Dad," but instead thanked him for making me plenipotentiary again, in spite of the CIA, General O'Meara, and his three hundred colonels.

Johnson and Bundy smoothed things over, but I knew nothing would change. Since 1903, when Theodore Roosevelt had signed a treaty guaranteeing Panama independence from Colombia and giving the US all rights to the canal, the hierarchy and the dynamic of the Canal Zone had been set. The US military ran things in Panama, and when they didn't, the CIA did. The election-eve incident validated all my concerns about the entrenched colonial patterns I faced.

The next day, Marco Robles won the presidency in a peaceful election, and the Seventh Fleet sailed home. The election failed to speed the pace of canal treaty negotiations. Pockets of frustration bubbled to the surface among the strongest anti-American factions in Panama that summer. In June, protesters threw a homemade bomb at the Peace Corps office in Panama City. On July 4, students splashed red paint across the US embassy walls.

The small changes I brought to US-Panama relations came from my warm feelings for the country and its people and my resistance to US imperialist tendencies. In an effort to improve communication among the American silos, I set up the Panama Review Committee consisting of O'Meara, Fleming, and me. I fought the Pentagon and the CIA on issues that were important to me and that I felt were important to Panamanians. Fed up with the American colonial routine, I refused to attend protocol functions in the Canal Zone, irking the establishment by sending my vice consul instead. I opened a new consul office in David, Chiriquí Province, the embassy's first foray far from the capital city.

I could call about three hundred Panamanians by their first name, and vice versa. There was one old-timer at the Panamanian foreign office who had been there forever as a gopher, doorman, and typist. He told me that I was the first ambassador in sixty years who could speak Spanish the way Panamanians did. That meant more to me than anything said in diplomatic circles.

I enjoyed enormous support from a deeply talented embassy staff led by my deputy, Rufus Z. Smith. I was a protocol-naïve, overly casual, non-career appointee; initially, my success depended on my staff's guidance and support. Smith graciously gave me full credit for pulling off our several modest diplomatic coups on the tough road back to equilibrium after the riots.

•••

One of the most time-consuming and least favorite parts of my job as ambassador was the social circuit. I had anywhere from two to ten cocktail party invitations a day. I found these gatherings dreadfully sterile and dull, so I developed what I thought was an artful approach to that scene. I walked in, immediately took a glass in my hand, made one round, and began to glide on a diagonal toward the door. When I tired of that act, I went up-country for the weekend.

Having lived in Panama before, I had many good friends throughout the country. I loved visiting farmers in the rural areas and listening to their problems and aspirations. My dear friend Fernando Eleta, who was now foreign minister, owned a large stud farm in Boquete, a picturesque town in the northwest near the Costa Rican border. I often went there to visit him on the weekends.

In those days, security concerns were minimal. The incredibly detailed planning now required for ambassadorial travel outside the capital did not become standard operating procedure until near the end of the 1960s. All I needed with me on these trips into the bush were a plainclothes security man and a radio operator with a single sideband set.

In September, I flew up to Bocas del Toro, a provincial capital on the southern tip of Colón Island in the Caribbean Sea. It was an old United Fruit center that had slowed down since its heyday but still produced bananas and plantains. About forty miles from Bocas del Toro was a large, prosperous ranch in Chiriquicito, where I had been invited to meet with a group of poker players disguised as cattlemen to discuss hoof-and-mouth disease.

My host and pilot was a young man named Juan Ameglio. Juan, a novice pilot with a new, single-engine plane, put us down as smoothly as could be expected on a short grass strip at his ranch. My security man and radio operator awaited my return in Bocas. I was the only American among the two dozen men on the trip. We had a wonderful, lazy weekend of poker playing and good talk about political banditry and animal husbandry. I caught dozens of the world's most delicious river fish, *boca chica*.

When we boarded Juan's plane for the return trip on Sunday, our cargo had expanded. Instead of two passengers, we were four, adding my good friend Fabian "Curro" Velarde as well as a friend of Juan's in the copilot's seat. We brought a huge, wet cardboard box full of iced *boca chica* fillets that must have weighed one hundred pounds. It had been raining off and on all weekend, making the ground soggy and the grass high.

Our overloaded plane did somehow manage to leave the strip with a wallowing motion, like a hippo struggling out of a marsh. With the stall horn blaring, we stayed airborne for five seconds at about forty feet. Then one wing dipped and we nosed down at a sharp angle, crashing headfirst into an enormous *cedro amargo* (cedar) tree. Flying fish filets and ice cubes clobbered us from behind.

Immediately there was the smell of burning wires, smoke, and a hissing sound. Curro was groaning next to me, and the pilot and copilot were unconscious. As we crashed, I had assumed a fetal praying position and was a bloody mess from a self-inflicted thumbnail cut between my eyes. Worse and more enduring was a deep hip bruise caused by the Colt .45 Curro was wearing on his belt when he fell on top of me.

Our friends from the ranch arrived in seconds, trying frantically to open the door, which had jammed from the compression. Finally someone arrived with a hacksaw and we crawled out of the wreck. I felt whiplash in every joint and was bent in pain. The others were worse off. Curro, while technically intact, seemed debilitated. A presidential press secretary and bon vivant, Curro never fully recovered from the crash; he died very young just a couple of years later. Juan and his friend regained consciousness but were badly banged up and had some broken bones. The four of us were woozy and gimpy, still in shock, trying to crack jokes and act macho.

With our plane out of commission, Porfirio Gomez, a dear friend who was head of the agricultural extension program, suggested going by boat to the airport at Bocas del Toro. The four of us survivors and a cast of about twenty friends set off on an old houseboat. Half the boat had been converted into a bar, which we turned into our floating recovery room.

The weather was blustery, and the sea rough. Our barge was powered by a small outboard motor that seemed to be propelling us in reverse against the heavy seas. The ten-mile trip from the ranch to Bocas del Toro took about four hours and ten cases of beer. As we inched along, the weather grew worse, the sea became slate-gray, and the sky almost black.

The provincial governor of Bocas del Toro, a wiry and stooped little fellow of Jamaican ancestry, greeted us most graciously on the dock. Seeing our makeshift slings and bandages and our crippled gaits, he was eager to hear our story. Then he warned us of an approaching storm that he described as "monstrous." "This will really be a dandy," he said in English, "and will surely blow down all our bananas and plantains."

With a population of ten thousand, Bocas had a quaint but dilapidated feel, with quiet streets lined by tall palms, old homes, and crumbling churches. The governor invited us to stay with him at the nicest house in town, owned by the sanitary engineer. It was a three-story home in classic United Fruit Company style, with unpainted wood and spacious balconies. We went up to the third-floor balcony overlooking the Caribbean, where we sampled our host's best rum and *patacones* (fried green plantains). I was only occasionally able to stanch the blood flow from the cut in my forehead and was now also bleeding out of both nostrils.

As we steadily sedated ourselves with rum, the winds intensified. The vintage house began to shake and creak. Then, ominously, the wind stopped. Our host shouted at us to head for cover, and we all stumbled down the stairs to the cellar. Given our impaired coordination, I can't believe we made it in time. The tornado hit just as we shut the basement door; it lasted three long minutes.

Torrential rain followed: six or eight inches in an hour. The cellar started to fill up. The sanitary engineer had stored his dead soldiers there, and soon we were up to our chests in water and hundreds of floating, clinking bottles. My old buddy Curro, by then barely conscious, shouted bravely above the clinking, "I'll drink to that!"

After the rain abated, we climbed out of the water like muskrats to find the town of Bocas del Toro decimated. The storm had wound its way through the town's streets, destroying two churches, two school buildings, and whole rows of homes. More than ninety buildings were destroyed and five hundred people left homeless. One four-year-old girl was killed when her house collapsed. The tornado hit at 11:30 p.m. while most people—completely unaware it was coming—were asleep.

The governor, a policeman, a Peace Corps volunteer living in Bocas, and I picked our way through the splintered and muddied town with flashlights to see if we could help. We saw that dozens of people were badly hurt. There were no medical supplies, no doctors, very few flashlights, and no hope of starting a fire.

I had reunited with my security detail and radio man when we docked in Bocas. Miraculously, the wet radio equipment worked. We got through at about 3:00 a.m. to the Southern Command Air Force headquarters at Quarry Heights in the Canal Zone. I told the colonel in charge what had happened and what I thought the needs were; he had his own checklist of questions. "Roger. Will inform Pentagon and Secretary of State immediately. Will have two loaded C-47's and two U-10's circling Bocas at daybreak. Please clear all debris from the landing strip. Good luck."

It was a long night with a lot of suffering; we would have traded all our bananas for an aspirin. At daybreak, four fully loaded US aircraft circled above the obliterated town. Most of the villagers were down on their knees in prayer when the planes touched down. The Air Commandos brought rations, medical supplies, and countless cots and blankets. These Air Force personnel were well trained, quick, friendly, and Spanish-speaking. Within three or four hours they had attended to the worst injuries and splinted all the broken bones, including those of my fellow plane crash victims.

There are more times than one might imagine when being a US government employee abroad becomes a source of tremendous pride—of country and competence, technology and character, and generosity. Few thrills, however, could surpass what I experienced that morning of salvation in Bocas. The chemistry among the Air Force crews, medics, and villagers, especially the children, was palpable. It was a glorious moment for US-Panama relations: the US military was in its finest hour, asking no questions and saving the day.

Returning to Albrook Air Force Base in the Canal Zone in a triumphantly empty C-47 marked the high point of my respect for the US armed forces in Panama. I was greeted with lots of attention from the media, who had caught wind of my double-catastrophe weekend. Curro Velarde's advice on how I should characterize our plane overloaded with *boca chica* fillets was, "*Bueno es el culantro, pero no tanto*," Panamanian parlance meaning, "You can have too much of a good thing."

Though I received a warm welcome from news outlets, I faced a very unhappy CIA station chief. Esterline thought it scandalous that the American ambassador puddle-jumped across the country in single-engine planes "flown by amateur cowboy pilots." My bosses at the State Department agreed. "Didn't you know," Esterline said, "that the CIA has several high-performance aircraft based at Paitilla Airport?" Beginning immediately, he assured me, he would put such "assets" at my disposal whenever I wanted to fly up-country.

Considering this the kind of offer I should exploit early and often, I scheduled a little diplomatic junket up the Pacific coast the following weekend. As promised, it was a beautiful asset. The plane was loaded with electronic gear and leather seats, and it looked very fast. Porfirio Gomez and I were the only passengers. As we took off and headed out over the bay just north of Panama City, there was a loud pop and a horrible ripping sound. Immediately the plane veered wildly to the right as I saw a piece of the tail fly past my window.

We made it back to the Paitilla runway via a scary corkscrew descent and a hard landing that realigned my spine and just about collapsed the gear. So much for the vaunted CIA assets, I thought, as we picked up another plane. Back in my office on Monday, I told the story in great detail to my perspiring station chief, informing him I would be switching back to single-engine planes with Panamanian cowboy pilots. Esterline did not object. From then on, our conversations began with my asking Esterline how his assets were.

That October, just two weeks after my dramatic return from Bocas del Toro, new President Marco Robles was sworn in. I attended the inauguration and sat with Robles's new cabinet, all of us decked out in white suits with thin black bow ties and shiny black shoes. After the ceremony, we walked en masse back to the presidential palace, called *Palacio de las Garzas* because of the huge African herons that roamed the courtyard.

At the palace, I presented Robles with a $2.4 million US loan for agricultural projects. A week later came another $2 million for research on Panama's long-range improvement plans and $3.5 million to pay outstanding government bills. The aid was an act of goodwill toward this new administration but also critical to improving the lives of Panamanians in rural areas. Now that the new Robles administration was in place, there was no excuse for the US not to move ahead with treaty negotiations. The Panamanians had not forgotten their grievances or their goals.

In November, after President Johnson himself was reelected in a landslide over Senator Barry Goldwater, I sent the president a telegram detailing the consensus of the Panama Review Committee, that formidable threesome of Ambassador Vaughn, Governor Fleming, and General O'Meara. I described the time between November and January as "a unique but fleeting opportunity to avoid a serious setback to our national interests here."

Inauguration of President Robles

The Robles administration had already come under attack by Communists and nationalists for its failure to progress on a new canal treaty. The discontent would no doubt build to a crescendo on the anniversary of the deadly riots on January 9, called Martyr's Day in Panama. Our committee felt it was crucial that President Johnson make a clear policy statement indicating a willingness to substantially revise the canal agreement. If not, we feared a government overthrow in Panama that would spell much bigger problems for the US.

American foreign policy regarding the Canal Zone was complicated by our intention to build a new sea-level canal in Panama, an idea that had been around for decades. When French engineers had originally tried to construct a canal through Panama in the late 1800s, they had used the sea-level model of the Suez Canal in Egypt. But the sliding mud and clay and changing elevations on the Panamanian isthmus had defeated the French, and when the Americans gained the rights to build a canal in Panama, Congress had voted to build a system of locks instead. The sea-level canal idea resurfaced like a fashion trend every few decades. In the 1960s the Johnson administration was quite determined to build one in Panama or, if the Panamanians wouldn't cooperate, in Colombia.

On December 2, I attended a meeting in the White House Cabinet Room with Johnson, McGeorge Bundy, Acting Secretary of State Averill Harriman, Assistant Secretary of State Thomas Mann, Special Ambassador Robert Anderson, Deputy Secretary of Defense Cyrus Vance, and Secretary of the Army Steven Ailes. In his talks with Panamanian officials, Ambassador Anderson had made it clear that the US would not relinquish the rights to the canal. But Anderson stressed to Johnson the importance of creating a new treaty with Panama, however small our concessions were.

Johnson wondered why we couldn't just mandate changes to the existing treaty by executive order. Anderson understood, as I did, that the canal was an emotional and patriotic issue for the Panamanians. After years of colonial-style occupation, they needed—and deserved—a new start with a new treaty. Assistant Secretary Mann insisted that the new treaty be negotiated in conjunction with our new, sea-level canal agreement.

On December 18, just a few weeks before Martyr's Day, President Johnson announced that the US would negotiate a new canal treaty with Panama. It was a major step in US foreign policy, which until then had excluded any possibility of a new treaty. That overture did provide the hope Panamanians needed to stave off rioting in January 1965, but fulfillment of their hope was seriously delayed. It wasn't until 1977—twelve years later—that President Carter signed a new treaty ensuring Panama's eventual ownership of the canal on December 31,

1999. A sea-level canal, still a favorite topic of conversation for civil engineers and environmentalists, was never built.

Around the same time as Johnson's historic announcement in Washington, I received a late-night telephone call at home in Panama City. A low, menacing voice told me I was going to be murdered. The same call came the next night. Jake Esterline had Panamanian security bug my phone and instructed me to ask questions to keep my caller on the line. The would-be assassin called three or four times a week late at night. My routine response to his description of my impending doom was, "*Interesante. Cuenteme mas.*" ("Interesting. Tell me more.")

My caller told me in Spanish that he was going to slit my throat; the next time he said he'd slit my throat with a hunting knife; then he told me how he'd slit my throat very slowly, and so on. At first he said he was coming for me in a few weeks, then next week, and finally "*mañana.*" By then the security team had determined that the calls were coming from Ecuador.

There was a nonstop flight the next day from Guayaquil, Ecuador, to Panama City. The few people on the plane were scrutinized thoroughly by the CIA. There was a slight fellow named Moreno, about five feet two inches, with an oversize moustache. He was carrying $50,000 in $100 bills, a phony Ecuadoran passport with a fake Panamanian visa, and a very large hunting knife strapped to his thigh. The most damning pieces of evidence were an exquisitely designed map of the area around my residence and a very flattering picture of me.

The Panamanian National Guard arrested Moreno without charges and sent him to the brutal maximum security prison on the island of Coiba in the Pacific. All they ever got out of him was that he was a member of the Communist Party of Ecuador. Many years later, I heard from a member of the military in Panama that Moreno had been killed on Coiba in a machete fight. I don't know what happened to that $50,000, but I imagine it didn't go toward prison improvements.

•••

The head of Panama's National Guard was a gentle and friendly fellow named Vallarino; Lilo was his nickname. He was low-key, often dressed in plain clothes, and I got along well with him. When he attended diplomatic events, he always brought two majors as his protocol aides: Boris Martínez and Omar Torrijos. These two didn't speak much English, but they had good posture and shiny buttons and were ubiquitous as the Panamanian military presence at official functions.

Torrijos was the *comandante* in Chiriquí province, a large and well-developed area on the western border. He was relatively unknown until he became part of a program sponsored by the Pentagon called Civic Action. The program was based on the theory that banana republics would become more stable if national troops were out performing public works rather than holed up in the barracks drinking, playing poker, and planning coups. Through Civic Action, the US military funded Torrijos and his troops to inoculate peasants, build roads, and install public bathrooms and showers. As a result, Major Torrijos became a year-round Santa Claus and hero among the rural people of Chiriquí.

I visited Torrijos and his Civic Action program while I was ambassador. The major was a quiet and agreeable guy with rugged good looks and chiseled features that would lend themselves well to busts and statues. He brought me along with a caravan of medical personnel who were pulling teeth and administering vaccinations in the countryside. Torrijos and I rode horses. He wore a cowboy hat and looked like the Marlboro man; I looked like Woody Allen.

Out of nowhere, a chubby little man on a mule clattered up a rocky, narrow trail. When he reached us, he mumbled something that sounded profane to Torrijos before being introduced to me as Lt.

Manuel Noriega. I had an immediate and visceral negative reaction to him.

I didn't know it at the time, but Noriega had been bad news from the very beginning. A mediocre student, he graduated late from the National Institute, where the January riots originated. He somehow wangled a scholarship to military school in Peru, where he excelled. The week after he graduated, he raped a teenage girl in Lima. He was assigned as a second lieutenant in Colón on the northern coast of Panama, where in his first month he raped another girl and almost killed her brother who tried to defend her.

Torrijos obviously thought Noriega could be useful to him. He was a tough *hombre*, and Torrijos made him his enforcer. In spite of the training they received at Pentagon schools in the US and abroad, the Panamanian military was, like all Latin American militaries, corrupt. Noriega helped Torrijos collect bribes and distribute payoffs. The situation became far worse when the military got involved in the drug trade, which happened some years after I left Panama.

With Major Torrijos on a Civic Action trip

The Civic Action program earned Torrijos widespread accolades for providing badly needed goods and services to the people of his province. With a taste for politics and tremendous support from *campesinos* around Panama, Torrijos seemed poised for big things, but I never could have guessed how big. Three years after I left Panama, he and Boris Martínez overthrew President Arnulfo Arias. Torrijos then exiled Martínez and ruled as Panama's de facto dictator for the next thirteen years. I would get to know him much better during his years in power.

•••

In February 1965, after less than a year in Panama, I was visiting Bob Fleming at his office in the Canal Zone when I received a call on the scrambler phone from the White House. It was my friend and supporter Bill Moyers. He said that the president wanted me to become assistant secretary of state for Latin America, replacing the towering and controversial Thomas Mann, who was moving up to become under secretary for economic growth, energy, and the environment. Once again, I was caught off guard and accepted immediately.

Still quite idealistic, I was excited to work on Latin American issues at the policy level. I hoped to use my elevated position in Washington to improve the floundering Latin American aid program, the Alliance for Progress. As usual, the reaction to my promotion among US diplomats and high-ranking officials was skepticism and doubt. In their view, I still lacked seasoning, despite my time in the Panamanian soup.

Most Panamanians were extremely flattering in their parting comments about me; of course, I would now be in a better position to forward their causes. Dr. George W. Westerman, editor and publisher of the *Panama Tribune*, generously wrote, "His personal warmth and understanding are qualities which inspire people and were the main factors in the establishment of normal relations between the U.S. and Panama."

President Robles spoke graciously to the press, emphasizing my affection for the Panamanians and my fairness in approaching problems, though he left out my exceptional talent for cards. I had spent many weekends on ranches and beaches playing poker with Robles and his cabinet, strong competitors all. Since I seldom saw Robles except during rural weekend getaways, the president referred to me as "*el embajador campesino*" (peasant ambassador). Foreign Minister Eleta and other cabinet members called me "*Colorado*" (Red). Since everyone in Panama has a nickname, I felt very Panamanian with two good ones.

I had been ambassador just short of a year, but I felt that the US relationship with Panama was out of danger and growing stronger. I left the ambassadorship in the capable hands of another former boxer, Charles Adair. Feeling energized by my heady promotion, I never suspected that I was jumping out of the frying pan and into the fire. I traded a plush mattress at the ambassador's residence in Panama City for a lumpy State Department office couch, my new bed for the next month. My timing in arriving at Foggy Bottom could not have been worse: three weeks after I became assistant secretary of state, President Johnson sent the Marines into the Dominican Republic.

7

1965–1966

The greatest instrument of diplomacy is honesty, except when you deal with Congress. With Congressmen you have to go through a kind of dance of the peacocks.

—Interview with the *New York Post*, 1975

IN MY NEW POSITION at the State Department, I was both assistant secretary of state for inter-American affairs and the coordinator of the Alliance for Progress, our foreign aid program in Latin America. When President Johnson inherited the Alliance in late 1963, it was floundering under the ethereal guidance of Kennedy's Latin America gurus Arthur Schlesinger Jr., Dick Goodwin, and Ed Martin. Critics of the trio claimed that they had around five weeks of combined total experience in Latin America.

When Johnson's former Senate colleagues made noises about appointing an assistant secretary of state for inter-American affairs who really understood the region, the president chose Thomas Mann, a fellow hard-nosed Texan whom he held in great esteem. Mann had been assistant secretary once before, during the transition from the Eisenhower to the Kennedy administration. In between, he had served as US ambassador to Mexico.

Mann was a pragmatist who ran the Alliance for Progress like the Marshall Plan: big loans and grants, asset allocations determined by Washington economists, and no real interest in accountability if the country's politics were right. Mann was remembered in Panamanian diplomatic circles as a gruff, humorless fellow who spoke Mexican border Spanish and was pro-military and pro-business. *Newsweek* called Mann "the tough Texas lawyer who as President Johnson's 'Mr. Latin America' chilled many a Latin heart with his passion for balanced budgets and currency stabilization."

After just over a year as assistant secretary, Mann was being promoted to the State Department's number three position, under secretary of state for economic affairs. However, Johnson still referred to Mann as his "one clear voice" on issues relating to Latin America. This sent me a mixed message as I assumed my new role with no voice but a huge amount of responsibility.

When I arrived in Washington to succeed Mann, I had more than fifteen years of experience in the Foreign Service but was a newcomer to Foggy Bottom and relatively unknown there. Unlike many young diplomats who started their careers as desk officers in the State Department, my jobs had taken place almost entirely overseas. I knew the workings of the Alliance for Progress firsthand from my travels through Latin America with the Peace Corps. That scathing letter from Venezuela's President Betancourt to President Kennedy denouncing the program was fresh in my mind as I prepared to take on the Alliance.

The arrangement with Mann had all the potential to be awkward and frustrating, and it lived up to its potential. Though technically

Mann had been my boss while I served as ambassador to Panama, I had never met him. I found him uptight and suspicious, and our relationship was icy and distrustful from the start. Publically, I was often asked how my views and approach differed from Mann's; by necessity, my standard response was, "I'm a Mann man."

A core group of Foreign Service officers who worked with Mann in Mexico during his ambassadorship had come back to Washington with him. Mann kept them close, and they became known at State as the Mexican mafia. My principal deputy, Bob Sayre, was a colleague and friend of Mann's from Mexico. One of Mann's top aides, Jim Johnston, dated and eventually married my administrative assistant, Maggie Conrad. The mafia had infiltrated my office, so everything I did was known to Mann. He kept close tabs on me, and I was expected to tow his line. Mann influenced policy decisions in Latin America more than anyone else in the administration during my time at the State Department.

Though I answered to Mann on a daily basis, my real boss was Secretary of State Dean Rusk. I had last seen Rusk when he interviewed me for the ambassadorship to Panama. Then he had seemed skeptical of my qualifications and had criticized my mustache and my youth. When I walked into his office in March of 1965, still mustachioed and a mere fourteen months older, Rusk was warm and complimentary. Obviously my track record in Panama had improved my standing with him. "I hear people in Panama refer to you as the peasant ambassador." I assured him that was true. My meetings with Rusk would be cordial and brief; he was consumed with the steadily escalating Vietnam War.

My superior senior staff made everything at State easier and more fun. Though he came from Mann's camp, my senior deputy Bob Sayre proved to be loyal to me and enormously helpful in navigating the bureaucracy. David Bronheim, a sharp Washington lawyer, became my deputy coordinator of the Alliance for Progress in July. Also providing insight and experience was Tony Solomon, who worked as my deputy before becoming assistant secretary for economic affairs.

Of tremendous talent and work ethic were my three special assistants: Diego Asencio, Margaret Beshore, and Charley Thomas. Diego had worked at the embassy in Panama and then as the Panama desk officer at State when I was ambassador; Margaret and Charley were both part of my A-team from Peace Corps-Latin America. Another Peace Corps stalwart, Leveo Sanchez, became my director of technical assistance for the Alliance.

The State Department building covered four square blocks and contained five miles of corridors. The Latin America division of State was the largest: I oversaw six hundred people in Washington and roughly two thousand employees overseas. The combined budget for State and the Alliance was $3.5 billion. The daily business of embassies in Mexico, Central and South America, and the Caribbean funneled through my office, and all of the ambassadors reported directly to me. Because I received at least five thousand pages of telegrams every day, I designated a poor soul to come into the office at 4:00 a.m. to screen the telegrams for me and whittle them down to the must-reads. When I arrived at 8:00 a.m., I had about 150 pages to peruse before my first meeting.

With Leveo Sanchez (right) and Rep. Edward Roybal of California (left)

I felt the need to get my footing quickly atop the complex pyramid of committees, subcommittees, programs, budgets, politics, and personnel. In those first weeks, I struggled to find a place where my talents and my interests coalesced and I could rise above the everyday paper parade to get some actual work done. Even with three superlative deputies and three superstar special assistants, most of whom knew the ropes, I had the sinking feeling of never quite being on top of my workload. I realized quickly that overseeing both the Alliance for Progress and the diplomatic mission in Latin America was the equivalent of two full-time jobs.

To get up to speed on each country under my purview, I asked the foreign aid and State desk officers, country by country, to prepare a briefing and meet with me for thirty minutes each. These sessions greatly increased my comfort level, especially in the cases where I realized that I knew more than my staff. If I had any advantage coming into Foggy Bottom, it was the fact that in the previous four years I had been on the road meeting all the important players in Latin America. From my Peace Corps work, I knew the presidents, foreign ministers, and ministers of agriculture and education, and I usually had a grasp of the country's assets, quirks, and challenges.

After the briefings on each country in my region, I was most concerned about the Dominican Republic. Its first democratically elected president, Juan Bosch, had been overthrown by the right-wing military in 1963, and President Kennedy had suspended US aid to the country. A leftist faction in the military had subsequently been gaining strength, and we feared it might try to take over, especially if reinforcements arrived from Fidel Castro. I asked the three people at State directly involved with the DR to come back to me in two days with more analysis.

The Dominican Republic, which shares the island of Hispaniola with the much poorer nation of Haiti, has a politically tumultuous history in which the US has played a significant role. Its capital, Santo

Domingo, was Spain's first capital in the New World. After years of Spanish, French, Haitian, and independent rule, the country fell into political chaos in 1916. Interested in preserving the nearby shipping routes to and from the new Panama Canal, President Woodrow Wilson sent Marines to the DR to bring order. The United States occupied the country for eight years with a tough military government that suppressed the opposition but also accomplished a great deal in the way of infrastructure development and economic growth.

After the US pulled out (a campaign promise delivered by President Warren Harding), the DR settled into its own brand of military government under the brutal regime of General Rafael Leonidas Trujillo. He was famous for naming all the country's biggest cities and landmarks after himself and his relatives. Trujillo slaughtered thousands of Haitians who crossed into his country, as well as anyone associated with the opposition. Amazingly, Trujillo enjoyed the support of the US from 1930 until 1960, when his agents tried to assassinate his vocal critic, Venezuela's President Betancourt. Trujillo himself was assassinated in 1961, and the Dominicans democratically elected Juan Bosch two years later.

After only seven months in office, Bosch was ousted by Trujillo loyalists in the Dominican military, a move that Kennedy had condemned but Johnson tolerated under the so-called Mann Doctrine. Tom Mann believed that military regimes in Latin America were just fine, so long as they kept the Communists out and maintained relations with the US. Now the DR's right-wing regime was looking shaky as leftist rebel activity in the Dominican military picked up.

After learning about the unrest in the DR in mid April 1965, I called our ambassador there, William Tapley Bennett Jr. I asked Bennett to come up to Washington immediately so we could discuss the complex political situation in the DR. Bennett said his mother was dying in Georgia and asked if he could stop to see her on his way to DC. I agreed, and the next day I left Washington for a weekend meeting of Latin American intellectuals and power players in Cuernavaca, Mexico.

No sooner had I unpacked my bags in beautiful downtown Cuernavaca than I got a call from Bob Sayre telling me that the leftist faction of the Dominican military was moving to take over the government and serious fighting had broken out in Santo Domingo. The president wanted me back in Washington immediately. Johnson had turned to Mann when the coup began, and the two of them, along with the National Security Council led by McGeorge Bundy, had driven the decision to mobilize the US Marines on aircraft carrier *Boxer* for a potential invasion.

The right-wing military junta who had overthrown President Bosch in 1963 were known as Loyalists and headed by Donald Reid. Reid's administration consisted of suppressive Trujillo types who were unpopular with the Dominicans. The opposition leftist military faction was led by Colonel Francisco Caamaño and augmented by a large contingent of civilian Bosch supporters who called themselves the Constitutionalists. During the coup that April, the leftist rebels captured Reid, and Col. Caamaño became provisional president. The Constitutionalists took over the airwaves and called for the killing of all police officers. President Johnson feared the country could become another Cuba.

When I landed at Washington National, I was met by Dominican desk officer Kennedy Crockett, who brought me up to date on White House actions. It was an awkward conversation, because these were meetings and decisions I should have been part of. Crockett had the task of writing up the president's "instruction" on the DR, readying the military to act. He explained that to be valid, the instruction needed my signature, even though I had not attended the meetings or been consulted on the decisions.

Not sure I agreed with an intervention, and certain I disagreed with signing a document I had no part in creating, I told Crockett I wouldn't sign. He was taken aback and tried his best to talk me into it. He argued that I would never be held accountable, that the authority ultimately lay with the president, and that my signature was only a formality. I held my ground, and by the time we reached my office, Crockett had given up. He scratched out my name on the instruction, replaced it with his, and signed it. In the ensuing pandemonium of the next several weeks, I'm certain no one noticed his revision.

Johnson was hot under the collar when I arrived at the White House for what would be the first of many daily meetings about the DR. He asked me what the hell I was doing in Cuernavaca. He followed up with, "Why the hell is Ambassador Bennett in Georgia?" Back to Santo Domingo went Bennett and back to the State Department went I.

Johnson ordered me to quickly drum up support from our friends in Latin America for an intervention in the DR crisis. He knew that with Vietnam in full swing, the public had little stomach for American military actions abroad, and he didn't want us looking like the heavy again.

Bob Sayre and I immediately launched a very active campaign to convince the Organization of American States (OAS) and several cherry-picked Latin American ambassadors in Washington to get involved. We lobbied for a diplomatic commitment from Brazil, Panama, Costa Rica, and Colombia to send their foreign ministers to the DR to help defuse the explosive situation there. We worked feverishly, making calls, taking meetings, and putting the best possible spin on an intervention, but the OAS wouldn't engage; the Latin ambassadors didn't want to touch it. Everyone saw this as a classic Big-Brother-with-a-big-stick operation and wanted no part of it.

I attended daily and sometimes twice-daily meetings with the president, Rusk, Bundy, Mann, Special Assistant Bill Moyers, Under Secretary of State George Ball, Deputy Secretary of Defense Cyrus Vance, Chairman of the Joint Chiefs General Earle Wheeler, Defense

Secretary Robert McNamara, FBI Director J. Edgar Hoover, CIA Director William Raborn, and others. I brought only bad news: I had been unable to garner support or even much interest in our anti-Castro cause. Meanwhile in the DR, Ambassador Bennett had been unable to get either side engaged in a conversation. Heavy fighting in Santo Domingo was spreading to the countryside.

There was a sizable American community living in Santo Domingo as well as a strong Peace Corps presence. We also learned that a large contingent of American meat-packers had been attending a conference there when the coup took place and were unable to get home. Reports of violence and Cuban involvement were increasing. Ambassador Bennett called my office to say that he had been forced to take cover under his desk when rebels fired shots into his office suite. The Israeli ambassador reported that a cabin cruiser had put ashore at his dock and was abandoned. He said the cruiser was capable of carrying fifty people and contained evidence that the passengers were Cuban terrorists.

We had an all-day White House meeting on April 28, four days after the coup and three days since I had joined the conversation about our possible intervention in the DR. The Pentagon pushed hard for troops on the ground; they had already positioned the USS *Boxer* off the coast of Santo Domingo. But we still had no international support and little solid information about the confusing political situation. Johnson didn't trust the CIA or their intelligence coming out of the DR. By the end of the day, it was decided that we weren't ready to send in the Marines.

Fifteen minutes after the meeting broke, I was standing in a corridor of the White House when Bill Moyers came running past me with a handful of telegrams. "We're going in!" The FBI had just intercepted a commercial telegram from the meat-packing group to their Chicago office. It read in part, "They're going to cut our throats." The telegram pushed Johnson over the edge. He ordered the invasion, called Operation Power Pack, to protect the lives of American citizens in the DR and prevent a Communist takeover.

That night, four hundred Marines were airlifted into Santo Domingo to begin evacuating Americans. The next day, 1,500 more troops arrived to get Americans and other foreigners out safely. The president also asked J. Edgar Hoover to send down fifty FBI agents to do the job of the CIA. Helicopters landed in the area between the US embassy and the Embajador Hotel, where American and other foreign nationals were ordered to await evacuation. In several waves, around six thousand evacuees from thirty different countries were ferried to Navy ships and taken to San Juan, Puerto Rico.

As foreigners were swiftly moved out, the Marines surrounded Santo Domingo to contain the fighting. The Pentagon wanted to prevent guerilla warfare in the mountains, which had been Castro's great advantage in his takeover of Cuba from his base in the Sierra Maestra. The Marines shortly had Santo Domingo sealed off in what was dubbed a "downtown Sierra Maestra" by Roberto "El Chato" Alemán, the Panamanian ambassador to Washington.

Initially, our goals were to evacuate Americans and other foreign nationals and keep Castro's Communists from infiltrating. We hoped that if we contained the fighting, the Dominicans would reach their own settlement.

Back in Washington, the meetings were constant, and a full night's sleep was but a dream. We set up a crisis task force at the State Department manned by five staffers twenty-four hours a day. Overnight I dramatically increased the DR's foreign aid to give the Alliance staff in Santo Domingo the means to buy plasma, food, and other emergency supplies.

I had come to believe that the US intervention was warranted, if only to save the lives of our citizens, but I disagreed strongly with the scale of our military presence. The question of troop levels was handled by General Wheeler, the Chairman of the Joint Chiefs. He was sending in another battalion—one thousand men—every day. Ultimately, we had forty-two thousand troops on the island. I said at one meeting that I thought it was outrageous to send so many troops to such a small area, especially when we had no mandate to intervene and no clear path to peace. I was put down pretty harshly by the president and never brought it up again.

Johnson went on television the night of the invasion to make his case to the American people: "What began as a popular Democratic revolution that was committed to democracy and social justice moved into the hands of a band of Communist conspirators." He closed with, "We will defend our nation against all those who seek to destroy not only the United States, but also every free country of this hemisphere." Despite the patriotic rhetoric, the reaction to our military intervention in the DR was bad on all fronts. The media was hostile, the public disgusted, and Congress up in arms. Johnson's stalwart liberals couldn't stomach it.

Amid the uproar, Johnson took full responsibility for the DR. He became chief strategist, Secretary of State, and Dominican desk officer, macro and micromanaging every aspect of the invasion. With his capacity to work two ten-hour shifts a day (sleeping from midnight to four) Johnson was a reinvigorated, one-man State Department.

During these frenzied days, Johnson called me regularly at five in the morning at my home. His comments usually started with, "Goddamn it, Vaughn." On his more charitable days, it was "Goddamn it, boy." Then he unloaded his problems and ideas for the day, and detailed my deficiencies—a pathetic performance on a TV talk show, or fainthearted lobbying of the OAS. Before I got dressed, I had my marching orders on about ten different points.

Though it could be painful, Johnson's constant communicating and probing was impressive; he mercilessly solicited opinions from every participant at our meetings and relentlessly extracted every detail of information on the topics that concerned him.

I was still working to squeeze even a drop of support from our Latin American allies. Their reaction to our unilateral intervention was outrage, especially in Mexico, where sympathy for Cuba prevailed. Leaders across Latin America thought the invasion was unwarranted, unprincipled, arrogant, and excessive. They considered the threat of civil war and Castro poor excuses for our bullying behavior. Though I didn't fully agree with our military approach, I worked hard to win hearts and minds for Johnson. For my efforts, I was lambasted by the Latin American diplomatic community as a former Peace Corps man who had turned his back on peace.

The media wasn't helping our cause. The coverage and the commentary were negative and hurt our efforts to build support at home and around the world. About five days after the invasion, the president called me: "What we really need to deal with these pinko journalists is a white paper." The paper Johnson wanted was to explain in detail everything we had done to forestall sending in troops: every diplomatic overture, every communication with the DR and its neighbors to avoid military action. He and I both knew that the extent of our coalition-building was my whirlwind four days with embassies around town before the invasion. It was going to be a short paper.

My first draft was three pages. When I gave it to Johnson later that day, he couldn't believe it. "I said white paper! This is a little note!" So I went back to my office to consult with Sayre, and with some creativity we came up with twice as many pages. That one immediately bounced back, too. I enlisted my assistant Margaret Beshore to surf cables by the hundreds in pursuit of tidbits to support our fabrication that the US had gone all out for a nonmilitary, multination solution in the DR. Then we inserted more bureaucratic expressions, flowery language, and wider margins.

About two weeks after my original draft, we came up with a rather thick volume of exaggerations and baloney that spanned almost 150 pages. We had it printed with a nice cover and sent it over to President Johnson on a Friday night. I carried a copy with me to the White House for a Saturday morning meeting on the DR. As I walked wearily into the Cabinet Room, I found the president sitting at the head of the table, alone, with only my white paper before him. He was stone-faced and didn't look at me as I came in.

Being a more junior figure among the participants at these meetings, I sat down toward the far end of the table, closing my eyes briefly. I had been hitting it very hard, getting at most two or three hours of sleep a night on my office couch. People kept telling me how awful I looked—"like a mortician's assistant" was one description. On my shoulders was the responsibility for our foreign aid program, our diplomatic mission, and now the creation of this white paper, an elaborate and largely unsupportable defense of our intervention.

All the usual suspects came to the meeting that morning: Rusk, Bundy, Mann, Moyers, Ball, Vance, Wheeler, McNamara, Hoover, and Raborn, with their staff assistants sitting along the wall. There were about thirty people in the room. Johnson sat sphinxlike until everyone had arrived and was seated. Then he leaned forward and launched into a full-out attack on me and my white paper. He said that I was a total incompetent; worse than that, I was disloyal, lazy, dense, and inarticulate. The president questioned my qualifications for holding any public position higher than a GS-3 (I was a GS-18.). He said I didn't understand what he wanted or what the White House needed. From every point of view, I had been a colossal failure.

The tirade probably lasted only three minutes, until the president ran out of demeaning adjectives, but it felt like an eternity. I could sense the blood draining from my head and extremities. No one at the table looked at me. I felt quite certain this was the president firing me; if he wasn't firing me, he was telling the world that I was grossly unfit for my position. Given the strange dynamic with Mann as the point man on Latin America anyway, I thought I had nothing left to contribute.

I rose somewhat shakily, put both fists on the table and leaned forward. "Mr. President, you shall have my resignation just as quickly as I can get to a typewriter."

"Sit down, you little shit," Johnson growled. I slowly sat down, and the meeting began. Within two minutes, a message was slipped down the table to me from Bill Moyers. It said, "Welcome to the club." Moyers was referring to the abuse that he and (especially) Jack Valenti, Johnson's special assistant, had suffered for years as those closest and dearest to Johnson. Leave it to Moyers, my friend on the inside, to boost my spirits when I needed it most. Predictably, the white paper went nowhere, and we continued to take a beating in the press.

A rare high point for me, and it was vicarious, came from the outstanding performance of the Peace Corps volunteers in Santo Domingo during the crisis. Many of the volunteers were nurses who went above and beyond to care for the wounded from both sides of the conflict. It was reported that when volunteers needed to move through areas of heavy fighting to reach injured residents, the rebels held up signs indicating a temporary ceasefire to allow the volunteers safe passage.

The administration was worried that volunteers would be killed or wounded, and at our White House meetings there was constant talk of evacuating them. When pressed, I always said I would take the issue up with Bob Satin, the Peace Corps' DR country director. No volunteers were hurt, and their actions did wonders for our relationship with the Dominicans. In fact, I never mentioned the administration's concerns to Bob. I knew he would make the right call, though he probably never could have convinced those volunteers to leave.

•••

We knew after several weeks that Ambassador Bennett had not been an asset in brokering peace. When a delegation from the new leftist Constitutionalist government led by President Caamaño came to see Bennett, he dismissed them. Bennett said they ought to put down their arms and go along with the right-wing Loyalists, who had just elected General Antonio Imbert as their president. The sides were at an impasse, but McGeorge Bundy said he thought he could break the stalemate.

On May 15, Bundy and I, along with Thomas Mann and Cyrus Vance, boarded an executive jet at Andrews Air Force Base and headed for Santo Domingo. I asked Bundy what his approach would be, and he said he had prepared a statement that clarified the issues and made a persuasive argument for a quickly negotiated peace in everyone's best interests. Though Bundy had little experience in Latin America, I couldn't question his intelligence, good intentions, or confidence.

Senior Loyalist military officials were at San Isidro Air Base when we arrived. Still angry about their dismissal by Bennett, none of the Constitutionalist leaders attended. The electricity was off throughout the city, and there was no air conditioning in the windowless conference room on the first floor of the control tower where we met.

We sat at a large round table with five or six officials, including new President Imbert, who sat next to the head of the Dominican infantry, General Martinez, a man about five feet two inches and two hundred pounds. On Imbert's other side sat the meeting's apparent leader, General Elías Wessin y Wessin, who had briefly been head of state after the coup. The most striking figure at the table was Admiral Francisco Rivera Caminero, minister of the armed forces. Living up to his mellifluous name, he was handsome and dignified in a sparkling white uniform.

Wessin y Wessin gave a short description of what he thought the solution was—basically, that his military needed to kill all of the opposition. Then he asked what had brought us there, and Bundy pulled out his eloquent speech and began to talk about a path to peace. Bundy was an impressive fellow and gave a compelling speech delivered with real feeling. While he spoke, I saw among these sweaty, uniformed figures not a glimmer of acknowledgment; they stared blankly forward. Although Wessin y Wessin had spoken good English, few of these men seemed to either understand or appreciate Bundy's Gettysburg Address.

When he finished, there was silence. After a few moments, Bundy said, "Well, do you think this is the right approach, the right time?" No response. After another long pause, "Do you want Jack Vaughn to tell you this in Spanish?"

Rivera Caminero answered, "No, we understand."

Bundy said, "Are you going to let us go back to Washington with no response from you? Do you have your own ideas?" All was quiet in the ever-hotter conference room.

Finally Martinez, the rotund little major general in charge of the fighting downtown, shook his head. "Meester, berry troubles. Berry, berry troubles." That concluded the meeting.

In the afternoon, we visited the US embassy, which was operating in emergency mode—things were in a state of total disarray. After viewing Ambassador Bennett's office, I noted with interest that the ambassador was too big to fit under his desk, and there was no evidence of bullet holes.

Late that night at the embassy, President Johnson called to discuss the possibility of installing a wealthy rancher named Antonio Guzmán as the head of a coalition government; Guzmán had been part of the Bosch administration, and the terms of his leadership included exiling most of the Loyalists. The embassy had only one phone that could receive overseas calls, and, in typical Johnson fashion, the president wanted each one of us on the phone in turns to give him our opinion of the Guzmán option.

The consensus was the climate would not tolerate a choice so far to the left. The Loyalists, vehemently opposed to anyone associated with Bosch, would probably hang on until the bitter end, ensuring more fighting and more civilian deaths. We also could not be certain that a Guzmán government would not turn Communist. Johnson abandoned the idea, and we all shuffled home from the DR.

Bundy and Vance were incredulous about our meeting with the Dominican military; I'm sure the experience was an eye-opener for both of them about how that country operated. The Dominican officials saw only one way to resolve the crisis: death to the opposition. I suspect that like most Latin American military leaders, they had been trained in the US and spoke decent English. Yet they had been raised in the Trujillo culture with the all-powerful role of the military and endemic corruption. Until their military man got on top, there was no solution.

By the end of May, Johnson finally got his wish for more regional support. Our allies Brazil, Honduras, Paraguay, Nicaragua, Costa Rica, and El Salvador sent troops in for what was called the Inter-American Peace Force. Shortly thereafter, the US began to draw down troops. Many agreements were forged and then collapsed as various envoys, including United Nations officials, attempted to broker a peace deal.

The conflict was finally settled through the good auspices of Ellsworth Bunker, US ambassador at large, who went to Santo Domingo with two negotiators from the OAS. On the last day of August, Caamaño and Imbert accepted Bunker's deal, and a truce was declared. With a plan set for elections, the last of our troops left in September.

On July 1, 1966, former President Joaquín Balaguer, one of Trujillo's protégés who had been living in exile in New York, became president in an election against Juan Bosch. Bosch had been waiting patiently in Puerto Rico, fully expecting to return to power, but the US didn't trust him. He was a philosopher, a democrat, and a good man, but not a good manager or politician. We couldn't be sure he wouldn't lose control a second time. The Johnson administration hand-picked Balaguer, a politically shrewd figure who managed to remain president for the next twelve years, and again later for ten years. Antonio Guzmán eventually did become president in the late seventies during Balaguer's brief time out of office.

Even though he came out of the brutal Trujillo tradition, a long view has shown that Balaguer was the right man for the DR—a good politician with staying power. By the end of his second presidency, he was a blind old man who seemed almost like a wind-up toy, sitting limply until he needed to perform, then straightening his shoulders and delivering a spellbinding forty-five-minute speech. Balaguer's longevity probably solidified democracy in the DR.

Johnson had taken on the DR crisis like a personal vendetta and, under the cloud of Vietnam, he tried to make the most of his quick Dominican triumph. He called the intervention his finest foreign policy achievement. US casualties were relatively low: 44 soldiers died and 283 were wounded. Though it cost incredible sums of money—both in aid and military expenses—thousands of Americans and foreign nationals were saved, and the DR became a politically stable country.

Despite this best possible outcome, the Latin American community remained hostile; the OAS and Mexico in particular harbored a deep resentment about our unilateral intervention. The DR cost Johnson the support of liberals as well, many of whom didn't believe Cuba was a significant threat. Members of Congress frequently commented that we lacked solid evidence of a Cuban presence in the DR. Another comment we heard from the media was that the Dominican coup had caught Castro off guard.

In fact, Cuba at that time was aggressively trying to expand its influence in the hemisphere. Though primarily interested in Venezuela, Castro pounced on any shaky regime: Grenada, Jamaica,

Bolivia, Chile, and the DR were all on his radar. Cuba maintained international swat teams that could move quickly into any situation. History shows that Johnson was right on the DR, but he paid the price for it politically among a skeptical and war-weary public and Congress.

Meeting as we did for hours and hours each day, I had ample time to observe the primary movers in the Johnson administration. I felt uneasy about McNamara and didn't trust him on Vietnam. I thought very highly of Rusk and Ball. Rusk was evenhanded and steady, and he loved the Peace Corps. Ball played the classic devil's advocate; he was the wise contrarian on almost everything. J. Edgar Hoover reminded me of Manuel Noriega; he had those flat, wide eyes that didn't send a message—like a hatchet man—and was truly nerve-racking to deal with.

The DR crisis left me with the impression that our leaders lacked a nuanced understanding of Latin America. Our intelligence from the CIA was virtually useless, our diplomats were a mixed bag, and key players in the Johnson administration were way out of their comfort zone dealing with Latin America—their expertise was in Europe. The episode cast a dark shadow that followed me through the next few years of my career as I worked in the realm of liberals who felt that my association with the DR intervention should disqualify me from peaceful pursuits.

•••

My first six months as assistant secretary and coordinator of the Alliance for Progress had been so consumed by the eastern half of Hispaniola that the rest of Latin America had dropped off my radar. By the fall of 1965, the Alliance had almost drowned off the beaches of Santo Domingo. Johnson worried that the program's already weak presence would sputter and die if we didn't do some CPR.

To signal renewed US support for the aid program throughout the hemisphere, the president instructed me to organize a high-profile PR tour of Latin America on the occasion of the Alliance's fourth anniversary that September. He told me to choose a good cross section of skeptical journalists and "show 'em the best of what has happened since you and Mann took over the Alliance."

I came to my post a devotee of Nelson Rockefeller, the father of our original foreign aid program, the Institute of Inter-American Affairs (IIAA). His strategy, created during World War II, made education and training the main focus; collaborative management with host countries was key. I had seen the great payoffs of training Latin America's future leaders through my work with Point Four in Panama.

The Alliance for Progress, Kennedy's version of our foreign aid program, made institutional reform its primary objective. Under the Alliance, a country received funding only after it developed a five-year plan in which virtually every institution, agricultural to economic, was changed to mirror the American model.

The Alliance projected an attitude of, "we are going to reform this country even if it kills you." Not only were the goals of the program irrational, but we didn't know how to achieve them. How do you reform the ministry of health in Paraguay? We didn't have a clue. Our State Department lacked depth of experience and expertise in Latin America. The Kennedy administration, and those who stayed on into Johnson's term, were oblivious to the region. They had never been there, even on vacation.

One pillar of the Alliance was agrarian reform. A University of Wisconsin program called the land tenure system sent a bunch of starry-eyed socialists to implement agrarian reform in Latin America. Based on the model of a medium-sized American family farm—multi-crop, self-sufficient, mechanized, and run by well-educated farmers with ready access to credit—it bombed throughout the hemisphere.

Several countries, most notably Bolivia and El Salvador, have yet to fully recover from the bungled agrarian reform efforts perpetrated under the Alliance.

Another miss was the industrial development program called import substitution, which encouraged the in-country manufacture of items that had traditionally been imported. The program set up government-run factories to produce these goods; they made a shoddy product at a high price. The results of the import substitution program were monopolies and bigger government. Instead of encouraging exports and fostering growth among private local businesses, as we do now, we created state-run economies that hurt countries in the long run.

The saving grace of the Alliance was a holdover from Rockefeller's program: training. Literally tens of thousands of Latin Americans received advanced, specialized training and degrees in the US and abroad and went back to become leaders in their countries. The University of California, Los Angeles, UC Berkeley, the University of Michigan, and the University of Chicago were major training centers. Kennedy and Johnson put more money into training for agriculture, administration, health, and engineering, and that really carried the banner for the Alliance.

Knowing well the pitfalls of our foreign aid program, I planned a trip to Latin America that would focus most on our investment in people, not institutions. Johnson wanted to equate the Alliance with his well-regarded Great Society program at home, which aimed to eliminate poverty and racial injustice through major initiatives in education, medical care, and transportation. Armed with very compelling talking points, my staff scheduled a seventeen-day, twenty-six-thousand-mile trip through seven countries: Mexico, El Salvador, Panama, Ecuador, Peru, Bolivia, and Chile. Johnson lent us his sleek JetStar for the occasion.

Accompanying me on my first overseas tour as assistant secretary were four journalists: John Goshko of *The Washington Post*, Hal Hendrix of Scripps-Howard, Jerry O'Leary of the *Washington Star*, and Jerry Hannifin of *TIME*. The talented State Department staff on the trip were Leveo Sanchez, Diego Asencio, Maggie Conrad, and Serban Vallimarescu, our senior public relations officer. I was thrilled to be out from under the cold stare of Tom Mann and back in the field, where I felt most comfortable and useful.

We started in Mexico, where I visited the presidential palace to sign a loan for more than $20 million to be distributed through private Mexican banks as $1,500 loans to small farmers. Even though Mexico had condemned our intervention in the DR just a few months earlier, we received a warm reception at both public and private venues there, and one of my speeches was nationally televised. Next was El Salvador, where a village serenaded our group with "The Star-Spangled Banner" performed by children on a motley collection of improvised instruments. A Peace Corps volunteer had taught them the melody by whistling it over a period of days.

In Panama, where I felt I could use my reputation to hit a bit harder, I told a group of several hundred wealthy businessmen that it was their duty to fuel Panama's economy by creating jobs for the poorest in their society. I said it was time to stop paying bribes and start paying more taxes. Remarkably, I left without even a heckle. I have always felt it is much better to shoot straight with our Latin American friends than to patronize them, which we often did in our foreign aid program. I think in this case the Panamanians respected a gringo giving them the hard truth.

In Quito, Ecuador, I signed a $3 million loan for artisan credits, and we invited hundreds of local handicraft workers to the ceremony. Instead of editing my speeches on the plane to Peru, and then Bolivia (I usually spoke off the cuff), I played poker and found my journalist companions more than game. On a terrible losing streak during the flight to La Paz, Bolivia, I drew four of a kind just as we turned for the runway. No way would I consider throwing in my hand and fastening my seat belt.

Our sympathetic pilot aborted his landing, pulled the plane up, and executed a ten-mile circle while I made a killing off the journalists. Ambassador Douglas Henderson and all the Bolivian dignitaries waiting at El Alto airport were curious about our last-minute maneuver. To their great credit, the journalists' explanations were widely evasive. The pilot's log said it all: "Final approach aborted; alpacas on thc runway."

An Aymara welcome

Having lost serious money, the journalists got their revenge during a colorful event in the little village of Batallas, about thirty miles northwest of La Paz. It was a place I had visited many times during my years with USAID. Just outside of town, a crowd of Aymara Indians blocked the road, forcing our caravan of cars to stop. The villagers walked down the line, peering into each car. When I stepped out to greet them, they hoisted me onto their shoulders and paraded me down the main street with piercing cries of, "*Ayaya Vaughn!*" ("Long live Vaughn!"). They showered me with confetti and draped paper garlands around my neck. Then this joyful group applied the coup de grace: multi-colored, knit earmuffs. None of the journalists missed the opportunity to snap my picture. The photos wound up in several publications, including *Newsweek* that November.

Journalistic revenge

At our stop in Santiago, Chile, an elderly woman in the slums presented me with an apple because she wanted to do something for "*un amigo de Presidente Kennedy*." Then we went to Nogales, Chile, where residents were rebuilding their town square after an earthquake. They told us they would name it "John F. Kennedy Plaza" and asked if we could ship them a statue. As we traveled to these Alliance projects, it seemed that we were making a pilgrimage to fragile shrines in memory of JFK. While I stayed on message, linking the Alliance to Johnson's Great Society, the locals that we met were still talking about "*Presidente*" Kennedy.

In dozens of speeches delivered in rural cornfields, urban housing projects, airport landing strips, and auditoriums, I emphasized the Alliance's potential. To presidents, government officials, businessmen, slum dwellers, subsistence farmers, and the public at large over the course of many fourteen-hour days, I underlined the needs of the "human sector." I stressed that the Alliance would stand or fall on its ability to aid people in achieving higher levels of individual competence. I pushed hardest the themes of education, training, and family planning. I tried to minimize (by ignoring) the Alliance's principal theme of institutional reform based on gringo models.

The trip netted the best press we ever had for the Alliance for Progress. The twenty or so feature articles harvested from that gambling tour of Latin America were deemed "very positive" and "helpful" by the US Information Service and were especially well received by the White House. We allayed fears and suspicions about what damage the DR intervention had done to our relationships in the hemisphere. My staff and I learned a tremendous amount about what was brewing in our host countries, and we became close personal friends with those four ace journalists.

After we returned, *TIME*'s Jerry Hannifin sent me a very kind letter about the trip: "As a reporter, I've never seen a top official of my government received as you were in the areas of Latin America that all the pundits assure we have ignored. I hope the ache has gone from your saddle sores, acquired from Aymara shoulders."

Johnson was thrilled with the results of our Latin American jaunt, and he wanted to keep the momentum going by showing a greater personal interest in the Alliance. To that end, the president asked that all US ambassadors stationed in Latin American countries come to the White House for a fifteen-minute pep talk and photo op when they visited Washington. After only two such appointments, Johnson became bored. He told me that henceforth, he wanted to see the ambassadors "in bunches."

In a matter of weeks, five of my ambassadors were in town at the same time. They were career officers: suave, sophisticated, and educated at the finest US institutions. This very handsome bunch, with big cuff links and chalk stripes, filed into the White House to meet with Johnson, who immediately launched into a story about the purchase of his first Texas ranch. One of the highest points in his life, Johnson said, was the day he first rode on horseback all the way around his new property. To his surprise, he came across a large herd of deer. Thrilled to own and eager to protect his very own Johnson deer, he went into debt building a cyclone fence around his new property.

Some years later, Johnson again happened upon his private herd. To his dismay, he found them runty, deformed, and sickly—obviously inbred. Looking around the room, the president said, "just like you career Foreign Service people." I had the feeling the president had been waiting years to tell that story. Johnson then asked the nonplussed ambassadors, "How many of you can claim to be on a first-name basis with a school principal or superintendent, small-town mayor, labor union leader, village priest, or small rancher in the country where you are accredited?"

There was a stunned and embarrassed silence. The president closed the brief encounter with a little lecture about the fraud of public servants lingering forever within the capital city cocktail circuit at taxpayer expense. This was not the way, he said, to represent the people of the United States or learn about your host country. Not surprisingly, that was the end of ambassadorial bunching at the White House on Johnson's watch.

•••

NOT LONG AFTER WE returned from our trip through Latin America, Dean Rusk called my office to say that New York Senator Bobby Kennedy was planning a swing through South America in November, and Rusk wanted me to brief the senator to prepare him. We all felt the trip was Bobby's way of building credibility for a presidential run, which made my assistant, Diego Asencio, even more eager to impress the senator. Diego was not aware of my difficulties with Bobby, which had been minor but numerous during my years with the Peace Corps.

Diego performed a considerable amount of legwork, pulling together briefs and talking points for Venezuela, Ecuador, Peru, Chile, and Brazil. Then he set up a meeting in my conference room for Bobby and five of his staff. About fourteen of my staff were with me to answer questions about the countries he would visit. When Bobby and company arrived, they sat at the opposite end of our long table. After some introductions, Bobby said he would like me to tell him what he could expect in each of these countries regarding the leadership, their attitude toward the US—especially in the aftermath of the DR intervention—and the status of our foreign aid projects.

I was several minutes into my description of Venezuela when Bobby interrupted me and asked what he should tell the media and politicians when he was asked why we sent the Marines into the DR. I gave him the standard White House line, the kind of thing Bill Moyers had said every day that summer: "To avoid bloodshed, to save American lives, and to make sure Castro didn't take over."

"Like hell I'll say that." Bobby had been one of the liberals critical of the DR intervention. I moved to the next briefing on Ecuador, and he interrupted me again. "What do I say in Ecuador when they ask me about the intervention in the DR?"

"I bet you won't even be asked that question." Indeed, on my recent trip through Latin America the topic had rarely come up. I moved on to Peru, and he asked his question again, obviously trying to goad me. For someone who had spent millions of dollars trying to murder Castro and urged spending additional millions on secret police academies to stem the Castro tide, Bobby's cynicism over Johnson's effort to avoid a Communist outcome seemed the height of hypocrisy.

"Senator, tell them exactly what your brother told the world at the time of the Cuban Missile Crisis, when you were serving as his advisor. He said that aggressive conduct, if allowed to go unchecked and unchallenged, ultimately leads to war, and, if threatened, the US must act in its own self-interest."

"How dare you refer to him as my brother! He was John Fitzgerald Kennedy, the greatest president of this century!" Bobby claimed that President Kennedy would never have supported a DR intervention. He capped off his rant by saying that our Latin America policy was "completely fucked up."

I told Bobby our Latin America policy was largely unchanged from that of the Kennedy administration. At that, he jumped out of his chair. I immediately stood up to challenge him. In the next beat, all the members of the meeting were on their feet. After a few tense seconds of aggressive posturing between Bobby and me, the senator stormed out, shouting, "I'm gonna get that guy!" One of Bobby's staffers brushed by Diego as he left, "That goes for you too, you SOB." I saw the blood drain from Diego's face—all hopes of working in a Bobby Kennedy administration snuffed out in a matter of minutes.

I was keyed up and uneasy after the harsh exchange. I knew a number of people in Washington who disliked Bobby as much as I did, but I had never seen anybody challenge him. Later that day as I worked at my desk my red phone rang—it was President Johnson.

"I just picked up a rumor on you and Bobby. Is it true?"

"Yes, Mr. President."

"Good going, son!" The president hadn't called me son since before the DR intervention.

Bobby left on his trip, and at his first stop in Lima, he was asked about the DR. He immediately sent me a telegram that read: "You lost. You owe me $5 or something." A story about our heated disagreement in my conference room subsequently appeared on the front page of *The Washington Post.*

Unfortunately, I would cross paths with Bobby again much too soon. His trip to South America coincided with the Inter-American Conference in Rio de Janeiro. I flew down to the meeting of thirty Latin American foreign ministers with Secretary of State Rusk, whose presence symbolized our renewed effort to make the Alliance a success. This conference hadn't taken place since 1954, and no sitting secretary of state had spent more than thirty-six hours in Latin America in recent memory.

Also of symbolic importance to me, and noticed by the press covering the event, was the absence of Tom Mann. Following my successful tour of Latin America two months earlier, Mann had been withdrawing from my daily existence and the major diplomatic events in the region.

Bobby and his entourage had arranged to spend the last leg of their trip in Brazil in order to make an appearance at the Rio conference. The US ambassador to Brazil, Lincoln Gordon, invited Senator Kennedy and his wife to a banquet at his residence in honor of Rusk. It was a gala affair with many notables from the US and Latin America, about one hundred people at tables of eight.

At the dinner, Bobby and Ethel Kennedy sat at the table of Gordon's wife, Allison, along with me, Dean Rusk, Averell Harriman, and several others. Seated directly across from Bobby was Brazil's minister of finance, Roberto Campos, a distinguished right-wing politician who later became Brazil's ambassador to Washington and the Court of St. James.

Ambassador Gordon gave his gracious remarks, first in Portuguese and then in English, and introduced several VIPs. After Bobby was introduced, he launched into a diatribe denouncing the foreign policy of both the US and Brazil. In his classic mean-spirited way, he slammed Brazil's government, class structure, and military. (Brazil had recently sent troops to the DR in a show of support for President Johnson.)

When Bobby finished, Minister Campos jumped to his feet. Fists clenched, the Brazilian statesman leaned toward Bobby, "This is your first trip to Brazil, is it not? How long have you been in our country becoming an expert? Do you really believe our Alliance for Progress programs are undemocratic? Shame on you!" Bobby slumped in his chair and smirked. I felt very sorry for Ethel and, for the first time, felt a twinge of pity for Bobby, too. He showed not only cultural insensitivity but also a lack of understanding of our foreign policy in Latin America. For all of his passion, Bobby had a limited supply of the three qualities I so admired in President Kennedy: a sense of humor, a sense of timing, and a sense of grace.

The two-week Inter-American Conference in Rio had begun with a bang for me and Walt Rostow, chairman of the State Department's policy planning council and soon to become Johnson's national security advisor. Together in a taxi tearing at breakneck speed from the airport, we were clobbered in an intersection by another cab going even faster. Both cars were demolished. I walked away from the wreckage with an extremely sore knee. Rostow climbed out uninjured, triumphantly holding high his mangled tennis racquet. Neither of us can remember how we finally arrived at our hotel that morning at about 3:00 a.m.

The next day, I escorted Rusk to a series of meetings with individual foreign ministers, the most memorable being our exchange with my friend, Panamanian Foreign Minister Fernando Eleta Almarán. Knowing Eleta and his opinions well from my time as ambassador, I had prepared Rusk for a full-court press. That is just what Eleta gave us, in spades. Possibly even more eloquent in English than in Spanish, Eleta captivated in both languages.

"Our little sliver of a country—split in two by your Canal Zone—has been totally dominated by the US military for half a century. When we have succeeded in forcing discussions on modernizing our treaty, we find that US negotiators play harder ball with us than they do with their Cold War enemies at the UN!" Eleta went on to say it was scandalous how little the US paid Panama for the lease of the Canal Zone. At the time, the level of our annual lease payment to Panama was not more than $5 million. Eleta pounded home at least a dozen reasons to justify a greater annuity from the US for having divided his country "in perpetuity."

He used for contrast the military deal the US had with Spain. "The Pentagon is paying the Spanish government in excess of thirty-five million dollars a year to lease areas occupied by three US military bases there. Yet you quibble endlessly with your friend, Panama, over our wholly justified requests to raise the pittance you pay us for *thirteen* bases in the Zone. Your negotiators seem offended when we suggest adjustments to compensate for inflation!"

After about twenty minutes, it was stone-faced Dean Rusk's turn. The secretary of state waited for a dramatic few moments while he surveyed the suite, Buddha-like, making eye contact with each of Eleta's retinue. Then Rusk set his jaw and unloaded: "I would remind you, Mr. Minister, of a defining difference between our very finite and limited agreements with Spain and our broad historic treaty with the Republic of Panama. We are dealing with apples and oranges.

"If for any reason the Spanish government should ask us to leave, we would have no recourse. We would close our bases and go. But in Panama, under the terms of the treaty between our two nations, you have waived your rights. Should your government ask the US to abandon any of the military bases in the Zone, our answer would be automatic and final. It would be that we intend to stay—and we shall stay." It was the first and only time I ever saw Dean Rusk angry, and I had never heard a colonial put-down delivered quite so coldly.

Panamanians have every reason to be proud of the eloquence, passion, and commitment of their foreign minister in arguing their case. I felt sorry for Fernando and his staff that day, the same way I had felt for their predecessors during my time in Panama.

One meeting I eagerly looked forward to in Rio was with Gordon Mein, the deputy chief of mission in Brazil. Several of his supporters in the State Department and I had been lobbying to get him an ambassadorship. He was a good man who had been passed over on earlier occasions for reasons only intelligible to the State personnel department. We had finally succeeded, and I wanted to bring him the good news personally. I invited him and his wife to my hotel room for a drink; I sensed they expected bad news. When I told them that Gordon would be the next US ambassador to Guatemala, they were surprised, thrilled, and a bit teary-eyed.

The next time I met Ambassador Mein was in 1968 at Andrews Air Force Base outside Washington, DC, where he was being returned home in a flag-draped coffin. He had been gunned down by terrorists on a street near his embassy in Guatemala City. The memory of Mein's appointment still haunts me.

•••

When I returned to the US in early December, I hoped to dig into my role in Washington and begin to make some changes. Mann's dark shadow had retreated somewhat from my office, and Vietnam still demanded Rusk's focus; I grabbed what independence I had and ran with it. One of the appointments squeezed onto my constantly overbooked calendar for early in the New Year was a meeting of the American Institute of Free Labor Development (AIFLD), one of the lesser known elements of the Alliance. It promoted free—as opposed to Communist—labor unions in Latin America.

The AFL-CIO ran the program, and it was a favorite project of the labor union's legendary chief, George Meany. Another enthusiastic stakeholder was the CIA; in the guise of labor specialists, a number of CIA agents worked out of AIFLD offices throughout Latin America.

What I understood to be the annual and basically self-congratulatory meeting of AIFLD in the elegant AFL-CIO headquarters in Washington turned out to be much more substantive. The group proposed doubling the AIFLD budget for the upcoming year and adding half a dozen new slots for CIA agents, and they assumed my approval was a given. As ambassador to Panama I had seen a rapidly expanding AIFLD/CIA program consistently stubbing its toe, and I would not say grace over a doubling of this effort.

Chairman Meany was furious. Alternately waving his cane and cigar, he accused me of pulling a double cross; he threatened to call Lyndon Johnson that very minute. I told him I would be pleased to get on the line to tell the president what a sloppy program he and the CIA were running. Meany instead went to Dean Rusk, who backed me up. By the time Meany called Bill Moyers to make an appointment with President Johnson, Leveo Sanchez and I had already briefed Moyers on the issue. He assured us the president would not have time to meet with Meany. Even without the funding increases they wanted from me, the AIFLD/CIA program continued floundering and misinforming.

Of all the botched and misguided institutional reforms that occurred under the Alliance, the one institution we didn't touch that desperately needed it was the judicial system. Until a country has an autonomous, apolitical, transparent judicial system, nothing will work. People can't live in peace or be democratic if they don't have courts with integrity, which don't exist today in Mexico and Guatemala and on down the line.

On the foreign policy side of my job, I agreed with Johnson and Mann's decision to extend aid to countries under military rule. More than half of the countries in Latin America had systems of government that we did not consider true democracies, but I didn't feel that justified turning our backs on their desperately poor populace. It was especially wrong to deny them aid, given that the roots of many military dictatorships could be easily traced right back to the Alliance for Progress: in the Third World, the military was often the only group organized enough to assume the daunting task of institutional reform.

While the Alliance's impact on the power of the military may have been unintentional, we were fully knowing and completely wrong in our decision to subsidize and train the Latin American military. The worst example was our Civic Action Program, which I had witnessed in Panama with Torrijos. In Panama, Bolivia, El Salvador, and Guatemala, the colonels who ran those civic projects received the same kind of public recognition politicians did, paving the way for ever more powerful military leaders.

Even if I'd had a tenure long enough to chip away at policy issues, I'm not sure I could have convinced Congress to eliminate Civic Action. As shallow as the understanding was in the executive branch, it was much worse in the legislature. Members of Congress rarely traveled south of the border, and most were completely caught up in Vietnam.

I tangled several times with Senator Wayne Morse of Oregon, who thought we should shun military governments; he also opposed our intervention in the Dominican Republic. He didn't understand that President Kennedy's suspension of aid to the DR had effectively pulled the rug out from under an already tenuous political situation. Others, like Congressman Daniel Flood, showed even more bravado in their misguided attacks. Rep. Flood demanded my immediate recall after I referred to the US as "Gringolandia" in a speech in El Salvador. He called the word "an epithet of derision" that showed my disloyalty to our country. I had actually used that term to great effect warming up a stiff diplomatic crowd in San Salvador.

These and other frustrations were on my mind when I met my old friend Johnny Johnston for lunch on January 18, 1966. Johnny was grudgingly working for me in Washington after being forced out as the aid mission director in Cuba when Castro took over. Vastly experienced and honest to the point of bluntness, Johnny provided me with an occasional reality check that I found entertaining and useful during my sequestration at State.

We talked so long that we were the only customers left in the small Georgetown restaurant late that afternoon. We sat at the bar reminiscing about the old days and griping about how badly things were going in the foreign aid business. A wide-eyed bartender interrupted us: "Someone calling himself President Johnson wants me to page someone named Jack Vaughn." Even in Georgetown, a page can hardly get classier than that.

"Would you like to replace Sarge?" Johnson said when I picked up. Before I could answer, he told me that if anyone found out, the whole deal would be off. He said it would move fast, and I should stay in touch with "Moyer" (what he often called Bill Moyers). "Are you interested?"

"Mr. President, I thought you'd never ask."

It had become obvious to everyone in Washington that Sargent Shriver would have to be replaced as director of the Peace Corps. For the last two years, he had been running Johnson's War on Poverty as his night job. If I thought my double duty at State was bad, Shriver's gig was even more grueling. He pulled off both jobs with panache, but the arrangement was madness, and Johnson knew he had to find someone to take the helm of the Peace Corps.

I certainly had not considered myself a candidate. Neither Moyers nor Johnson ever broached the subject with me, even though I had developed a good rapport with the president and Lady Bird by then. With the high standard set by the politically savvy Shriver, lobbying was considered a key skill in leading the Peace Corps; I had almost zero political background. Also, there were strong contenders among senior people at the Peace Corps, like Warren Wiggins and Associate Director Harris Wofford.

Bill Moyers aspired to the position; he wore that on his sleeve from day one. Johnson once told me that Moyers would be Shriver's replacement when he could spare his talents, which were considerable. A number of senators, political figures, and university presidents were also considered prime candidates.

Like my ambassadorship to Panama, I felt this appointment amounted to a conspiracy between Johnson and Moyers. I don't think they even asked Shriver about it. Johnson and Moyers probably felt comfortable with me because I'd been at the Peace Corps from the beginning, and I got along well with the volunteers and the staff. I found out later that Johnson had asked Mann about the appointment. Mann said that the move would be a good one because Bobby Kennedy had his knife sharpened for me, as did Senator Morse, and they planned to take me down in the upcoming months. If Bobby's animosity helped me get the Peace Corps job, then I really did owe him one.

When I returned to my office that day, Moyers called and said the nomination was fast-breaking. The announcement would be made at 5:15 with the president, Shriver, and me at the White House. "Don't tell anybody," he warned. Keeping my lips sealed and my excitement in check, I walked over to the White House a little before five. I first saw Moyers, who sat in front of his old-fashioned typewriter composing the president's statement.

I walked into the briefing room to find a throng of media already assembled and Shriver and the president chatting at the podium. Feeling dazed, I walked up to the two men, who welcomed me warmly. I had never seen Johnson so relaxed before; the backdrop for our meetings had always been grim—the DR intervention, a Vietnam issue, or some scandal in the Democratic Party. Shriver's mood was equally upbeat. He seemed delighted to be getting out, and who could blame him?

Johnson read Moyers' pitch-perfect statement, saying that by becoming director of the Peace Corps I would "return to [my] first love." The flashbulbs popped, and the news appeared on the front page of *The New York Times* and *The Washington Post*. Johnson announced concurrently that our distinguished ambassador to Brazil, Lincoln Gordon, would succeed me as assistant secretary of state. I breathed a huge sigh of relief. After ten tense months working for Mann, Rusk, and Johnson, I would be running my own show at the Peace Corps as its second director. Free at last!

At the press conference with President Johnson and Sargent Shriver

8

1966–1969

Everybody knows that Sargent Shriver was the first director of the Peace Corps. Only my wife remembers who the second one was.

—Interview with the *Battle Creek Enquirer*

Though President Johnson had announced me as his choice for director of the Peace Corps, my dream job wouldn't become a reality until I received congressional confirmation. I had breezed through the Senate Committee on Foreign Relations twice before, first for my ambassadorship to Panama, and again for my appointment as assistant secretary of state.

When Johnson nominated me for the Panama post, I had been working in relative obscurity in the Peace Corps and had not accumulated much of a public record for Congress to scrutinize. The positive outcome of the Panamanian crisis had smoothed the way for a quick confirmation to my position at the State Department. The senators had not drawn their sharp knives.

This time would be different. As assistant secretary of state I had butted heads with a number of members of Congress who disapproved of the Dominican intervention. One of my most vocal critics, Senator Wayne Morse, sat on the Foreign Relations Committee. Morse spoke out against my nomination in advance of my confirmation hearing, saying that by recognizing the right-wing Dominican military, the Johnson administration had "walked out on freedom."

When the scowling Senator J. W. Fulbright, the Foreign Relations Committee chairman, asked for my opening statement at the confirmation hearing that February, I took the offensive on a topic I knew would be the major bone of contention.

"I was really very unhappy at Senator Morse's comment that when the chips of democracy are down in Latin America we walk away. Unhappy because I don't think it is true, and I don't think the facts will bear that out… I think we must realize our objectives are long range, and, therefore, we are going to suffer through a lot of unsatisfactory political arrangements until such time as we can achieve the broad base of education and sophistication and the understanding which permit a constitutional democracy to work."

Morse was the first of the senators to chime in. "Mr. Vaughn, I have taken note of your views on my views on Latin America, and I want you to understand that I know nothing that could possibly concern me less than your views on any of my views or on any other subject.

"I want you to know that as far as I am concerned I shall vote against your nomination because, in my opinion, your work as assistant secretary of state for Latin American affairs disqualifies you for any appointment. I think that there is no question about the fact that you and Mann and Rusk have given bad advice to our president."

Two brave souls provided counterarguments to Morse. The first was US Representative Dick Ottinger of New York, a guest at the hearing and a former colleague of mine at Peace Corps-Latin America. Dick had managed the launching of programs in Colombia, Chile, Ecuador, Peru, and Venezuela with great success. He graciously described me as quiet but persuasive. "[Jack] will not be the flamboyant leader. He will be the man who gets the things done that ought to be done."

Senator Bourke Hickenlooper of Iowa, who had always been in my corner, spoke kindly as well. "I don't know just how much advice you have given or how much of it has been received, but I do have a feeling that your record has been excellent, especially in Latin America."

I had solidified my good relationship with Hickenlooper several months earlier when I told him about the huge rainbow trout in Bolivia's Lake Titicaca. I told the senator—one of the few who travelled to South America—how a friend of mine had planted the trout in Titicaca right after WWII, and the fish had grown to gigantic proportions. People from Iowa usually have not seen a rainbow bigger than five pounds. Hickenlooper went down and caught a forty-eight pounder that he mounted and proudly displayed in his office.

Hickenlooper did voice concerns about the Peace Corps' lasting impact. He questioned whether the two-year volunteer tours were drops in a Latin American bucket prone to tipping over with each new military coup, civil war, or drought. The senator made a valid point; the Peace Corps had always struggled to measure tangible benefits, and the question of lasting impact remained out of its grasp—the organization was barely five years old.

Senator Joseph Clark of Pennsylvania asked if we had set up a system to train local counterparts to continue the work of Peace Corps volunteers, a common question among members of Congress and taxpayers hopeful that the Peace Corps would be a temporary aid measure. I replied that we were not yet doing enough, and I explained the cultural barrier to such a system.

"The pull to work and live in the capital is so strong. This is where the power is. This is where the twentieth century is. This is where the good jobs are, and the status. After [rural villagers] have come into the city from the backcountry and have tasted this and feel that they are modern people, it is awfully hard to get them back on the farm." Until these underdeveloped countries were producing young people with the ability and interest to serve their countrymen, I explained, they would need the Peace Corps.

The senators spent a good deal of time belaboring the question of whether the Peace Corps endorsed, supported, or fomented revolution in its host countries. Senator Frank Lausche, Democrat from Ohio, hit that issue particularly hard, wanting to know if I thought volunteers should be involved in social reform and if that might create political upheaval. I felt it boiled down to semantics: What does a revolution in Chile mean to US politicians, and what does it mean to a Chilean mother of six living in a one-room hut?

"I have never suggested that the Peace Corps was going to set revolutionary forces in motion. What we are talking about is getting people involved and trained to participate effectively in local government [and] local institutions—getting people to the point of being effective citizens. Really, in most underdeveloped countries of the world this is revolutionary, because the people have never participated before."

The strangest questions during the hearing came from Senator Lausche: "Have you had any complaints about the oddity of dress of some of the Peace Corps workers?" I answered that at times I had made my own complaints about volunteers not dressing as neatly as they should. Recently in Malawi, President Hastings Banda had complained publicly that the volunteers teaching secondary school dressed too casually. The volunteers had quickly sharpened up their wardrobes with ties, slacks, and dresses.

Lausche persisted, "Doesn't it go beyond neatness; doesn't it go really to the charge that there has been oddness of the greatest character?" I looked quizzically at the senator, wondering what he could be getting at. "Don't you have many of what you call the mustached people around?"

Laughter erupted in the room, and I responded, "Senator, that is the meanest thing you've ever said to me." Senator Morse, who also wore a mustache, said, "That is one thing Vaughn and I agree on."

After explaining to the hippie-phobic senator that personal grooming often posed a challenge in living quarters with no running water or electricity, I offered my commitment to the clean appearance of Peace Corps volunteers. One of the reasons I banned beards when I became director was to eliminate this distracting chatter by politicians and host countries about the volunteers' facial hair.

Naturally, the committee members inquired about how the Peace Corps spent taxpayer money. At the time, the annual cost per volunteer averaged about $8,000, down from the original $9,500. But because we were adding new countries at a great clip, our budget for 1966 came to $114 million—more than triple our first year's spending. The Peace Corps sponsored 10,380 volunteers in forty-six countries after starting five years earlier with just 526 volunteers in thirteen countries.

As Warren Wiggins planned, the organization had grown quickly and spread widely, if not evenly, among the world's poorest nations. The largest groups of volunteers worked in India, Brazil, Nigeria, the Philippines, Malaysia, Turkey, Ethiopia, and Colombia, all of which hosted more than five hundred volunteers.

Left to right: Hubert Humphrey, George Ball, me, Sargent Shriver, Dean Rusk, and President Johnson

Senator Morse, true to his word, voted against my nomination, stalling my confirmation for a few days, but not derailing it. My swearing-in coincided with the celebration of the Peace Corps' fifth anniversary, and the White House hosted a gala that night crowded with Peace Corps staff, politicians, and diplomats. Also in attendance were around fifty returned Peace Corps volunteers proudly escorting ambassadors from their countries of service, a unique moment of parity between young dreamers and senior diplomats. Shriver and I blew out the candles on the Peace Corps cake, a great photo-op and the symbolic end of an era.

Later that week, the Peace Corps bid a raucous and heartfelt goodbye to its powerhouse leader, Sargent Shriver. More than 1,500 staff, politicians, and friends crowded into the Sheraton-Park Hotel for the "Shriver a Go-Go Party." Harry Belafonte performed, and Shriver spoke, stirring up the crowd as he could so effortlessly. On the topic of the organization's new director, he assured people I was up to the task: "Jack's a fighter."

Shriver's departure that night reminded us how much we had inherited from him. He had received a recycled and disputed idea for a volunteer corps, redefined it—with help from Warren Wiggins—and turned it into a national movement. With Bill Moyers, he had extracted large sums of money from a Congress in a penny-pinching mood.

He had assembled a team of talented, motivated, and passionate people who worked better and harder because Shriver was their boss. He ran the Peace Corps like today's start-ups: full of young energy, big ideas, bigger risks, and tireless idealism. He wanted it to be different, better, more flexible, and responsive than the government—and it was.

Following Shriver as the Peace Corps' leader was ego-shattering. For months I was routinely introduced as Sargent Shriver's replacement, or sometimes even as Shriver's assistant. Though we said we would, Shriver and I never met to talk about issues of transition or even for a catch-up lunch while I was director, but we stayed in touch and remained friends for the rest of his life.

The Office of Economic Opportunity more than filled Shriver's plate, and I jumped into the Peace Corps with both feet. I understood quickly, especially having stayed in touch with so many of my Peace Corps colleagues, what the major growing pains of the organization were in 1966—and there were many.

•••

SARGENT SHRIVER AND I had in a sense both left the Peace Corps in March 1964. While I headed to Panama City, he left for Johnson's War on Poverty. As he assumed responsibility for the Office of Economic Opportunity (OEO), Shriver slowly faded from the daily operation of the Peace Corps. Though rarely occupied, Shriver's fifth floor office at

Peace Corps headquarters remained the same, with modern paintings, photos with presidents and kings, honorary degrees, and keys to foreign cities all stacked on the floor along the walls. He claimed that hanging pictures spoiled the plaster and gave the misleading aura of permanence.

Shriver's personality and image lived on at the Peace Corps, even though he spent ten to twelve hours a day at his second job. He came into the Peace Corps office every morning to read his mail and hold a meeting; he spent the rest of the day and evening at OEO. Rumors flew furiously about who might replace Shriver: could it possibly be famous football coach Vince Lombardi, or would it be Donald Petrie of Avis Rent-a-Car?

Somehow the Peace Corps had stayed on message, received positive press, and continued to grow in 1965, thanks mainly to Shriver's deputy director, Warren Wiggins. The Peace Corps famously has a five-year limit on staff tenure—Shriver's idea to keep the organization sharp and fresh. Wiggins, who had been my boss in Bolivia and at ICA Washington, offered to stay past his five years to help me with the transition. His loyalty and superior management skills put me forever happily in his debt.

While I reveled in the support of Wiggins, Tedson Meyers, and other veteran staffers when I arrived, I also celebrated my autonomy. The Peace Corps was totally mine. I usually missed Dean Rusk's Monday morning senior staff meetings, but the secretary of state unfailingly expressed his confidence in me and my staff. Vice President Hubert Humphrey, now the chairman of the Peace Corps Advisory Council, also gave me the all-clear to take the ball and run. It was a beautiful change from the strict programming at the State Department.

The Peace Corps had grown considerably during the time I was away, and in 1966 we reached our peak with 15,556 volunteers and trainees in fifty countries. We had every reason to work longer hours, but many staffers were maxed out, deflated by the departure of their inspiring leader and exhausted from years of twelve-hour days. The changing of the guard could not have been easy for them. Shriver, the back-slapping, aggressive, hail-fellow-well-met had been replaced by me, the soft-spoken pragmatist. I began my time at the Peace Corps quietly orienting myself and making staff changes at a rapid clip. At meetings, I listened and questioned; pep rallies and lectures were not my style.

Five associate directors at the Peace Corps oversaw divisions from training to evaluation to health. When a problem arose in the field and a country director wanted to make a change, he encountered a gauntlet of divisional approval before receiving a final sign-off from the top. I thought the chain of command desperately needed thinning. The Peace Corps director should have an unobstructed line down to the country director in the field, and decisions should be made at the point of maximum knowledge.

One of my first major staffing changes was to phase out all of the associate director positions and treat the directors of the Peace Corps' four regions—Africa, Latin America, Far East, and North Africa-Near East-South Asia—as deputies. Cutting the associate directors out of the chain eliminated game-playing and jockeying for power.

After a few weeks of quiet retooling, I sensed rumblings of unhappiness around the building and understood that I needed to address the whole staff. People quickly saw that I was as devoted to Shriver as they were and that my ideas weren't all that different from his. However, it was the dawning of a new era for the Peace Corps, and we were going to have to get even better. I said we would play fewer bureaucratic games and that the days of one-upmanship were over. We would work in concert with a clearer line of authority. We would become leaner, more efficient, and more effective. What I was getting at, but didn't say to the group, was that I wanted to make the Peace Corps as great as Shriver had always said it was.

I faced major challenges in the areas of volunteer and staff selection, volunteer training, program planning, and management. The Washington office comprised an eclectic group of intellectuals, world-beaters, and individualists—not management types. Shriver, despite a concerted effort, had been unable to hire an effective director of administration. Due to his aversion to firing people, there were now three former office administrators shuffling around the office with little to do and one current administrator trying unsuccessfully to perform the job.

In 1966, the Peace Corps employed seven hundred staff in Washington and four hundred abroad. We had no standard operating procedures, no handbook, no guide for new employees. Kamikaze new hires came in ready to win the world but with no clue how to manage, budget, report financial transactions, or adhere to government regulations—administrative skills typical Washington bureaucrats could perform with their eyes closed.

The answer to my office management problems came to me from Liberia. Fresh from a tour as assistant country director, Douglas Stafford was a young, self-deprecating former standout at IBM. Doug took control of our group of cowboys, trained them, and got their fiscal reports in on time. The Peace Corps' newfound management abilities were key to our growth into a mature organization.

Efficiency and cost-cutting were other priorities in our transition from a start-up to an institution with staying power. I elevated our planning and program review director to a senior position held by Sol Chafkin, and later by Paul Sack, to ensure that we were funding the best programs and eliminating those that lacked impact.

I worked with the Peace Corp's brand new office of the controller, led by Morris Kandle and later by William Whalen, to keep our costs as low as possible without taking any punch out of the work we did. Waste was sometimes easy to find: I discovered that the Washington office received fifty copies of *The New York Times* every day. I made it two.

I found more money for our programs by relaxing the rigid rule of separation between the Peace Corps and the State Department. After five years, the difference between the Peace Corps and other US agencies had been well established, and I felt comfortable encouraging a new collaboration, especially a lucrative one. Ambassadors had what was called the ambassador's fund, as much as $200,000 a year of discretionary spending. The Peace Corps could use that money to buy cement, lumber, nails, and screws for our projects. There were times when the extra money from the ambassador's fund made all the difference in our shoestring budgets.

I co-opted not only money but also manpower from the State Department. I brought Margaret Beshore with me as head of talent search, our flashy name for overseas staff recruitment. Maggie Conrad, my assistant from State, came to run my front office. Carolyn Thomas, who had worked for me in the Latin America division, also moved in to bring her efficient touch to my phone calls, my correspondence, my visitors, and our various crises.

While we worked to minimize costs, in some cases I realized we were underpaying key staff members. One of them was Stan Scheyer, our wonderful medical director who oversaw the health care for thousands of far-flung volunteers. I thought Stan deserved more than $8,000 a year, and I asked him to write a letter that I could send to the Surgeon General requesting a raise. When Stan's letter arrived at the Surgeon General's office, it was sent down to an official in the Bureau of Health Services, who sent it to their Peace Corps liaison, who forwarded it to the Peace Corps medical director for consideration. Needless to say, Stan happily approved the request.

We sought out seasoned pros like Stan to fill senior positions, but the Peace Corps was still a young person's organization: most volunteers and a good number of junior staff were recent college graduates. We used these bright twentysomethings to dream big and work the long hours necessary to accomplish the seemingly insurmountable quantity of work to be done.

But sometimes we suffered the consequences of their inexperience. On one occasion I had written an urgent brief for Dean Rusk on a tenuous political situation in one of our host countries. I gave the document to Carolyn Thomas to copy. Our lingo in those days was to "burn a copy." Carolyn handed the original to a new assistant with those instructions, and the young woman rushed it down to the incinerator.

When I had left Peace Corps-Latin America in 1964, returned volunteers were just beginning to trickle into the ranks of staff, bringing their invaluable experience, sensitivity, and drive. Now, two years later, more than 250 returned volunteers were working for the Peace Corps in Washington and overseas. I wanted to hire more, particularly as recruiters and overseas staff.

In some cases, these volunteers had worked in a country where they had not had adequate Peace Corps support, where the host village didn't know they were coming, or the job they had been trained for didn't exist. A volunteer who has gone through that experience will make certain it doesn't happen to another. With former volunteers influencing the programming overseas, we were more consistently putting round pegs into round holes, with all the key locals involved, from the minister of education to the village chiefs and local school teachers.

One of our staffing shortcomings was the dearth of women in senior positions. I saw talented, overqualified women working as assistant training officers or assistant selection officers because they had been stuck in a system that inexplicably wouldn't promote them. That imbalance was easy to correct—I promoted women to management positions in Washington and appointed the first women country directors.

One standout in Latin America was Betty Hutchinson, a consummate diplomat who had been serving as deputy director in El Salvador before I made her director there in 1966. Another, Carolyn Payton, served admirably as director of the Eastern Caribbean region and subsequently became the Peace Corps' first woman and first African American worldwide director in 1977.

•••

Brent Ashabranner's Indian airport shuttle

AFTER DELIVERING CLOSE TO sixty speeches and informal talks at fifteen college campuses during my first two weeks as director, I took my first overseas trip to visit volunteers in Ethiopia, Tanzania, Kenya, Thailand, and India, one of our largest programs, with seven hundred volunteers. Brent Ashabranner, the India country director, made a giant impression by picking me up from the New Delhi airport on an elephant. An educator and keen observer, Ashabranner seemed tough and honest; I liked him immediately. Soon after that visit, I brought him to Peace Corps headquarters as director of training and university relations.

On the India trip, I met two remarkable women who struck me as startlingly similar: Ms. Lillian Carter (Jimmy's mother) and Mother Theresa. I met Ms. Lillian shortly after I arrived in Bombay. At sixty-eight she was one of our oldest volunteers, working as a nurse in a leper colony outside of Bombay. It didn't matter what the local Peace Corps rep had in mind for my itinerary; Ms. Lillian had her own plan for me. I visited her site and listened to her political analysis of Bombay. Years later it was clear to me where Jimmy got his political instincts and drive.

Next I spent a few hours in Calcutta with Mother Theresa, who looked old even then. She headed an organization called Missionaries of Charity that helped the desperately needy in her community and around the world. Mother Theresa was a flatterer, very controlled, and calculating in what she wanted to achieve from my visit: US government funding for her programs. She showed me some of her projects and answered my questions selectively. She was a politician in the same class as Ms. Lillian.

While I was visiting India, Indian Prime Minister Indira Ghandi was in Washington arguing her case for major aid to her country, which had suffered tremendously from drought in the last two years. President Johnson responded in part with a commitment for agricultural assistance through an expanded Peace Corps program. Warren Wiggins sent me a telegram in New Delhi with the news, and we subsequently launched a major recruitment effort for the India program, more than doubling it in the next year. Many of those who went to India were liberal arts graduates (AB generalists) who received crash courses in agriculture and animal husbandry. It was astounding how much a history major from Princeton could learn about poultry in three hundred hours.

India was just one example of our rapid expansion. That year we started programs in Botswana, Chad, Libya, Micronesia, and South Korea and were poised to add many more. In each country, we started as big as we could, following the Wiggins philosophy. I knew I would need strong, sharp super-managers to head each of my four worldwide regions. Shriver's old guard were reaching their five-year limit and moving on. To fill their shoes, I looked for current Peace Corps staffers who had overachieved, no matter how big or small their job descriptions.

Bob Steiner, my North Africa-Near East-South Asia director, had launched the Afghanistan program in a tough, unfriendly atmosphere and been extremely successful in turning the mood around. The new Africa director, C. Payne Lucas, came from the staff of a small program in Niger, where he had endeared himself to the president, Hamani Diori. I chose Bill Moffett as Latin America director; he was an old Latin America hand who came from the outstanding Chile program. Director of the Far East Ross Pritchard was one of the few and most talented of Shriver's senior staff who stayed on. We aggressively recruited Harvard professor of education Russell Davis to oversee the highly concentrated volunteer areas of East Asia and the Pacific.

Warren Wiggins generously worked as my deputy for almost a year, offering creative brainstorms and helping me copy Shriver's rolodex. It was the last time I worked with Wig. He was one of my heroes, a big idea man who could also juggle the details. He never received enough credit for his contributions to the Peace Corps.

When I faced the towering task of replacing Warren Wiggins, my thoughts turned to former elephant jockey and current director of training and university relations, Brent Ashabranner. A USAID veteran, Brent had far-ranging overseas experience, from Addis

Ababa to Lagos. His jaunty persona was topped off with a sprinkling of bright red hair.

Because the deputy director position was one appointed by the president, I called the White House's head of patronage, John Macy, to tell him Brent was my choice. Macy, clearly surprised by my announcement, told me about his list of twenty-five candidates for that job, all submitted to him by the White House and other political operatives. They were mostly defeated congressmen or retired ambassadors and governors, any of whom Macy assured me would be quite appropriate. "We especially need someone with a name, because you're unknown."

I didn't even bother to look at the list; I just told Macy I was sorry but I had made up my mind. President Johnson had never told me I could pick my own deputy, but I had assumed that was part of the package, and now I was going to make sure it was. I told Ashabranner he was hired, but nothing official could happen in terms of salary, title, or swearing-in.

Macy and I went back and forth for weeks. Being a dyed-in-the-wool bureaucrat, Macy refused to let it go. Finally, I played my trump card. I explained to Vice President Humphrey how Ashabranner's talents, which were many and strong, and mine, which were few and wobbly (especially in the bureaucratic realm) were a perfect fit. "Fine, I'll settle this." And he did with one call.

•••

With my Washington staff issues settled, I turned to the volunteers. We enjoyed an enormous volume of applications: in 1967 the Peace Corps was the largest employer of new college graduates, and we accepted just one out of every five applicants. Despite our selectivity, we lacked any research-based criteria for choosing volunteers.

Lacking better methods, we relied strongly on the reports of the academic psychologists who evaluated applicants and trainees. During volunteer training, psychologists peered over trainees' shoulders, clipboards in hand, watching for aberrant behaviors, from mild rebellion to drug use. The FBI ran background checks on everyone, mostly to determine if the applicants had ever smoked pot.

On Friday afternoons, I received a thick packet of FBI files, for which US taxpayers had spent thousands of dollars. A typical report said that it had been reliably reported that a volunteer smoked pot. The question confronting me was what amount of pot smoking should eliminate an applicant. Were three joints too many? I found the situation uncomfortable and somewhat absurd, and I tended to give everyone the benefit of the doubt.

I felt that one of the best ways to tackle the question of volunteers' success was to make our volunteer training more thorough, practical, and realistic. As director of the Latin America region, I had pushed hard to increase the number of hours of language training from 50 to 150, but I still felt our training was lacking and that our weakness in this area put volunteers at a serious disadvantage. One of the first volunteers sent to work in a Chilean slum didn't speak enough Spanish to get himself on the right bus to work, a story reported in *TIME* Magazine. I told the reporter, "At times [the volunteers] miss the mark, and when they do, it's certain we helped them miss."

At the beginning, Shriver had no good options for training venues other than US universities. Who would know more about young people, about teaching, about the world and foreign languages, than our top universities? Schools like Michigan, UCLA, and Berkeley basically designed Peace Corps orientation and training courses. When I became director, our trainings still took place over a few weeks at American universities and emphasized academic and psychological instruction rather than practical training.

I immediately bumped the language training from 150 hours up to 300. We moved toward the technique developed by the famous Dartmouth language professor John Rassias, a gifted teacher and comedian who developed a highly effective method of oral language acquisition. We kept adding to and boosting our language instruction so that by the time I left the Peace Corps, fully half of the three-month volunteer training was devoted to language. We taught not just the standard Spanish, French, Portuguese, and Urdu, but also the minor tribal languages like Twi, Tswana, Sara, Pushtu, Waray-Waray, and Bicolano—145 languages in all.

It took about four hundred hours of intense language training for a volunteer to feel comfortable speaking a new language—not fluently, but proficiently. For the more difficult, tonal languages like Thai and Korean, it took up to seven hundred hours. By the time volunteers touched down in their host countries, they could be expected to easily say, "I'd like a llama steak." Not everyone was cut out for learning a language quickly or well. We gave applicants language aptitude tests, and low scorers were placed in countries with a relatively easier language.

The importance of language proficiency went beyond the practical to the heart of the Peace Corps' mission: communication. As an example, the peasants in the Andean region of South America feared and disliked white people; for centuries the Spaniards and then the Europeans had exploited them. If a volunteer arrived speaking Spanish, he was thought to be just like any other white man, not to be trusted, his tongue checked to see if it was forked. A volunteer who arrived in the Andes speaking Aymara or Quechua was invited into a local home for lunch the first day. If I made any important change at the Peace Corps, it was improving the foreign language training for our volunteers.

Another crucial upgrade to our training program was moving it overseas. Not only were many university training programs impractical, but the schools also began to take advantage of their relationship with the Peace Corps. During one negotiation of a training contract with the University of Michigan, the school tried to charge us a few cents for every volume in the university library. Our trainees weren't going to set foot in the library; the school just viewed this as easy government money.

Our first attempt at overseas training took place in the summer of 1967, when a group of volunteers assigned to Ghana trained entirely in that country with former volunteers and staff. It made tremendous sense and led to better prepared and more confident volunteers.

By the end of my time at the Peace Corps, at least half of training was conducted abroad. The volunteers received intense foreign language instruction: six days a week, twelve hours a day, for six weeks. They lived with local families, which ensured near-immersion conditions. In-country training gave the future volunteers a clear picture of what they were getting into: the boredom, the frustration, the lack of privacy, the diarrhea. We lost on average twenty-five percent of future volunteers during training, the majority of those during the weeks of in-country training. Those who made it were superstars.

•••

EVEN MORE IMPORTANT THAN having language-proficient volunteers was hiring overseas Peace Corps staff who spoke the host languages well, if not fluently. In the case of returned Peace Corps volunteers we hired, this was a given. Staff we selected from outside the organization were put through the paces. I devised a short quiz for applicants to Spanish-speaking countries that would have made the dean of romance languages at Penn proud:

Please translate these three sentences:

El salió de su padre. (He left his father.)

El salió por su padre. (He went to get his father.)

El salió a su padre. (He resembles his father.)

This test stumped many sweaty applicants and separated those with true fluency from those at the llama steak level.

The Peace Corps suffered from a high failure rate in selecting overseas staff; when I arrived, there were many overseas vacancies. In one particularly desperate case, a lone staff member oversaw 150 volunteers in an area the size of Montana. We tended to hire lots of professors, ministers, and former priests. I think they saw more of what they needed spiritually and personally in Peace Corps service than they did in the routine of a university or seminary.

Some of the problems in attracting and keeping staff were related to family. When a successful professional wanted to work for the Peace Corps, his spouse had to agree to go into an environment vastly different from any she had ever known, leaving the support of friends and relatives. She was required to live modestly, communicate in a language she didn't know, place her children in questionable schools, and operate outside US diplomatic and business communities.

The successful spouses of in-country staff provided enormous support to their families, hosted volunteers in their homes, stepped in as needed, and were often left to cope alone while their husbands traveled to visit remote volunteers. Finding talented couples willing to take on the challenges was daunting.

Country directors and their staff created projects for volunteers, coordinated with host governments, attended to the health and safety of the volunteers, and managed the crises, accidents, and road blocks that cropped up over and over. They organized training conferences and relocated volunteers when things weren't working out. Every two years, the country staff made formal pitches to Washington headquarters for new programs and more volunteers.

The best country directors possessed an extraordinary set of skills: spoke the language, had technical know-how to support volunteer projects, firmly grasped the host country's culture, and endured constant, rugged travel. To be cool and laid back was vital; to be politically savvy was invaluable; to earn the volunteers' trust and respect was key. Doing all that and working fifteen-hour days defined the outstanding Peace Corps country director. Our skill in selecting those highly successful directors was hit-and-miss.

One country director in Bob Steiner's region, North Africa-Near East-South Asia, had been struggling for months to create viable programs and manage his volunteers. Then we learned he had ordered a king-size mattress to be delivered to him by air. His staff let us know of his increasingly odd behavior, and then we learned that the director had fallen victim to island fever. Our staff psychologists had seen the condition before in volunteers, but this was our first case among the staff. Bob and I sent someone from Washington to bring him home.

A couple of weeks later, his fever apparently lifted, the fired director and his congressman from California appeared in my office demanding reinstatement. I explained our position and called Bob in to give specific examples of this director's poor performance. The conversation grew heated and louder as Bob and I refused to budge. Finally, the congressman indignantly demanded Bob's resignation. That was it for me—I pointed to the door, "Sir, you may stand up and leave by that door, or I will throw you out of it." They rose and left without a word.

The first country director in British Honduras (now Belize) became interested, as some misguided overseas directors did, in providing the volunteers with vacation facilities. He must have felt that the volunteers rated a chance to get away from it all on an occasional weekend or during school vacations. The Peace Corps didn't approve this project, so the country director had struck upon the ingenious idea of building a hotel with petty cash.

In those days, Peace Corps regulations required that petty cash purchases not exceed $100. If an item cost more than that, it had to be budgeted and justified. This director had discovered that with enough $99 payouts, you could build a pretty nice recreation lodge, especially if you use only local materials and volunteer labor. Eventually this place featured twenty-five bedrooms, a rec room, and a dining room, all built with petty cash.

I found it a pleasant place to be: a lot of vines, swings, catwalks, hammocks, and palm trees—quite a show. The country director who had perpetrated this scheme had already finished his tour and returned to university work by the time I became director. When I happened across his lodge on my visit to Belize, I told the new director that it would have to go. If volunteers in Africa couldn't stay in hostels, then volunteers there certainly couldn't behave like Tarzan on their weekends off.

Though most volunteers managed to do well even without a great country director, having one could sometimes make all the difference. Togo, a small West African country, had suffered through three seemingly well-qualified directors who had failed to get the program off the ground. Morale among volunteers had hit rock bottom, and many headed home well before their two-year mark. We were getting calls from the press, and the US ambassador had become hostile toward us. I reluctantly agreed with my regional director that we should send in still a fourth country director, despite the risk of an embarrassing repeat disaster.

Into this mess went director number four, Mike Furst, and his spirited wife Shirley. An experienced agricultural extension type with an affable manner and talent for both learning and teaching, Mike arrived with no fanfare. He brought fluency in French, a knack for politics, a light touch, and an easy laugh. Most importantly, he kept his commitments. In a quiet and diligent way, Furst brought legitimacy to the program. In months, the Togo program went from being the joke of West Africa to one of the best in the region. Appropriately, volunteers received most of the credit, but those of us in Washington knew that Furst had been the key.

Another overachieving country director, Larry O'Brien, completely turned around our school construction program in Gabon. When Larry, a former philosophy professor from New York, arrived with his pregnant wife and small child, the Gabon program consisted of twenty volunteers working at two sites alongside paid local workers. Larry rightly felt this arrangement wasn't true to the Peace Corps mission and certainly could not be called efficient.

Using his magical amalgam of cultural sensitivity, pragmatism, and toughness, Larry turned the program on its head, putting two volunteers in each of twenty sites across the country. He convinced locals to contribute to the construction effort for free, and when the schools were completed, none of the villagers referred to them as "the Peace Corps schools"; they were "our schools." "That's how I know we've been a success," Larry told me when I visited Gabon.

By and large, we found our success rate in overseas staff selection soared when we picked from our impressive and growing pool of returned Peace Corps volunteers. In 1967, our sixteen thousandth volunteer returned from service, making the number of returned volunteers greater than the number in service. On my office wall I hung a board listing Peace Corps staff, with returned volunteers in red. When I started, about twenty percent of the names were red; I wanted at least half the board red by the time I left.

Superstars from this pool of returned volunteers included Jon Darrah, our regional representative in Chiang Mai, Thailand, and Hal Crow, country director in Colombia. Another was Steve Knaebel, a volunteer in Venezuela who came back to Washington as a recruiter and later became a Spanish teacher at Camp Crozier, our training facility in Puerto Rico. Steve had a mastery of Spanish and Latin American humor that was rare among gringos.

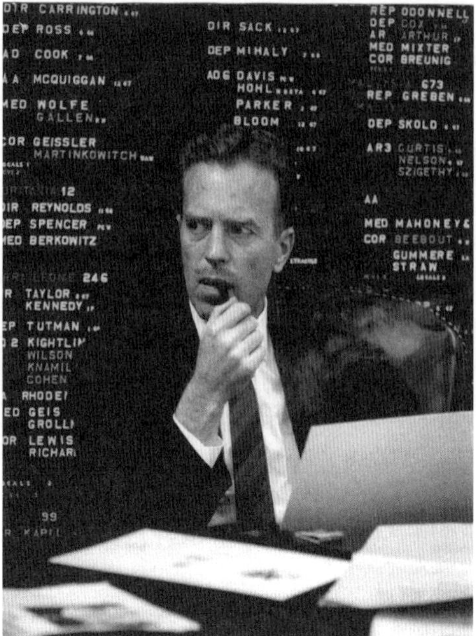

Steve's boss when he worked in Washington as a recruiter was a fellow returned volunteer from Venezuela (and fellow Stanford grad) named Chuck Butler. A hard-charging former college quarterback and a workaholic, Butler excelled as a super salesman on his recruiting trips. His over-the-top drive gave me pause, but his record as a volunteer and recruiter was so outstanding that I decided to send him out as the first Peace Corps director to Tonga, a Polynesian archipelago in the South Pacific.

It's fair to say that returned Peace Corps volunteers who became staff could be more demanding, more hair shirt, than staff hired from the outside. This was certainly the case with Butler. In Tonga, he set a volunteer allowance of sixteen dollars a month and six chickens. By contrast, volunteers in the rural Philippines received sixty-five dollars a month. The living allowances in each country were determined by the country directors to allow the volunteers to live at the same level as the people they served, with a little extra for travel. Butler's volunteers, barely able to eke out an existence, eventually convinced him to increase their allotment to twenty-five dollars a month and eight chickens. Unfortunately, Butler went seriously astray when he built a comparatively opulent house for himself with discretionary funds, and I had to fire him.

Butler's fall from grace was an exception to the rule of outstanding performance among returned volunteers who became overseas staff. On the whole, I don't think the Peace Corps would have survived if not for returned volunteers filling out the ranks in large numbers and with great competency; they pulled us through some tough situations. We could count on them to understand the experience, fully commit to its success, and exert the kind of tough management and inspired leadership necessary to pull it off.

•••

In about half a dozen cases, we sent a major Peace Corps contingent—around six hundred volunteers—to a country at one time. The first country to host Peace Corps volunteers on this scale was the Philippines, where we sent teachers and teachers' aides. The program echoed the famous Thomasite teaching program under Theodore Roosevelt at the turn of the century when the US took the Philippines from Spain. Those first Thomasite teachers (who arrived on the USS *Thomas*) established English as the national language and created a modern school system. After the Philippines, the Peace Corps went to Ethiopia and Nigeria with hundreds of volunteers working as elementary and middle school teachers.

Augmenting our teaching programs was the School-to-School initiative, aggressively pushed by President Johnson, in which American schools raised money to build new schools in Peace Corps villages abroad. Volunteers nominated a community that had never had a school and rallied the locals to provide resources: land, labor, locally available building materials, and teachers.

The first effort took place in 1963 in Casa Blanca, Colombia. We spent $3,000 on that school, and it took about three years to build. The next one took a year and a half and cost only $2,000. A year into my time as director, we were building these schools for $1,000 over a period of six months. In 1969 alone, the Peace Corps built 350 schools.

The sponsoring school in America chose from a list of potential communities around the world and raised $1,000. The resident Peace Corps volunteer supervised the construction of a three- or four-room schoolhouse. The new school maintained a relationship with its sister school in the States: students traded letters and artifacts, and the volunteer returned to visit the American school with pictures and stories. Quite often, the new school was the most substantial structure in the community and became not only a school but a civic center, athletic facility, and social gathering place. The program enjoyed great popularity, and politicians liked getting involved; Governor George Romney of Michigan raised $50,000 for fifty new schools.

One of our most interesting experiments in high-volume volunteer programs took place in the US Trust Territories of Micronesia, a group of small islands covering three million square miles in the Pacific Ocean due west of Hawaii. Given in trust to the US by the United Nations after World War II, these picturesque islands were largely neglected and underdeveloped and had become a source of consternation at the UN.

The situation seemed ideal for the Peace Corps: small, isolated Third World communities where the volunteers' presence would be felt and seen and useful in bringing people into the twentieth century. Our talented head of volunteer recruitment, former Malaysia director Seymour Greben, launched a campaign with brochures that lured volunteers with pictures of pristine beaches, shimmering blue water, and the slogan, "The Peace Corps goes to paradise."

After a rigorous selection and training process, we ended up with four hundred volunteers headed for Micronesia in October 1966. They were joined by six hundred the next summer, and at one point we had a volunteer for every one hundred Micronesians spread across one hundred islands. Nowhere else in the world could we have achieved this ratio with so few volunteers. Most volunteers came as AB generalists to work as elementary and secondary school teachers. Another large contingent took on daily responsibility for the public health system. They tackled environmental health, hygiene, water seal latrines, the water supply, and controlling filariasis, leprosy, and tuberculosis. Still others worked in agriculture, engineering, and architecture.

The most meaningful part of the Micronesia venture turned out to be the dispatch of about fifteen young lawyers to help the territories establish their legislature. These volunteers had an opportunity afforded to few lawyers in the world: to start from scratch making laws and processes tailored for indigenous communities. They regularly ran up against the Department of the Interior, a team led by Stewart Udall, who were more formidable than any bureaucrats I knew. The volunteer lawyers took them on and won in virtually every confrontation. There were rumblings from some in Congress that our volunteers were advocating politically on the part of Micronesians against the US. In truth the volunteers were doing what they had always done: working in the best interest of the local people in a nonpolitical, democratic way.

I visited Micronesia in March 1967, about five months after the first volunteers arrived. Fascinated by the great progress of the volunteers, I also felt irrepressibly drawn to the endless island beaches. Micronesia was a shell hunter's dream, and I fell victim to my long-standing weakness for exotic seashells. In my zealous pursuit, apparently I gave some of the volunteers the impression that I was more interested in looking for seashells than visiting with them.

Shortly after I returned to Washington, I received an enormous air mail package containing a man-eating clam, a mollusk that must have weighed seventy-five pounds. Some anonymous volunteers had dispatched the giant package to me cash on delivery; it cost me over $200 to retrieve it from customs.

Seaplane arrival in Micronesia

Disgruntled volunteers were a constant part of my workaday existence. Expanding as quickly as we were in tough and unpredictable environments, often with untested staff at the helm, volunteers sometimes felt they had been let down, unprepared, misplaced, or mismanaged. I worked from day one as director to cut down on these kinds of problems, but inevitably we still had some real loser country directors out there, some programs that didn't adequately address the needs of a community, and training that fell short. I received an enormous volume of personal letters of complaint from volunteers in every corner of the world—and their parents.

•••

Hubert Humphrey's presidential defeat in the fall of 1968 raised fear and speculation at the Peace Corps. With Humphrey, our continued good fortune would have been assured; under Nixon, all bets were off. I deeply admired Humphrey. Some of the most wonderfully informative and entertaining evenings of my life were my late drop-ins to Humphrey's office to brief him on the Peace Corps. On topics ranging from alcoholic MDs in VA hospitals to tales of Minnesota politics, Humphrey was a master storyteller.

In the anxious months following Humphrey's defeat, the Peace Corps hunkered down, looking for some early signal from the incoming administration. Would they keep us? Would they downsize us? Names of my potential replacements bounced around, but nothing stuck. Though few political operatives in Washington knew it—or believed it—I was a registered Republican. I suspect it was in my DNA. Shriver used to joke that Richard Graham, later a founder of the National Organization for Women, and I were the only Republicans on the Peace Corps staff. I doubt that my political affiliation was known to the Nixon administration.

In December, Assistant Secretary of State for the Far East Bill Bundy (brother of better-known McGeorge) offered me the ambassadorship in Manila. The need was urgent because the incumbent, G. Mennen "Soapy" Williams, was on the verge of a persona non grata exit. Soapy had gotten crosswise with President Marcos and his well-shod wife Imelda by acquiring old art treasures considered part of Filipino patrimony. I would have jumped at that assignment in earlier times, but I still held out hope that I might stay on as Peace Corps director under Nixon.

President Nixon moved into the White House on January 9 without offering the Peace Corps any clue to our future. Ironically, volunteer applications surged with the start of the Republican administration, which had committed to negotiating an end to American involvement in Vietnam. I started attending the Monday morning meetings of the secretary of state, now William Rogers, hoping to pick up some helpful crumb of a rumor about how we stood in the eyes of the new regime. All I gained from those gatherings was a glimpse at the mounting tug-of-war between Rogers and National Security Advisor Henry Kissinger.

In March, we finally received a call from Rogers' office setting up an afternoon session with Peace Corps management at our headquarters. Our meeting that day turned into a lively and impressive tour-de-force. The secretary seemed pleased and acted very much at home. Reflecting on the quality of the senior people guiding the Peace Corps at that time, I can't imagine any observant visitor not being captivated by the sparkle and commitment of that group. There were no stereotypes and no two alike.

At the end of his high-spirited, three-hour visit to our office, Secretary Rogers made a short speech to me and my staff, saying the Nixon administration was highly satisfied with what the Peace Corps had achieved and that he hoped I would stay on as director indefinitely. We heaved a collective sigh of relief and popped a bottle of champagne—a rare splurge at the Peace Corps. The next day, my old traveling buddy Jeremiah O'Leary reported in *The Washington Evening Star* that Nixon would be keeping me on, at least until I hit my five-year limit in 1971.

Several days later, my assistant Carolyn told me that a *Washington Post* reporter had called for my comment on a story about my replacement. I was dumbfounded.

When the article appeared, it identified the new Peace Corps director as Joseph Blatchford and included his passport picture, in which he looked like John McEnroe as a child. My successor did in fact play tennis with the president of PepsiCo, Don Kendall. President Nixon had reportedly promised Kendall early in the campaign that he would appoint Joe Blatchford as Peace Corps director, and to the surprise of the State Department, he had. Rogers never called me to apologize or explain.

A week after I was fired via *The Washington Post*, there appeared in the same paper a scathing article by syndicated columnist Mary McGrory titled, "The Pink Slip Administration." She chided the Nixon patronage gang for dumping so many nonpolitical senior staff like me. The article prompted a call from Rogers wanting to know whether I had put McGrory up to it. My response to the strangely overwrought Rogers was that I didn't even know Mary McGrory—but I certainly liked what she wrote. Her article spawned a rash of similar attacks on the Nixon administration's personnel policies across the national media, inciting Rogers to send me an accusatory follow-up note.

The mood around the Peace Corps became terribly gloomy. We all felt we had a wonderful thing going, and suddenly everything changed. A couple of weeks of political purgatory passed before Under Secretary of State Elliot Richardson, a handsome and sophisticated ex-boxer, came to my rescue. What Richardson offered immediately eased my doldrums. Naming the six or seven ambassadorial posts still open in the Western Hemisphere, he told me to take my pick. I made my decision easily. The Peace Corps had brought me into close contact with the president and foreign minister of Colombia, and I felt that Carlos Lleras Restrepo and Alfonsito López Michelson were the kind of men I would enjoy dealing with.

As I packed up my effects at 806 Connecticut Ave., it struck me how lucky I was to have followed the great Sargent Shriver. Mine had been a lower-key tenure, with many fewer requests for autographs, but just as busy, thrilling, challenging, and fun. I relished the friends I had made, especially among the young people at the organization. Ever since those tough-talking, scared teens had joined the ranks of my regiment in World War II, I have felt I get along better with younger people than my peers or elders. Maybe it has to do with their higher tolerance for my romantic ideals and bad jokes.

My final cable to Peace Corps staff worldwide read, "Before you I had not known of a group or an idea so ripe for dealing with the ills of our time. Before you I had not been associated with individuals who gave me so much pride and kindness. I send you my love, repeat love, and best wishes. May you find Peace."

Mine was the best job in the world and the favorite of my career. During my time as director, the Peace Corps added twenty countries, dozens of talented and wonderful staff members, countless dialects, and many more hours of practical skill and language training for our intrepid volunteers.

Regrets I have related to the Peace Corps are few, but one oversight still haunts me. In the early days when we were desperately trying to find mutually rewarding jobs for AB generalists, we missed the environmental angle: the ease of training and continuity, and the tremendous need in virtually every country. Not until a volunteer in Chile named Duty Greene planted a million trees and appeared on NBC news with former Peace Corps staffer Douglas Kiker did I understand that I had failed to see the forest.

Before leaving for Colombia, I made my obligatory stop at the White House. Protocol requires that new ambassadors arm themselves with a very useful status symbol: a color photo confirming a close—if not lifelong—relationship with the US president. A crew cut and serious H. R. Haldeman, later of Watergate fame, escorted me into the Oval Office, curtly announced me, and departed.

"Good afternoon, Mr. President." There was no response, and when I looked closer I saw that Nixon was asleep in his chair. I approached his large desk and said good afternoon a little more assertively, and he awoke with a twitch. Lurching to his feet, he came around his desk to shake my hand. The president admitted that he may have nodded off, but to his credit he knew where I was headed. "When you get down there, ambassador, just remember: you can't trust any of those little sonsabitches south of Key Biscayne."

9

1969–1971

I have had calls from Parade, Esquire *and* Harpers *to do an article on Latin America. I have had several irate calls from the State Department to shut up.*

—Letter to my wife, Leftie, 1970

In the northwest corner of South America, straddling the Panamanian isthmus, Colombia is the most complex and sophisticated country in Latin America. Liberated from the Spanish by Venezuelan Simón Bolívar and his rebels in 1819, Colombia had the first constitutional government in South America. With the continent's second largest population, after Brazil, the country boasts seven cities of over a million residents. Despite Colombia's many assets, from its bright and diverse people to its natural resources like petroleum, coal, gold, and precious stones, years of civil war and other conflicts chronically upset the country's stability. Colombians had a knack for electing intelligent, talented presidents, but peace eluded them.

In 1948, simmering tensions between liberal and conservative political parties in Colombia were driven to a boil by the assassination of popular liberal presidential candidate Jorge Eliécer Gaitán. Probably not by coincidence, a Cuban university student named Fidel Castro was visiting Bogotá at the time and became involved in protests over the killing. During the ensuing riots known as the *Bogotazo*, upwards of 180,000 Colombians were killed, and an enduring civil war was born.

Colombia's revolution was business as usual when I became ambassador in 1969. The widespread *violencia* of the previous two decades had evolved into an alphabet soup of antigovernment, leftist guerilla groups—FARC, ELN, EPL—and right-wing paramilitary gangs. The United Nations had been of no help getting the violence under control,. ditto the Organization of American States.

The US routinely confused the Colombians by advancing separate agendas through the Pentagon and State Department, much the way it operated in Panama. All through the 1960s as the Alliance for Progress worked to reform government and provide economic opportunities for the poorest Colombians, the CIA and US Army were working behind the scenes to train, advise, and supply the Colombian military to wipe out peasant populations suspected of leftist insurgency.

Drugs were not yet an overwhelming issue; at that time, the only recognized opiate of the masses was communism. Castro and the Soviets, Chinese, and East Germans had become major players in Colombia with their never-ending Cold War antics and enormous shipments of weapons and money. Murder had become one of Colombia's leading industries.

Two other challenges of my ambassadorial post could be found in Washington in the form of President Nixon and National Security Advisor Henry Kissinger. Nixon never recovered from his 1958 goodwill tour of Latin America. After witnessing lively protests in Uruguay and Peru over the US support of anti-Communist dictators, Vice President Nixon faced more angry mobs in Venezuela. That leg of his trip began inauspiciously when an unwelcoming committee at the airport hurled spit at Nixon and his wife. As their motorcade traveled through a poor suburb of Caracas, a mob attacked. They shouted anti-American slogans, smashed windows, and rocked the car violently, trying to overturn it. Venezuela's foreign minister was injured, and secret service agents threw themselves over the vice president as the car sped away.

In contrast to Nixon, whose distaste for Latin Americans was palpable, Kissinger's attitude towards the region was one of disinterest. He found Latin American leadership boring and beneath him, which was hard to figure since Kissinger had for many years written Nelson Rockefeller's speeches on Latin American themes. Until John F. Kennedy, Rockefeller had been the only senior US politician in the last century for whom Latin American leaders felt any affinity. As was so often the case, our best foreign policy tool in Colombia was the Peace Corps. The country hosted more than six hundred Peace Corps volunteers in 1969 and was thought (especially by me) to be one of the most successful programs in the world.

While I worked as Nixon's plenipotentiary in Bogotá, I received only two notes from Secretary of State William Rogers, both addressed to my predecessor. I preferred to communicate with congenial Under Secretary of State Elliott Richardson; it was he who swore me in as ambassador. I thought more highly of Richardson than of anyone else in the Nixon administration. Over the next ten years, he would occupy four cabinet positions, a feat unmatched by any US official.

A week after my appointment as ambassador, Colombian President Carlos Lleras Restrepo, a wonderful leader and friend, came to Washington for a state visit. President Lleras, Colombian ambassador to the US Misael Pastrana Borrero, and I attended a brief

White House press conference and photo op with President Nixon. Then the four of us walked down the long corridor to the Oval Office; Pastrana and I trailed the two presidents by a couple of paces.

Without a word, President Nixon entered his office with Lleras and slammed the door, nearly hitting Pastrana and me on the nose. Making the best of it, the Colombian ambassador and I traded stories and talked Colombian politics while we waited outside. The incident typified Nixon's flat-footed diplomacy, and this time the joke was on him: Misael Pastrana was elected president of Colombia the following year.

In addition to working under an administration indifferent to Latin America, I also carried the yoke of our increasingly defenseless war in Vietnam. We were still four years away from the Paris Peace Accords, and anti-Vietnam sentiment was stronger than ever among Americans at home and abroad. Peace Corps volunteers, as usual, were vocal.

One morning a 6:00 a.m. phone call from the CIA station chief alerted me that hundreds of Peace Corps volunteers were gathering outside the US embassy. "Can the local Peace Corps staff possibly handle this?" my station chief wanted to know. "Can't we round up the ringleaders before it gets out of hand? What should we tell Washington and the local police?"

I told my station chief to give me an hour. If it was the ambassador's attention they were after, who better than I to pay the protesters a visit? As my limo pulled up in front of the embassy, I saw masses of volunteers lining the sidewalks looking calm and well turned-out. Their signs were in English, and their chants in Spanish. These were my people—my primal impulse was to join them.

Roughly four hundred pairs of eyes were on me as I emerged from the car. I shook hands with the volunteers closest to me, then started down the crowded sidewalk past the entire group. I sensed no hostility; they were quick to joke and tease. One volunteer thrust her placard at me, and I took it for a spin down a short length of sidewalk. The symbolic passing of the baton drew shouts and applause from everyone.

EL ESPACIO

Diario de la tarde, Bogotá, martes 19 de mayo de 1.970

Caught in the act by the local paper

In a few minutes, after nothing more than the momentary transfer of a homemade poster from the steady hand of a concerned volunteer to the moist palms of a passing Nixon representative, the protest came to a peaceful end. The volunteers broke into groups as I circulated, trying to greet and congratulate each one.

Agence France-Presse jumped the gun and released the wire report, "American Embassy Under Siege." Our embassy quickly sent a vague account to the State Department downplaying the event. The return cable read, "Need clarification." I thought it the perfect response; US foreign policy in both Vietnam and Latin America badly needed clarification—and correction. Knowing that ambassadors had been fired for lesser infractions than joining a protest against their own embassy, I didn't clarify and was relieved when State let the matter drop.

Despite the chill in Washington and the violence in country, the Colombia post suited me perfectly. From the earliest days of our friendship, President Lleras Restrepo treated me as a brother and, often, as a student. Topics of his monologues ranged from Lincoln to Castro to Kennedy. He was intellectually anchored to Lincoln, both of them forever impacted by civil war.

Lleras' greatness grows when we judge him against the backdrop of his inherited nightmares: from Khrushchev to Castro to the endlessly violent fallout from civil war to coping with foreign-backed insurgencies like FARC and ELN and their half-dozen vicious mutations. A genial, gifted, and, when needed, reassuringly tough *hombre*, Lleras remained a towering figure in Colombia until his death in 1994.

In addition to a good relationship with the host country's president, the other ingredient to a successful ambassadorship is a strong deputy chief of mission. A good DCM serves as a confidant, alter ego, buffer, and full-time manager of the embassy while the ambassador is out cutting ribbons. My deputy, Bob Stevenson, was a Harvard-educated Vermonter who could cope in all seasons. Broad-gauged and savvy, Bob's greatest quality was his common sense.

•••

Life at the ambassador's residence had its perks. I started my days with a jog on the back forty of our expansive and lush grounds. There was a Monterrey pine on the side of the house that must have been 180 feet tall; every three or four days the gardener cut a bough from it that he placed on the nightstand, and the whole bedroom was affected.

I came home each night to a fruit plate on which I could identify only about half of the varieties. Because of the dramatic altitude variations in Colombia, fruit like mangoes, cherimoya, plums, peaches, pears, and grapes were in season year-round. The tangerines were almost as big as grapefruit. I picked mangoes from the trees, falling out of one once after being startled by the resident goat, Helen Clapp. Helen thought she was a fighting bull, posing, snorting, and plowing through the garden fence to eat my Bibb lettuce.

During lunch one Saturday at the residence, I received a call from the CIA station chief asking if I was all right. He had picked up a rumor about a kidnapping in South America and wanted to make sure I wasn't the victim. Several hours later we learned that the US ambassador to Brazil, Charles Elbrick, had indeed been kidnapped by MR-8, a Marxist group. They held Elbrick for three days in Rio de Janeiro before freeing him in exchange for fifteen imprisoned leftists.

Kidnappings and violence were already commonplace in Colombia, but with a precedent-setting ambassadorial snatching, my security detail exploded. Armed guards, selected from Colombia's military elite, followed my every move. They accompanied me on morning jogs around the residence, and whole trucks of soldiers flanked me on field trips. A guard now always sat beside my driver, assault rifle on the floor. He mostly tuned the car radio and periodically chanted into his own radio, "*C-uno a C-dos, me escuchas?*" The answer came back: "*C-dos a C-uno, royer.*"

Our meeting rooms at the embassy had passcodes for entry, antibugging devices, and armed Marines standing guard. I knew things had gotten out of control when my security team received a shipment of waterproof guns at the beginning of the rainy season.

During one visit to Cali, Colombia's second largest city and one of its most dangerous, a window crank came careening out of a third-floor window of the US consulate building and hit the roof of my car as I stepped out of it. The incident triggered a panicked response that included the full force of the Cali police. They quickly seized my suspected assassin and whisked him to police headquarters, where, after extensive questioning and likely questionable interrogation techniques, he was cleared of wrongdoing. The incident in Cali caught the attention of *The Washington Post*, and a reporter called me for a comment. "No, it wasn't an assassination attempt. It was a beautiful woman throwing flowers to me, only she forgot to take them out of the pot."

Despite Cali's infamy as the kidnapping capital of the world, I visited often and stayed with my friends John and Mary DeWitt. Warmer and less rainy than Bogotá, which sits on an Andean plateau at 8,600 feet, Cali was a bustling city with distinguished universities and the Latin American headquarters for American companies like Colgate Palmolive, Goodyear Tire, Stanley Tools, and Gillette. John and Mary threw parties with a great mix of guests, from corporate titans to Peace Corps staff and Colombian politicians.

In other travels, I refereed lightweight and flyweight matches at the National Amateur Boxing Championships in Cartagena—great fun with spirited crowds and high-caliber fighters. While in town for the tournament, I also served as a judge for the Miss Cartagena competition. I was encouraged to find that only the latter was fixed.

Out of habit I found myself at many Peace Corps outposts, including one small mountain village where a new school had been constructed. At the dedication, the local hosts served *aguardiente* (firewater), the Andean drink of choice, in gourds strung with rope. Guests wore the gourds around their necks so that the hosts would know refills were needed when their gourds tipped over. The Colombian brand of *aguardiente* is called *guaro*, made from sugarcane with more than thirty percent alcohol content, always served neat. As I walked from the town center to the school with machine gun-toting soldiers in trucks leading and following me, I made sure to keep my gourd up.

Cartageneras bellas

Another dedication took place in Barranquilla, a large port city near the Caribbean Sea, at a new bridge over the mighty Magdalena River. The project, a collaboration of USAID, Peace Corps, and communities on either side of the bridge, connected Barranquilla to the beautiful Isla de Salamanca, a national park. It was an impressive structure, and the dedication involved much fanfare, including soldiers in uniform (and not just those guarding me), Peace Corps volunteers, local dignitaries, school children, lively bands, and food vendors spread out along the length of the bridge.

After the speeches and ribbon-cutting, the Peace Corps volunteers asked for a photo at the apex of the bridge where both the Colombian and American flags flew. As we posed, with the volunteers standing around and behind me, one volunteer in the back placed his hand on the bridge railing. It shifted and fell hundreds of feet, noiselessly splashing into the Magdalena. Now we understood that the soldiers lining the sides of the bridge were more than just ceremonial; none of the railings were secured. With that final detail apparently scheduled for *mañana*, we were lucky not to have made any sacrifices to the Magdalena that day.

•••

Beyond its well-earned reputation as a land of emeralds and never-ending wars, Colombia is a country of universities—there are well over one hundred. As an agent of the American government, I had been unceremoniously ejected from many Communist-leaning Latin American campuses, most dramatically in Bolivia by the Cochabamban lynch mob. During my Peace Corps years, the treatment was the same: "The volunteers can stay," the rectors would say, "but you must leave the campus before the protesters arrive." In Colombia after a speech at a Medellín university, I was walking out of an auditorium when a distant figure tried to get my attention by throwing a tire iron from the roof.

The State Department's inability over the years to build a mutually trusting relationship with at least a few of the better Colombian universities greatly frustrated me. Our often bullying posture toward Latin America and our uncompromising Cold War policies proved too alienating. Improving our troubled relationship with Colombian universities was one of my major objectives as ambassador. Much the way I did in the wake of Panama's anti-American rioting, I began to look for a symbolic way to bridge our ideological and cultural divide.

In the summer of 1969, an unprecedented opportunity for binational bonding literally fell from the sky: Apollo 11. Even before Neil Armstrong, Buzz Aldrin, and Mike Collins returned to Earth, a popular Bogotá bar had been renamed *Apolo Once*. The astronauts had captured the imagination of the Colombians, as they had the world. The American mission to the moon offered the total package: world-class technology, romance, and great courage.

In September, a State Department telegram arrived: "What impact would a short visit to Bogotá by the Apollo 11 crew have on the Colombian public?"

My immediate answer was, "We cannot do without them."

The only representation of American culture on display when I arrived at the residence in Bogotá was a traveling modern art exhibit with works that ranged from the abstract to the alarming; they provoked puzzlement more than understanding. Thrilled by the chance to introduce accessible, inspirational American space explorers to Colombians, and motivated by my desire to build a dialogue with Colombian universities, I instructed my public affairs officer, Walter Bastian, to play up the Apollo 11 visit for all it was worth.

The three astronauts, accompanied by their wives, a throng of NASA public affairs people, and a handful of Voice of America reporters, departed on September 29 aboard Air Force One for their Giantstep-Apollo 11 Presidential Goodwill Tour. The trip took them to twenty-four countries over thirty-six days. They stopped in Mexico City first, followed by Bogotá, where they touched down to a huge expanse of red carpet on the tarmac and a custom-built stage decked out in red, white, and blue. The crowd at the airport was estimated at seven hundred thousand; it went on forever in all directions, surging, and roaring.

As I greeted the men at the bottom of the airplane stairs, I was surprised at the youthful appearance of Armstrong. With his crew cut and trim, diminutive frame, he could have been twenty-five. Armstrong and I walked together onto the stage to deafening applause. As we waited for the audience to quiet, I asked Armstrong if he spoke Spanish. "Some," he said. My introduction of him and his companions was brief and proud. Then, in flawless Spanish sprinkled with Colombian expressions, Armstrong lifted off. He said all the right modest things to his awestruck audience.

We climbed aboard open jeeps, perched on the seat backs and holding onto the roll bars, to parade slowly toward the presidential palace. As inappropriate as such a comparison may be, the astronauts were said to have outdrawn Pope Paul VI when he visited Bogotá earlier in the year. Of course, the astronauts were three to the Pope's one, to give the Pope his due. The two-hour parade to the Palacio de Nariño, though spectacular and emotional, was but a preliminary. The main event, from my PR perspective, would come that night at a gathering at the embassy residence for hostile Colombian university faculty and staff.

Neil Armstrong and his wife, Janet

In planning the event, Walter Bastian and I concentrated on faculty members falling into a number of negative categories: hardline Communists, those who had refused prior invitations to the residence, and those who had turned down educational exchange offers. We ended up with a list of about five hundred reportedly or notoriously anti-American academics, many of them graduates of Russian and Cuban universities, whom we felt wouldn't come to the residence for any other cause than the moon.

More than half of the invited guests arrived on my doorstep that night. I watched them emerge from the receiving line, autographs in hand, exhilarated and inspired. Many hours later, guests still lingered with the indefatigable Apollo 11 crew. I realized then that surrogates sometimes make the best ambassadors. In matters of cultural attitude adjustment, the Harrison Fords, Michael Jordans, and Barbara Bushes can do it better than anybody in striped pants.

We knew attitudes had changed that night, but we didn't know if the Apollo 11 effect would last. During the balance of my time in Colombia, I saw ample evidence that, post-Apollo, the lines of communication between Colombian universities and the US were greatly expanded. Academic exchanges, lectures by visiting American professors, and even Peace Corps programming all became easier, lighter, and less suspicious in the aftermath of Neil, Buzz, and Mike.

I presented President Lleras with a gift of four moon rocks and the Colombian flag that had been taken to the moon by Apollo 11. Lleras was very gentle with me, as he always was, and we talked for a couple of hours about coffee fungus, citrus wilt, cattle, university students, airport congestion, President Johnson, and Colombian presidential politics.

•••

Sorting through the endless pile of paper that greeted me when I returned from a trip, I usually found a handful of very appealing items mixed in with all those dreary cocktail invitations and bureaucratic tasks. Among the saving graces on one occasion were a request to donate a trophy for a horse race, a reminder to buy tickets for the bullfight season that began in January, an invitation to hunt jaguar (ditto for quail and partridge), and two complimentary tickets to a soccer game on Sunday between Brazil and Colombia.

Part of my job was hosting a near-constant parade of visiting American government officials and politicians, or businessmen from companies with a presence in Colombia, among them General Motors, Texaco, and Chase Manhattan Bank. One of my more colorful guests was Secretary of Commerce Maurice Stans, who wore a sharkskin suit and diamond pinky ring. Stans went on to become finance chairman for Nixon's Committee for the Re-Election of the President.

Even before they arrived, Stans' team was ordering us around. His staff director called my office from Buenos Aires several times a day with orders and questions in preparation for their stop in Bogotá. Finally, in a burst of ego and frustration, I told this man that if he didn't stop calling me, the visit would be canceled. Stans came through the embassy like a freight train, confiding to me that he depended on "mainlined" B-12 shots every three days. I took a four-day trout fishing trip in the foothills to recover.

Since my ambassadorship in Panama, a worldwide Peace Corps tradition had developed in which volunteers were invited to the ambassador's residence for Thanksgiving dinner. As director of the Peace Corps, I had heard wild stories about these feeding frenzies, but had never seen one up close. On that first Thanksgiving Day in Colombia, it happened to me. Volunteers stood at the ready an hour before the specified time. Pleasant, humorous, and mature, this large pack of skinny Americans quietly devoured every last bite on the buffet. The household staff was in awe.

With the exception of Peace Corps types, I usually enjoyed the company of Colombian guests more than my gringo visitors. One afternoon, I had lunch at the residence with the Cardinal and Papal Nuncio, then snuck off to a stag dinner with presidential candidate Belisario Betancur. Another morning I gave away an ambulance to a children's hospital before dining with the minister of agriculture at the Jockey Club, where we talked cattle.

In social settings, my Panamanian background served me well; Colombia shares a number of traditions with its neighbor to the north, including cumbia music. I arrived in Bogotá knowing how to dance the cumbia—step back-together-change, with a circular arm motion—a skill that greatly endeared me to my kitchen staff, off-duty Colombian officials, and *campesinos.*

Cumbia in the campo

In the spring of 1970, the Colombian presidential elections were the topic of all conversation. In April, the president, Senate, and Chamber of Representatives would for the first time in history be elected on the same day. The four presidential contenders—all supremely confident—were Misael Pastrana Borrero, Belisario Betancur, Evaristo Sourdis Juliao, and Gustavo Rojas Pinilla, Colombia's former military dictator. The race came down to a duel between Pastrana and Rojas.

In the weeks leading up to the elections, all seven universities in Bogotá closed for the rest of the semester. Our political section started using the word "tense" in every cabled line to the State Department.

It took me almost an hour to get to the embassy because the streets were full of teenagers in miniskirts and loud sashes hawking their favorite candidate's handbills (mostly Rojas). We set up a press room with coffee and sympathy for the fifteen or so US reporters covering the story with their loosened ties and short pencils behind the ear.

On April 15, four days before the election, I sent our last political cable on the election, predicting *Pastrana gana*. On the day of vote counting, there was a failure of the Colombian communications grid. When the system came back up, Pastrana was declared the winner by a slim margin. Rojas supporters, called Rojistas, claimed the vote had been rigged. A rumor briefly flew that Rojistas had poisoned the water supply. The suspicious election gave birth to a new guerilla movement in Colombia named *Movimiento 19 de Abril*, or M-19. Despite the controversy, Pastrana served a full four-year term.

That spring, I found myself at a personal crossroads. After years in an unhappy marriage, I had met the love of my life, Margaret "Leftie" Weld, a returned Peace Corps volunteer. My wife, refusing to grant me a divorce, had followed me to Colombia and was finding ever new ways to complicate and delay legal proceedings. I decided the only solution was to quit my post.

The news of my resignation in June, just a year after I began my tour, took a variety of slants in the media. The Bogotá press reported that I had fought with President Nixon. The Associated Press credited my opinion that the Nixon administration didn't care about Latin America, and my irritation with the elaborate security detail surrounding me. *The Washington Evening Star* reported my plan to return to Montana to write a book.

I had been candid with friends about my frustration over Nixon's non-policy in Latin America. Instead of lower tariffs on hemispheric exports to the US (a Nixon campaign promise), there were increases in Pentagon and CIA activities. My attitude toward Nixon mirrored his toward Latin America: distaste, distrust, and avoidance. But my real and only reason for leaving Bogotá was Leftie.

My official statement, and that of the State Department, denied any disputes with the administration and cited a desire to return to private life. When Assistant Secretary of State Charles Meyer asked if I would stay through the presidential inauguration on August 7, I said no even before he had finished the question.

By standard procedure, I gave testimony before the Latin American Subcommittee of the House and shared final reflections at a hair-down session with the Bureau of Latin American Affairs at State. I felt I owed them a candid appraisal of what had soaked in during all these years trying to get on the right frequency with Latin Americans.

Among other observations, I said that there were far too many American officials abroad. If the Israelis and Japanese, for example, could comfortably manage their diplomatic presence in Bogotá with five or six professionals, why must the US maintain over two hundred? What catastrophe would befall us if we cut our numbers to forty or fifty people, I wondered, beyond a dramatic increase in the embassy's and consulate's efficiency? The argument fell flat then, as it would today. Inmates can run the asylum, but they cannot change it.

Word of my testimony about our missteps in Latin America reached the media, who clambered for an op-ed. Their calls were followed closely by those of State Department officials asking me to put a lid on it, which I did. Instead of dwelling on foreign policy, I hotfooted it to Juarez to write the final chapter of my protracted divorce. After a summer of garage sales and job interviews, I met Leftie in London with the shirt on my back and a Colombian emerald engagement ring nestled in the bristles of my extra toothbrush. We were married on October 20, 1970.

•••

When I returned to Washington in the late fall of 1970, civil rights leader Whitney Young approached me about becoming president and CEO of the National Urban Coalition. The Peace Corps' Africa director, C. Payne Lucas, had recommended me as a tough manager, which was what Young said the coalition needed at this critical moment in its short history. John Gardner had recently resigned as coalition chairman, replaced by the prominent lawyer Sol Linowitz, who served a largely symbolic role.

America's epidemic of urban riots began in Los Angeles in 1965, when police discrimination and brutality crossed the line, and the black neighborhood of Watts rebelled violently. Six days of bloodshed and arson resulted in thirty-four deaths, thousands of injuries, and millions of dollars in property damage, the worst riots in Los Angeles history up to that time.

Watts signaled the beginning of rioting in cities across the country with similar urban dysfunction. Blacks and other minorities rioted in Chicago, Cleveland, San Francisco, Newark, and Detroit, among others. Then on April 4, 1968, the champion of nonviolence, Dr. Martin Luther King Jr., was shot to death on the balcony of the Lorraine Motel in Memphis. The assassination ignited an intensely violent reaction in more than one hundred cities, with terrible damage occurring in Baltimore, Louisville, Kansas City, and Chicago. None of those riots, however, matched the mayhem in Washington, DC, where I was serving as director of the Peace Corps at the time. The mood at headquarters was numb and sad; some staffers talked of leaving international work to focus on the problems at home.

Washington, like Los Angeles and other major cities, maintained a system of residential segregation that cordoned blacks off from economic opportunity, education, and dignity. The Dr. King riots in Washington carried all the weight of years of both covert segregation and overt discrimination and abuse. More than twenty thousand rioters overwhelmed Washington's police, and President Johnson called up thirteen thousand troops to secure the city. Marines with machine guns stood guard on the steps of the Capitol, and Army troops circled the White House. Four days of violence, April 4 to 8, 1968, effectively shut the city down.

The physical toll in Washington came to thirteen people killed and roughly one thousand buildings damaged by fire, including hundreds of stores. Some inner city neighborhoods were economically decimated. The psychological toll, of course, could not be measured. It was a wake-up call for white residents and the political establishment.

The riots moved John W. Gardner, secretary of health, education, and welfare, to resign from his position in the summer of 1968 to chair the new National Urban Coalition, a group formed to solve the root causes of urban unrest. Across the country the coalition created local chapters with broad bases of public and private support to tackle problems at the community level. Gardner, a great thinker and humanitarian, enlisted a who's who of business, labor, minority, political, civic, and religious groups to attack the key issues of the inner city: housing, unemployment, health care, and police-community relations.

In 1970, Andrew Heiskell of Time Inc., industrialists Henry Ford II and Edgar Kaiser Sr., labor leader George Meany, banker David Rockefeller, civil rights leaders Whitney Young and Julian Bond, Mayor Richard Daly of Chicago, and Mayor John Lindsay of New York City sat on the coalition's steering committee.

As a nonprofit organization, the coalition was sharply restricted in its ability to engage in lobbying and national politics. During his tenure, Gardner became convinced that political activism on the national level—not the coalition's grassroots approach—would fundamentally change our institutions. When he resigned in 1970, he took the coalition's small lobbying arm with him as the foundation for Common Cause, a liberal-leaning group dedicated to influencing national politics and policies through citizen involvement.

After the departure of the charismatic Gardner, Whitney Young described the coalition as "in crisis" and needing a president who was a "hard-nosed manager." Why he approached me instead of qualified black leaders who must have abounded in his national network, I shall never know.

My job would be to hold together and grow what was originally an emergency response to the urgent social problems our government was not equipped to handle. The idea—ambitious, potentially heroic, and addressing the greatest challenges of the day—naturally appealed to me, and Young was a sharp and persuasive advocate. Had I known the players and the game a bit better, I may have paused (or reversed) before running onto the field.

At my first meeting with the coalition's steering committee members that November, the problems were transparent: labor leaders were suspicious and resistant to change, bankers and business leaders were panicked, local government officials were cynical, and black leaders were totally political. Of the loosely organized group, the black leaders were the only ones who seemed to have coalesced—with each other. I could not immediately see my role as a hard-nosed manager in such a climate. Better selections for CEO may have been political geniuses and master persuaders like Bill Moyers or Sargent Shriver, both of whom were reportedly considered for the position.

Knowing a bit about the challenges before me and fearing the worst, I brought to my wobbly coalition a pair of colleagues from the Peace Corps. Larry O'Brien, former director in Gabon and later head of Peace Corps evaluation, became my director of program operations. Larry was a great political strategist who thought like an anthropologist. Jon Darrah, a volunteer in Malaysia and then a Peace Corps fellow in Washington, became my invaluable special assistant.

The coalition launched many noble initiatives during my tenure, all of which ultimately had the feel of rearranging furniture on the Titanic. We established a community-oriented healthcare delivery system in six cities that provided care to all, regardless of their ability to pay. Minorities composed the majority of the boards for these unconventional HMOs, and the project eventually received $4 million in federal funding. Larry orchestrated the flagship program in Philadelphia, one of our greatest successes.

We provided technical assistance and seed money for low- and moderate-income housing. And, noticing the struggle of small, minority-owned businesses, we created a fund to help them compete for contracts with larger companies.

In my speeches across the country, I made all kinds of wild pronouncements and recommendations, hoping to give the coalition the reputation of a forward-thinking, risk-taking, nonpolitical organization, even if we weren't. I advocated for the creation of a lobbying group dedicated exclusively to the interests of children. We released an alternative to President Nixon's budget, tacking on a ten percent tax increase to support new programs for the poor. In my fervor, I called agriculture subsidies nonsense and our military budget ridiculous. At least once I proved prescient, when I pointed out the madness of lumping Health, Education, and Welfare into one governmental department.

That department—HEW—and the Office of Economic Opportunity (OEO) were coping with many of the same pressing issues that we were. The message from coalition representatives across the country was, "We do not believe HEW and OEO are doing nearly enough." In theory, with our broad-based support from businesses, churches, and the community, the coalition would operate faster, more progressively, and with better results. In practice, our organization followed the same failed patterns of HEW and OEO; it took few risks, compromised, and then threw money at the compromises.

The National Urban Coalition basketball team

As the memories of burning cities after Dr. King's death faded and local special interests began to vie for attention and money from the coalition, we slowly began to unravel. Major contributions from the private sector dried up following Gardner's move to Common Cause, which proved a much more satisfying outlet for businesses wanting to make a difference. With funding a major concern, we were faced with questions like whether to start charging subscribers for *City*, our sleek and costly magazine. Now courting individual donors to keep our doors open, I made countless fundraising trips to the forty-eight cities with local coalition chapters.

A serious blow came in March, when Whitney Young, who had championed and hired me, drowned while swimming at the beach in Lagos, Nigeria. Only forty-nine years old, Young was the executive director of the National Urban League and an advisor to Presidents Johnson and Nixon (and Kennedy before them). Johnson had awarded him the Presidential Medal of Freedom. With Young's death, the coalition lost a strong leader and a rare advocate at the White House.

President Nixon's reluctance to engage with the pressing matters of race and inequality certainly slowed our progress. The landmark Kerner Report, published at the end of President's Johnson's term, contained alarming figures: unemployment among black people was twice that of whites, and black infant mortality rates were triple those of whites. The report controversially cited racism as a major contributor to the plight of black Americans and famously concluded that the US comprised two societies, black and white, separate and unequal. Apparently unmoved by this mountain of evidence, Nixon commented that the Kerner Commission had blamed everyone but the rioters for urban unrest.

With most black leaders justifiably distrustful of the Nixon administration, the coalition struggled to launch cooperative public-private programs. The only positive interactions we enjoyed with the White House came from our relationship with Nixon's urban affairs counselor, Daniel Patrick Moynihan. How that talented Democrat landed there is a mystery to me, but given the White House's flat rejection of the coalition and its initiatives, Moynihan's influence with the president was critical to us.

We did manage to involve the Nixon administration in one of the coalition's most successful pilot projects, a work-study program for Vietnam veterans. The veterans worked half-time jobs for full-time pay while pursuing their education. The range of education spanned from high school or trade school to graduate level study. The administration originally turned a deaf ear when we suggested taking the idea national with federal funding, but Moynihan applied pressure, and the White House came around, naturally seeking full control and credit for Nixon.

Moynihan invited the coalition's senior staff to the White House ceremony marking the program's transition to the federal government. Officials of all the major veteran organizations were present in their bemedaled uniforms, bursting with pride and middle-age paunch.

The four invited work-study veterans were the picture of diversity: one was black, one Native American, one Hispanic, and one white. I stood chatting with the black veteran when President Nixon, who had kept us waiting for over an hour, burst in.

The president headed over to me and my companion, a slightly built, eloquent, and handsome Army infantry veteran. Under our pilot program, he was studying for an MBA at Dartmouth College while working part-time in a hotel. The president thrust out his hand to the vet. "Where you going to school, son?"

"Dartmouth, sir."

"Big Green!" Nixon hunched forward in that awkward way (parodied by cartoonist Herblock), looking like a cheerleader off the playing fields.

"Yes, sir, Big Green," was the quiet response from a young man whose focus was certainly not directed at his college athletic program.

•••

My growing disgust for Nixon made me question my deep Republican roots, and I watched with interest as the field of potential Democratic candidates came into focus in the spring of 1971. One of the early movers was an old acquaintance of mine, Senator Fred Harris of Oklahoma. I knew Fred as a friend of the Peace Corps and a smart, progressive fellow. I had also worked with his wife, LaDonna, whose father was Irish and mother Comanche Indian. A vocal supporter of Native Americans, she founded Oklahomans for Indian Opportunity (OIO), which later became Americans for Indian Opportunity.

At the Peace Corps, Shriver and I had both sought ways to improve the scant representation of minorities among volunteers. While we employed a dozen or so wonderful black staffers, we were never very successful at recruiting black volunteers. With Hispanics, we did a little better, and they performed especially well as volunteers in Latin American countries. Native Americans were the least represented: we had none.

In 1966, when I became Peace Corp director, LaDonna and I worked on a joint project with her group, OIO, to entice Native Americans into the Peace Corps through a specially tailored selection and training process. Financed by a grant from the Bureau of Indian Affairs, we recruited qualified Native Americans and waived the usual stack of reference letters in favor of in-depth interviews with the candidates. The seventy-six who completed applications were subjected to heavy-duty psycho and other analysis that whittled the group down to thirty-four who were invited to training; eleven accepted.

LaDonna felt that the traditional Peace Corps training presented an obstacle to Native American applicants: faced with the rigors of psychological evaluations, hours of language training, and the confidence and swagger of their Ivy League counterparts, the Indians from impoverished backgrounds with less education might "self-select" out of the whole ordeal, she said. Instead, we provided a customized, five-week "pretraining" course in Oklahoma run with the expertise of OIO. From there, the applicants entered traditional Peace Corps training before leaving on assignments in countries with significant Indian populations like Peru, Ecuador, and Bolivia.

Despite our prep program, the regular Peace Corps training traumatized the Native American recruits and failed to prepare them adequately for the demands of their posts; many of the jobs to which we assigned them were not a good fit. The first year only two applicants made it through training. The second year we did better, bringing twenty-three through training, but only four of them remained overseas after the first year. The report from my lead evaluator, Larry O'Brien, placed the blame squarely on the Peace Corps. Larry's findings were so damning that my successor, Joe Blatchford, tucked the report away as "confidential, authorized eyes only."

We ran the program in 1967 and '68 with the best intentions and the sound advice of LaDonna and her senior staff and psychologists from the American Indian community. Of the many questionable projects I undertook at the Peace Corps, this was the greatest flop. The only positive to come from it was a closer relationship with the Harrises, who impressed me as forward thinkers and true believers in change. None of us held the project's failure against each other.

Larry O'Brien had also forged a good relationship with the Harrises, and he began writing speeches for Fred as the Oklahoman's bid for the Democratic nomination began to take shape. Larry urged me to come on as campaign manager, an offer that appealed to me the longer I stayed at the coalition and the more I saw of Richard Nixon. Of all the rumored and actual presidential prospects on the Democratic front, I thought Fred clearly the sharpest. At thirty-seven, he had been the youngest member of the Kerner Commission and understood the complexity of race and poverty. I also thought the charismatic LaDonna would be a tremendous asset to the campaign.

Peace Corps staff and volunteers had always told me that Senators Harris and Birch Bayh of Indiana were the only junketing US politicians willing to spend quality time with them. The senators listened, commiserated, asked questions, and met the volunteers' local friends. The Harris and Bayh approach contrasted with the traditional hurry-up visits of most members of Congress who came for snapshots and handshakes before racing back to the ambassador's residence for a hot bath and a hot toddy.

My connection with Fred and LaDonna Harris, my interest in the presidential race, Larry's encouragement, and my convenient location in Washington made me nominal campaign manager from the start. I made it official that July, resigning from the National Urban Coalition and prompting the media to comment that Harris's fledgling campaign would be run by a bunch of amateurs. Reports described me as a "former director of the Peace Corps, former ambassador, and former Republican." Hoping not to add to my list of formers too soon, I called upon every contact I could think of to light the labyrinths of the District for Fred.

An old art school on R Street near the embassy of the Dominican Republic became our headquarters. Three staffers from the National Urban Coalition made the move with me: Jon Darrah, office administrator, Larry O'Brien, issues man, and Ed Moose, the coalition's San Francisco coordinator, now our Western campaign manager. I also brought along my wonderful secretary, Mary Jane McConnell. In our freshly repainted headquarters we found large stacks of posters proclaiming "Spiro Agnew Cares." After updating of name and picture, we distributed them to our regional offices.

•••

When Senator Fred Harris decided to test the national political waters, he had but one claim to fame: he had pulled off the Oklahoma political upset of the century when he defeated legendary football coach Bud Wilkinson for a US Senate seat. Fred's stunning victory had been made possible by the impressive political machine of the recently deceased Democratic Senator Bob Kerr. (Fred had served out the remainder of Kerr's term before taking on Wilkinson.) Unfortunately, by the time Fred decided to make his run for the White House, the Kerr machine had rusted.

This time, the candidate depended on his personality, smarts, and galvanizing speaking ability. His blunt, down-to-earth manner, curiosity, intelligence, and open, pleasant demeanor made him a natural and refreshing politician. Fred also had serious weaknesses, which could be broadly classified as immaturity. Some of us dreamed that our candidate might develop star power because he was so Oklahoma—different from his more traditional rivals. The other Democratic contenders (of whom there were eventually fifteen) fell somewhere between wimp and limp. Men like Edmund Muskie, George McGovern, and John Lindsay seemed un-ignitable.

The candidate

In mulling over his prospects and strategy for a future presidential run, Fred had consulted with Bobby Kennedy, a leader among the Democratic candidates in the 1968 presidential primaries. Fred had asked the political veteran how best to structure a campaign as a populist candidate. Bobby's advice had been simple: appearance is everything. You must dress and look the part at all times: a little disheveled, loose necktie, shirt sleeves rolled up, shoes unshined. Bobby's calculating advice did not surprise me, and, to his credit, Fred didn't take it. The Fred Harris I came to know did not usually seek advice, and if any came his way, he was almost certain to ignore it.

The campaign's biggest asset by far was our finance chairman, young New York investment banker Herbert A. Allen. Herbert's wife, Laura, hailed from Oklahoma and knew the Harrises well. Laura and her parents vacillated between hopeful and amused at the thought of Fred Harris in the White House along with LaDonna, whom Fred called his "Indian advisor." Herbert's casual but no-nonsense style, bold ideas, and flair turned the campaign into a great adventure. Most losing causes are not as exciting as Herbert made this one.

Despite my political inexperience, I fell into my campaign manager role quite naturally. I couldn't imagine better training for navigating a presidential election than running the National Urban Coalition. Everyone was an expert, everyone wanted to be in charge, someone was always insisting that we revise the strategy, and we always needed more money. From the start we encountered trouble with the senator's congressional staff, who wanted to run the show, but not as badly as Fred himself wanted to run it. "Whom do we have to rein in today?" was a daily agenda item.

Work days at our historic townhouse headquarters started in my office, where we political amateurs squeezed around a table in front of an antique fireplace. On the mantel sat a chalkboard with our numbered list of objectives for the day. Like all campaign staffs, ours was young, ambitious, and idealistic. We loosely employed former congressional staffers, political aides, civil rights activists, and Ivy Leaguers. In October, our highest profile staff member, Sam Brown, came aboard. Sam had organized the Moratorium to End the War in Vietnam, the most effective movement to rally public opposition to the war.

Few of us stayed seated at headquarters for long. In the summer of 1971, Fred traveled nonstop through nineteen states, shoring up the support of youth, minorities, and the poor and working-class voters in anticipation of announcing his candidacy for the Democratic nomination in September. At that time, Maine's Edmund Muskie was ahead in the polls, though Edward Kennedy (who was never officially a candidate) surpassed him the next month. Fred planned to enter primaries in Florida, West Virginia, New Mexico, and California, where he felt his populist message would be well received.

Fred spoke convincingly about the importance of independence and empowerment. A natural raconteur, he enjoyed telling the story of LaDonna's financial windfall years earlier. When Fred was studying law at the University of Oklahoma, he and LaDonna lived in a mobile home with their newborn baby, subsisting on peanut butter sandwiches and boiled potatoes. One day they were surprised and thrilled when LaDonna received a large government check in settlement of a claim made by her Comanche tribe. Their debts were paid, and new clothes were purchased.

Several months later, another check arrived from the Bureau of Indian Affairs for the Harris's baby. Baby Harris, a quarter Comanche, received half the amount her mother had. With great exuberance, Fred said, "What should we do with the money?"

"What do you mean *we*, white man?" was LaDonna's reply.

Fred's campaign messages focused almost exclusively on social and economic issues. Under his platform, which he called "new populism," every American would be guaranteed a decent income and greater social security benefits. Big business would get smaller. To that end, he proposed an antitrust bill to break up the country's largest corporations dealing in steel, cars, containers, oil, and aluminum. He thought the best way to control inflation was to take away the power of companies like General Motors to raise prices "without regard to market pressures."

Fred won every straw poll of dirt farmers or union workers, but in normal polling he never managed to break out of "all others." His message greatly appealed to his target audiences, but not as much to potential high-dollar campaign donors. As Herbert and I saw our expenses mounting and our funds dwindling, we put great stock in a fundraising luncheon Herbert had arranged in New York City. Fred's big-league stage was the 21 Club, where some forty heavy hitters from Wall Street and environs would hopefully be swept up by the new populism.

It could have been the third martini Fred downed with early arrivals at the restaurant; more likely, it was exactly how he felt about the state of the nation and his hopes for the party. He began his speech to New York's elite, "Gentlemen, we've got to get the rich off our backs." If he said anything after that I don't remember it. I do recall that applause was limited mostly to 21 Club waiters. Fred told me afterward that he "went for broke," and I congratulated him on his success.

Fred liked to manage his own campaign, especially on the sly. He followed up his New York fiasco with a five-day chartered plane swing through states we had not included in our plan or our printed and distributed campaign schedule. He cut a swath from DC to Miami with speeches and overnight stops along the way. The jet was wide-bodied, the hostesses aboard slim-bodied, and the drinks free. Not surprisingly, the campaign media on board demonstrated a keen interest in the new candidate.

That was the last time our candidate ran his own show, because there was no more show to run. A steaming Herbert Allen arrived from New York the day after a triumphant Fred returned from Miami ready to convert more Republicans. Herbert's and my conversation lasted but a few minutes—our decision was made for us. Fred had run his campaign into bankruptcy. We kept repeating, "It's over," as if we were Roy Orbison.

On November 10, forty-six days after declaring his candidacy, Fred announced his withdrawal from the campaign, saying with classic bluntness, "I am broke." McGovern went on to win the nomination, but he possessed little of the stuff that made Fred so engaging. He had no chance against Nixon. Our four regional campaign managers accepted the bad news stoically. The remarkable manager in San Francisco, Ed Moose, had already lined up two fundraisers in his territory—one with Dinah Shore and another with Sammy Davis Jr.—and Fred was determined to show up for such big celebrities.

Moose and Fred set off for an elegant dinner at Dinah's house, but Fred insisted they stop off for a little Mexican food en route, making them an hour and a half late. Arriving at the event as the last celebrity left, they found nobody in the kitchen with Dinah. There was, however, a nasty note. When word of the Dinah Shore disaster spread, the star-studded event in Las Vegas hosted by Sammy Davis Jr. was cancelled.

Fred kept right on attacking, but with a smaller team each cycle. He ran for the nomination again in 1976 against many of the usual suspects, including a relative unknown named Jimmy Carter. I noted with some interest that Fred tightened his budget that time around, traveling by RV and staying with campaign supporters. I never saw Fred after our campaign went belly up, but I had formed what would turn out to be a lifelong friendship with Herbert Allen and his family, which made the whole madcap adventure worthwhile.

10

1972–1977

The days are long and hot, and I've had so many French sandwiches that I could croque, Madame.

—Letter to Leftie, 1974

After Fred's primary campaign imploded, I began to question why I had ever abandoned the joys of a steady income. At age fifty-one, perhaps it was time for job security—or at least predictability. In keeping with one of the happiest themes of my life, an old colleague from the Peace Corps presented me with my next move. Jules Pagano, an adult education expert, called from Coral Gables to ask if I would be interested in joining the newest branch of the State University System of Florida, Florida International University, as dean of international studies. Coral Gables sounded lovely to me and Leftie. Exhausted from the campaign, I had the urge to become tenured and take a sabbatical. Plus, I was low on argyle socks.

I accepted the university job as soon as the offer left President Chuck Perry's mouth. Perry, a Fiorello LaGuardia type whom I affectionately referred to as Carlitos, had at thirty-two become the youngest university president in history. A natural salesman, he championed the school from the moment the state legislature passed a bill authorizing its creation in 1965. Perry made FIU a widely known acronym even before the school opened its doors in the fall of 1972.

The bill creating FIU passed the legislature after years of opposition lobbying by the high-profile University of Miami, a private college whose supporters feared that students would defect to Florida International University's cheaper program. A comparison-shopping undergrad would indeed find a compelling bargain: in 1972, a year at U of Miami cost $2,420 while full tuition at FIU was $570.

Florida's State Board of Regents approved my appointment in March 1972. The *St. Petersburg Times* reported that I would be the highest paid of any dean in the Florida state system, except those in the medical school. I never knew $30,000 a year could have so much cachet.

For the first several months, Carlitos Perry and his senior staff ran FIU out of the control tower of the abandoned Tamiami airport, due west of downtown Miami. To house the growing staff and impending student population, the school set up a colony of double-wide trailers on the desolate airstrip.

While the university boasted that one third of its faculty had lived abroad or had significant overseas experience, I found mostly monolingual gringos when I arrived. I hired my dauntless compadre Jon Darrah as assistant dean of international studies, and we arranged for Peace Corps-style Spanish language training for our small group of staff. We found well-qualified teachers among the university's Cuban work-study students, who drilled our group with mixed results.

A stack of faculty résumés sat atop my desk when I moved into our double-wide on the Tamiami airstrip. Unfortunately, I didn't have the money to hire any of them. The state legislature, interested in funding programs that would benefit the local community, was hard-pressed to justify financial support for the university's international programs.

Jon Darrah

Without funds to build a team of teachers and administrators, I had to jump into the broad-gauged hustle of starting a department from scratch. Acting as a kind of international consultant, I advised people hoping to establish or expand businesses abroad, in one instance meeting with a group of American entrepreneurs trying to start a professional soccer team in Central America. In order to raise our profile, I sat on the board of a Miami bank and sent Jon to participate in the local United Nations.

A steady stream of old friends and acquaintances from Latin America came to visit our new Center for International Studies. We hosted the Prime Minister of Barbados and President José Figueres of Costa Rica, who was serving his third and last term as president. Figueres took Leftie and me out on a friend's yacht, where he told us how he was saving Costa Rica's faltering economy through a lucrative coffee export deal with Moscow.

A good friend from my earliest Peace Corps days, Monseñor José Joaquin Salcedo, was a regular visitor to Miami. A priest and founder of Acción Cultural Popular, Salcedo broadcast educational programming to the *campesinos* of Colombia and Venezuela through his popular and progressive Radio Sutatenza. He had helped the Peace Corps with our educational television project in Colombia in the sixties.

A visionary and an eccentric, Salcedo had once rocket-launched a parachute-strapped cat across his backyard when Jon and I visited him in Colombia. (The cat survived.) When he ran afoul of the Colombian government with his grassroots activism, he retreated to his home in Miami Lakes. Leftie and I often visited him and the coterie of young men who flocked wherever he held court. Despite his many trips to Miami, the only English he ever spoke was "two eggs over easy."

Through Peace Corps friends Hal Crow and Basilio Liacuris, I became involved with the creation of the Inter-American Development Institute, a fancy name for a small group that raised funds for Salcedo's projects. Committed to protecting endangered Indians, Salcedo ran a program to help the Guaymí in rural Panama, and I often flew into Panama City for meetings related to that work.

Every time I visited Panama, I was met by a bulletproof car containing a box of expensive Cuban cigars. A note taped to the cigar box read, "Need to see you urgently for *unos cuantos minutos*." Ten hours later, I was dismissed in a state of inhalation injury from first, second, and third-degree cigar smoke after a marathon meeting with Panama's self-proclaimed Supreme Chief of Government, Omar Torrijos.

I asked Torrijos' aide-de-camp how the general always knew when I was arriving in Panama. He explained that Torrijos tracked his friends and enemies, and that every incoming passenger manifest from Miami International Airport was checked by his secret police. Names that matched Torrijos' list were teletyped to him as the plane left Miami, giving him two hours' notice of visitors. "You should be *encantado* to be on the good guy list. Did you notice how you breezed through immigration and customs?"

A complicated, cowardly, manipulative, drug-addicted alcoholic, Torrijos had come to power in a 1968 coup with coconspirator Boris Martínez. Torrijos had expelled Martínez four months later with the support of the US and ruled Panama autonomously until his death in 1981. To the surprise of the United States, Torrijos turned out to be a master politician who would eventually outsmart us to take the Panama Canal.

Torrijos possessed two unique talents: he could harangue the poor to greater effect than any demagogue I have known, and he could con my fellow Americans to a degree that left me dumbfounded. His success in co-opting US senators brought him almost to the level of the tobacco lobby and became the linchpin to his successful negotiation for the canal.

Torrijos' monologues during our meetings were full of the latest speculation and gossip about what he (or his multiple spies) thought was going on in his insecure, drug-saturated, Mafioso world. Items on his agenda stretched from the Castro brothers in Cuba and the Ortega brothers in Nicaragua to the Nixon-Kissinger crowd in Washington. He was predictably at odds with either the governor of the Canal Zone or the commander-in-chief of the Southern Command. His major themes were always drugs, Communist intrigues, and canal-treaty negotiations.

In late 1972, I had one of my most memorable airport pick-ups by Torrijos himself in his new bulletproof Mercedes van fitted with two elegant reclining chairs and driven by his daughter. Torrijos was drunk and fuming. The previous day, his brother, Panamanian Ambassador to Spain Moises "Monchi" Torrijos, had been busted a second time for smuggling heroin in his diplomatic pouch.

He said the CIA had agreed to stop opening Panamanian diplomatic pouches after exposing Monchi once before. But in the most recent case, it was the FBI that blew the whistle on Monchi. "Don't the CIA and FBI compare notes?" Omar grumbled. "Let's be realistic: you know we don't pay our diplomats that much, and he was only moving five kilos!"

We drove for hours as Torrijos ranted and raved between drinks from a bottle of Chivas Regal he kept between his legs. Across the isthmus and back we went, then down along the Pacific coast toward the Azuero peninsula, stopping for a midnight seafood dinner at his beach house in Farallón. I mostly listened, but also asked questions and offered my opinion when asked. It was easy to feel like Torrijos was agreeing with me, because he never contradicted anything I said; he did this to great effect with everyone.

My impromptu meetings with Torrijos continued for the next seven years. Once when Leftie and I were vacationing on Sanibel Island in Florida, Torrijos called our cabana to ask me to fly down for the day. Why Torrijos chose me as one of his sounding boards was never totally clear. I reasoned it was because I was a nonthreatening, Spanish-speaking relic of the Kennedy-Johnson years. I also happened to be a frequent visitor to Central America at a time when there was scant communication along the Nixon-Kissinger axis.

•••

Having taught at Michigan, Penn, and Johns Hopkins, I came to FIU bristling with bias about how a new university should be oriented: toward teaching! I felt that universities missed the mark by chasing big sports and big research, a problem FIU wasn't well established or well funded enough to have—yet.

In an effort to appease the University of Miami, the founders of FIU had agreed to admit only juniors, seniors, and graduate students for the first several years. Most of the record-breaking 5,500 students on opening day at FIU in September 1972 were graduates of Miami-Dade Junior College. Their average age was twenty-five, many worked full-time, and almost half were married. These were not the future football stars of America. The FIU of today, Division I and fully overtaken by big-time sports, was many decades in the making.

With Chuck Perry in Sutatenza, Colombia

Big research also came slowly. President Perry asked me to tap my Washington contacts to fund international research projects, but I found little interest among my bureaucrat friends, and I confess I didn't push very hard. Instead, I reveled in teaching a graduate seminar designed for internationalists of all ages and stripes; about half of my students were foreign correspondents based in Miami.

I loved those weekly exchanges over strong coffee and stronger rhetoric at the "dean's seminar." We set an awful lot of theoretical foreign policy, and I learned a great deal, especially about the increasingly complex issues around Cuba and the Cuban presence in South Florida. When a professor can teach a seminar of manageable size with no term paper in which he learns more than his students, the result is academic nirvana.

Leftie enrolled us in a beginner course at the famous Fairchild Garden. In Washington, I had dabbled in African violets, which had flourished in the low light coming through our apartment windows. But I didn't truly flip over gardening until our classes at Fairchild. After each class I bought six or eight *Crotons* and *Schefflera.* Eventually we ran out of room on our condo balcony and had to drive around with plants in the car. Ever since those evening classes among gentle old ladies and killer mosquitoes, gardening has been a consuming passion.

Just about the time the university completed construction of its first building, a five-story mammoth aptly named Primera Casa, academia began to get real. Committee in-fighting, clique formation, status disputes, and bureaucratic nonsense started to gum up the works. Gossip spread like yellow fever as almost everyone, from staff to faculty and students, now worked and studied in one building on campus. As nonacademics, Jon Darrah and I felt the tension we created with colleagues by doing things our way—decisively and without regard for process and formality. We had no patience for the artificial boundaries between disciplines and departments.

They say no university president should stay in office beyond five years; in doing so he would spend most of his time defending his own mistakes. Given the enormous scope of our mandate at FIU, such a warning was especially appropriate for our senior start-up group. Sure enough, most of us were gone by the time Carlitos Perry left in 1975. Perry, with his flair for pomp and circumstance, went on to run golfer Jack Nicklaus's Golden Bear enterprise and later headed Family Weekly Publications, publisher of *USA Weekend.*

Shortly after the start of the school year, I had taken a part-time consulting job with Children's Television Workshop (CTW). The opportunity came to me—you guessed it—from two Peace Corps media veterans, Bob Hatch and Stuart Awbrey. Now working their PR magic at CTW, they suggested to Joan Cooney, the network's cofounder, that I was just the one to smooth the way for CTW's efforts to take *Sesame Street* overseas. The fact that I had been involved with the Peace Corps' major educational television venture in Colombia seemed to be the clincher for Ms. Cooney.

•••

In 1966, Joan Ganz Cooney was working as a documentary filmmaker in New York City when a dinner party conversation with her friend Lloyd Morrisett, a vice president at the Carnegie Corporation, led to a groundbreaking idea. Cooney's passion was educational TV; Morrisett's interest at Carnegie was early childhood education. At that time, virtually every household in the country had a TV or two, but children's programming consisted mainly of mindless and violent cartoons interrupted by commercials targeting children.

Cooney and Morrisett conceived a series for preschoolers that would be highly entertaining yet free of violence and commercialism. Backed by Cooney's exhaustive research, the show would give young children the essential building blocks for their education in a format they would find irresistible. The target audience for this new venture was low-income, inner-city preschoolers, but the charm and humor of *Sesame Street* appealed to virtually everyone.

In 1968, Children's Television Workshop officially launched with Joan Cooney as executive director, one of the very few female executives in television at the time. She built a staggeringly impressive team of educators, researchers, and creative geniuses who worked collaboratively to produce a uniquely rich and effective program for three- to five-year-old children.

Turned away by the big three networks, *Sesame Street* found a home on PBS, where it premiered on November 10, 1968, to great reviews and greater popularity. To Cooney's surprise, she soon began receiving phone calls from television producers around the world interested in airing the show. She hired Mike Dann, a former CBS executive, to handle the overseas flying of Big Bird. By the middle of 1972, *Sesame Street* was being watched in fifty countries. The show aired in its original form, and many countries used it as a tool for teaching English.

When I came on as a consultant, a new type of program—a coproduction between CTW and foreign producers—was in the works in Mexico, Brazil, and Germany. In coproductions, foreign production teams created their own Muppet characters and rented our animated sequences for dubbing in the native language. The "wrap-around" segments with live characters conversing on the street were produced locally with realistic backdrops, native actors, and local expressions and humor.

My first assignment as a part-time consultant was a curriculum development conference in Caracas, Venezuela, for eighteen Latin American countries interested in *Plaza Sesamo*, the Spanish-language coproduction, and *Vila Sesamo*, the Portuguese version. Like *Sesame Street* in the US, the foreign coproductions began with research and curriculum development, a process vital to the effectiveness and relevance of the shows.

I traveled to the conference with Norton Wright, a former producer of *Captain Kangaroo* with ample international experience, who had conducted the first feasibility studies for *Sesame Street* in Latin America. He warned me that some of the conference participants, who were mainly education ministers and high-ranking academics, looked warily upon *Sesame Street* as American cultural imperialism. Beyond that, some took issue with Mexico City as the chosen production hub for *Plaza Sesamo*, calling the country of insidious telenovelas "the television tyrant to the north."

The conference felt like old home week; I had many friends and acquaintances among the foreign officials. What made the job easy, though, was the quality of the product we were selling. In Mexico City, Norton had set up a highly professional team of creative talent, skilled technicians, and education experts. To find writers with the right punchy, witty sensibility, he had mined the staffs of top advertising agencies. To keep the feel multinational and multicultural, he had hired actors from throughout Latin America.

Though I was new to this field—the network, the show, and the production process—I was an immediate convert and an enthusiastic spokesman for the cause. To those officials who complained about using one show to serve a diverse and complex hemisphere of nations, each with its own accent, colloquialisms, and traditions, I asked them where else they could find a better or less expensive tool for their children to succeed in school and in life. In America, I said, we listen to the BBC news; the program doesn't change our culture, but rather gives us greater knowledge and perspective.

Nowhere was high-quality, immediately accessible education more needed than in the Third World, and many Latin American countries recognized this gem when they saw it. The discussions in Caracas resulted in some tweaks to the curriculums, making them more relevant to a Latin audience: we added nutrition education in Brazil and information about hygiene and gastroenteritis throughout Latin America. Media giant Televisa worked with CTW to produce *Plaza Sesamo* for Spanish-speaking Latin America; in Sao Paolo, TV Globo collaborated with us to create *Vila Sesamo*, a series in Portuguese with a samba beat.

With the exuberant reception of its first coproductions, CTW was in a very expansive mood, and I was thrilled to benefit from it. Compared to academic committee jousting in Florida, CTW was a breath of fresh air. At none of those endless FIU committee meetings did we ever take on the topics of teaching or learning. Instead, my fellow deans and I dealt with petty politics and budget items; we did not neglect perks, tenure, and publishing. That spring when Joan Cooney said in her Arizona twang that I would be doing CTW a favor to join their talented team full-time, I jumped at the chance.

Though it meant moving from higher education to preschool, going to *Sesame Street* in 1973 felt like entering the big leagues. As the new director of international development at CTW, I was joining a well-oiled and multitalented team that included Norton Wright, director of international production; Lu Horne, producer of international materials; and Peter Orton, vice president of worldwide distribution.

The huge success of *Plaza Sesamo, Vila Sesamo,* and *Sesamstrasse,* a collaboration with Norddeutscher Rundfunk (NDR) in Hamburg, Germany, were tributes to the talents of Cooney and her staff. We provided our overseas partners with carefully researched teaching materials and offered assistance in casting, production, and technical training. We thought cross-culturally in all areas: music, comedy, national symbols, health, and safety.

For countries outside the Spanish, Portuguese, and German-speaking world without the resources to create their own coproduction series, we offered a specially tailored, culturally neutral international library of Muppets and animation with separate voice, music, and effects tracks for easy dubbing. Renting CTW's world-famous Muppets and animation represented enormous time and cost savings for our foreign customers. Original animation cost CTW between $8,000 and $10,000 a minute to produce.

Despite our best efforts, cultural neutrality was a goal not always achieved in the eyes of our overseas partners. In Mexico, we received complaints about an episode where Big Bird takes over Mr. Hooper's store to sell jelly beans and ends up selling more than he expected. The show was intended to teach basic math, but our Mexican producers called it blatantly pro-capitalist.

Then there were those who had their problems with Mexico: in Spain, officials rejected *Plaza Sesamo*, fearing contamination by Mexican accent. They were not dissuaded when we told them that the *Plaza Sesamo* actors hailed from six different Latin American countries. Spain became the first country to dub CTW's international library of Muppets and animation in its native tongue, Castilian. The show, Ábrete Sésamo, was not a major hit. It wasn't until 1979 that Spain launched its own coproduction, *Barrio Sésamo*, with greater success.

In Japan, *Sesame Street* had been airing in English, and we hoped to convince network executives to create a coproduction in Japanese. At NHK, the public broadcasting company in Tokyo, my colleagues Jim Drake, Tom Kennedy, and I discovered there is no such thing as one big sales pitch in Japan. Instead, beginning at the level of janitorial staff, we had to pitch our way forever upward to the executive suite over several days. After many identical meetings screening our pilot and explaining why a joint production was just what the emperor ordered, it seemed we had made very little impact.

At our final meeting with representatives at the highest level, we were told that NHK would use *Sesame Street* only in its original form as a supplement for teaching English in elementary schools. Their decision quashed my hopes of hearing Ernie and Bert bicker in Japanese.

In a last-ditch effort to salvage the Japan venture, we took our deal to the largest private channel, TBS. They weren't interested. Our disastrous day was capped off by a loud fight between Drake and our Japanese consultant, Tadashi Yamamoto, in the lobby of the Tokyo Hilton. Later that night, I created a drugstore uproar as I engaged in the obscene gesturing required to describe talcum powder in a foreign medium.

We had better luck in Seoul, where *Sesame Street* was being used to teach English to adults. Television executives were interested in producing a dubbed Korean version for their younger audiences using CTW's library and our expertise in voice casting, among other things. For our pitches to smaller markets like South Korea, I developed a strategy of setting up *Sesame Street* screenings for the wives and grandchildren of the presidents and cabinet members, a wonderful way to generate momentum and gentle pressure.

My trip to the Philippines presented a slightly different dynamic: President Ferdinand Marcos's wife, Imelda, a mother of four who held tremendous power in her own right, would be the primary decision-maker. Known for her toughness, Imelda had survived a knife attack the previous year that required seventy-five stitches.

Imelda Marcos

The screenings and pitches went very well in Manila, and at the end of my visit I sat down with Madame Marcos to seal the deal. Our intent was to create a *Sesame Street* coproduction in Tagalog, now called Filipino, the most pervasive language in an extraordinarily polyglot country. Imelda and I had no real disagreement on approach, substance, format, or even price. We even agreed to bring a few Peace Corps volunteers into the production phase.

At the end of our negotiations, Imelda told me the agreement would have to include a sizable up-front "contribution" (amounting to about half the cost of our production deal) from CTW to her favorite "charities." She could not believe that Joan Cooney, one of her idols, would be bothered by such a small "down payment for success," as she termed it. I assured Imelda that Cooney would be bothered, as would I, and our deal fell apart.

•••

In Europe, Germany's *Sesamstrasse*, produced early and successfully in Hamburg, served as a pioneer. An excellent illustration of a country making the show uniquely its own, the series sometimes veered quite far from the American version. The German educational advisors felt strongly that children be taught early to question authority, quite the opposite of our thinking at home. They also asked to incorporate sex education for the three- to five-year-old audience, an idea that took a good deal of vetting and revising before it won approval by the supervising CTW staff. Along with its more mature subject matter, *Sesamstrasse* also used rougher language than its American counterpart.

Deviations in coproductions were expected, and usually approved, even if we didn't fully agree or understand. The CTW staff built foreign coproduction teams and taught them the formula and process to creating the shows. We ensured that politics stayed out and that shows were curriculum-centered and appropriate (especially in the case of toddler sex ed). We watched and consulted but rarely interfered with foreign coproductions. Our staff trusted foreign production teams to do the right things because CTW had trained them; we also made sure that educators and government officials at the highest levels stayed involved with the series.

At first, the British and the French had scoffed at our show; the BBC famously banned it, although commercial channels aired *Sesame Street* in about half of British households. With the great success of our coproductions, it became more difficult for critics abroad to make the hackneyed case of cultural imperialism, especially when the "imperialists" were mild-mannered kids, Muppets, and cartoons speaking in the host country's language.

Eventually, the Brits embraced CTW, particularly with the introduction of *The Electric Company*, a show focused on grammar and reading that the BBC began airing in 1975 to combat illiteracy among ten- to sixteen-year-old potential dropouts. The executive producer of BBC School Television Service said of *The Electric Company*, "It has punch, and this is just the time we need it in Britain."

France also took an arduous journey toward acceptance. The notorious French bias against so-called American culture was compounded by the absolute dearth of children's programming on their four government channels. I began courting the advisors to the Minister of Culture, three women in black faille suits who looked like sisters and apparently served as the arbiters of French television.

Over expensive lunches at Maxim's on the rue Royale, I tried to convince them that *Sesame Street* as we were presenting it was a cultural blank slate. The French production would have no perceptible trace of America, only a formula for entertaining and educating that would prepare a generation of French toddlers for success. The ladies waited until after the meal and their last ten-dollar *pousse-café* before giving me a puckered "*non*."

The vice president of finance at CTW, Tom Kennedy, began to question the expense account billings from my trips to Paris to pitch our program. "How could you possibly spend this much for lunch?" My one-word answer was, "Maxim's." I traveled back to Paris several times to visit with the ladies, each time buying more elaborate desserts. Then one summer day after an unusually costly luncheon, the three of them in unison came forward with a "*oui.*"

Norton Wright and I were handed over to a French production team to negotiate the deal. The talks were conducted entirely in English, but our counterparts took liberal asides in French to discuss the finer points of taking us for all we had. Naturally I kept my fluency under wraps until we had reached a mutually satisfying agreement. When we stood to say our goodbyes, I gave my most eloquent French farewell to our stunned new partners.

Bonjour Sesame, a French version of Muppets, animation, and live-action sequences from our international library, debuted in September 1974. Within weeks of premiering on Television Francaise Une to a potential audience of three million children, *Bonjour Sesame* was ranked at the top of French TV viewing. All traces of US influence removed, Bert became "Bart," Ernie became "Ernest," Cookie Monster was "Macaron," and Herry Monster was "Hyacinthe."

Once France fell, so to speak, other reluctant nations like Holland and Denmark followed suit. At the Milan Film Festival that fall, *Bonjour Sesame* and other foreign CTW productions earned top honors. In 1978, France took the plunge with a coproduction called *1, rue Sésame.*

Children, parents, and critics in all parts of the world were captivated by CTW's beautiful mix of whimsy and learning, but bringing the magic of *Sesame Street* to the Third World was by far the most gratifying aspect of my job. I knew from my Peace Corps experience that too many elementary school dropouts could permanently cripple a society. Third World preschoolers rarely arrived at school prepared to succeed; once there, they faced powerful incentives to drop out. *Sesame Street* provided an immediate and inexpensive boost for those kids. In Latin America, only Cuba turned down *Plaza Sesamo.* Even in Chile, when a US-backed military coup ousted Marxist President Salvador Allende, *Plaza Sesamo* remained on the air.

On one trip to Mexico City, I found a woman waiting for me in my hotel lobby with a dozen roses. She asked if I were "John Cooney," assuming that the head of CTW was a man. She told me how her only child—a girl with serious mental retardation—had never shown any progress in spite of all of the special care she and her husband had sacrificed to provide.

Then came "the miracle." Her daughter watched all fifteen hours of *Plaza Sesamo* that aired every week, never missing a minute. After several months she began to show a remarkable change in interest, awareness, and involvement with what she was watching. She began to mimic, smile, and have moments of understanding. The program, in the words of this woman, had made her daughter into a "real person."

When I caught up with the articulate, persuasive, and no-nonsense Joan Cooney to tell her this story, I was reminded of the best guarantee for success in a job: having the right boss. Cooney was the maypole with a team of keen and exuberant talent dancing around her. The superstars at CTW included Jim Henson, Dave Connell, Jon Stone, Ed Palmer, and John Page. I had the luck of working most closely with Norton Wright. A four-time lightweight boxing champion at Yale, Norton squared off to spar with me in the halls of CTW, deflecting my left jab with his notebook.

I spent the majority of my time traveling with Norton and producer Lu Horne, settling down in my office across from Lincoln Center only occasionally. After two years of almost nonstop travel to negotiate deals and set up coproductions, Norton and I had the process down to a science. Norton always said that his goal in setting up countries with the studio, equipment, and staff to create their own shows was to work himself out of a job, something he did with wisdom and style.

With the international coproductions of *Sesame Street* running like clockwork and both *Plaza Sesamo* and *Vila Sesamo* in their second seasons with new characters and a shorter, half-hour format, the pace of my work began to slow. I loved my job but couldn't help being intrigued when a search committee from the Planned Parenthood Federation of America approached me about becoming its next president.

Planned Parenthood, which had recently lost its great leader Dr. Alan Guttmacher to leukemia, had spent a year whittling down a list of two hundred potential replacements to twenty finalists. The search committee wanted someone positioned to steer not just the organization's domestic endeavors, but also its international projects; they liked my overseas experience and probably overestimated my political clout. I became Planned Parenthood's third president in March 1975.

•••

In 1916, four years before my own unplanned entrance into the world in Montana, a courageous young nurse in the crowded immigrant slum of Brooklyn's Brownsville opened the doors of the nation's first family planning clinic. The nurse, Margaret Sanger, was arrested and jailed under the Comstock Law, which banned the distribution of information about contraception. Undaunted, Sanger went on to coin the term "birth control" and turn her organization into a national movement that became Planned Parenthood in 1942.

Sanger died in 1966 right after a major triumph: the Supreme Court struck down a law prohibiting the use of contraception by married couples in Connecticut. The momentum for family planning peaked in 1973 with *Roe v. Wade*, a decision that saved millions of lives by allowing women seeking abortions to come out of the back alleys and receive quality care.

In March 1975, when I succeeded the late Dr. Guttmacher as president of Planned Parenthood Federation of America-World Population (PPFA-WP), euphoria still reigned among pro-choice groups over their Supreme Court victory. But opposition to the decision rippled across the country, and an ominous phenomenon occurred: two conservative religious groups—Catholic and Protestant (mostly Southern Baptist)—came together in their outrage over abortion and formed an aggressive political lobby.

Caught off guard, the pro-choice movement allowed its newly organized opposition to shift the conversation from women's rights to abortion. Planned Parenthood supporters were labeled "pro-abortion," and the fervent, self-righteous members on the other side festooned themselves in "pro-life" and "antiabortion" rhetoric, placards, and bumper stickers. Few people could have predicted then how strong this movement would become.

The conservative coalition struck a chord with its constituents and gained power as it went to work creating barriers to federal funding for contraception and abortion. Slowly the gains made by Sanger, Guttmacher, and their many supporters were diluted or overturned. Our clinics and doctors began to come under attack, and new legislation was introduced to erode the progress that the pro-choice movement had made.

As I had at the National Urban Coalition, I stepped into Planned Parenthood just on the downswing of its greatest momentum. In both cases, I found it irresistible to be on the right side of history when the chips were down. Planned Parenthood seemed to me completely American in its position on freedom of choice. The organization's philosophy remained the same under my leadership as it was in Margaret Sanger's day: "To free women to be in control of their bodies, with every baby wanted and loved."

In 1975, Planned Parenthood was the largest secular volunteer organization in the world, with twenty thousand unpaid workers, most of them women. We provided medically supervised family planning services to more than nine hundred thousand people. Seven hundred clinics in the US and close to one hundred in foreign countries offered counseling, sex education, and a full array of clinical services, including Pap smears, breast exams, contraceptive care, and vasectomies.

PPFA-WP was a $155 million business, providing a quarter of all fertility services in the US. Reproductive healthcare, information, and contraceptive devices were offered to everyone, regardless of their ability to pay. Half our funding came from the federal government, and half was raised through direct-mail solicitation and private contributions.

Planned Parenthood's overseas operation, Family Planning International Assistance, was largely funded by USAID and involved in eighty-one projects across twenty-two countries. We distributed condoms in Turkey, provided sterilization in the Philippines, and trained *campesinos* in Central America to educate their neighbors about birth control. In 1975, we set up our first professionally staffed overseas offices in Ghana, Costa Rica, Bangladesh, and the Philippines.

In Colombia we partnered with my old friend Monseñor Salcedo to distribute condoms through the Catholic Church, a surprisingly uncontroversial program. In making his case to potential funders, Salcedo gave the example of a typical rural family with seven children. The mother, age twenty-nine, has endured eleven pregnancies and needs a rest; the father makes two dollars a day. Is it wrong to suggest contraception? "My people believe 'abstinence' is some kind of diet," Salcedo said.

Our New York headquarters on Seventh Avenue housed one hundred staff members and four vice presidents: Frederick Jaffe, Jeannie Rosoff, Hans Blaise, and Dr. Louise Tyrer. I was particularly fond of Louise, who started around the same time I did as vice president for medical affairs. Feisty and colorful, she was worldly and wise about family planning in the US and abroad. Louise was an ally, an exception to the political and territorial senior staff.

I avoided office politics by traveling constantly, visiting many of the 187 affiliates and 500 clinics in our seven regions: Northeast, Southeast, Great Lakes, Mid-Atlantic, Mid-West, Southwest, and West. At that time, we had affiliates in forty-six of the fifty states. In the Los Angeles area alone we had clinics in Pasadena, El Monte, Canoga Park, Mar Vista, Pomona, Baldwin Park, and the Wilshire District.

When I became president, Planned Parenthood was losing money. Through an enormous fundraising campaign spearheaded by our smart and hardworking chairwoman, Tenny Marshall, we made it into the black in 1976. We raised $640,000 in direct contributions, almost twice as much as the previous year. Tenny capably steered an enormous board, many of them wealthy women who made up for their lack of humor with deep passion and pockets.

A constant challenge was bailing out small, financially strapped affiliates. A clinic needed around two thousand patients to break even, but our smallest served only four or five hundred. At headquarters we usually became aware of an affiliate's financial woes during the final crisis phase, when we were asked to provide a replacement for a recently fired executive director or accept defaulted fair share payments. It was a scenario repeated over and over.

To me it seemed like madness to regularly prop up these tiny operations when some were within an hour of each other. I urged the smallest affiliates to think creatively about consolidation. During visits with local directors, I said, "in your board meetings look at yourselves and look at the neighbor forty miles away to see if there aren't some things you can do together and move toward a more rational grouping." The idea was enormously unpopular among the proud local leaders who had worked tirelessly to build their own affiliates.

Sensitive to the financial strains on our organization, I felt our New York landlord was overcharging us for subpar office space. He even shut off the heat on the weekend, freezing our staff and our office plants. I identified an affordable and attractive building in Austin, Texas, that I felt would be an ideal headquarters for us. Located in the center of the country, closer to most of our affiliates, the space was bigger and much cheaper than our New York office. The thought of moving panicked many of the staff, though, and the old New York establishment on the board clearly bristled at this potential upset to the status quo. We didn't move.

In my speeches across the country aimed at boosting funding for affiliates and advocating public policy reform, I pushed three major themes: improved access to quality contraceptive care for the estimated 4.5 million women who did not have it, more and better sex education for young people, and research into male contraception.

In 1970, Planned Parenthood had begun a five-year plan with federal government funding to eliminate the unmet contraceptive needs of the estimated seven to eight million women at or below the poverty level. By 1975, when I joined the organization, we had been able to reach at most half of that group, leaving more than four million others without the healthcare and contraceptive counseling they needed.

This shortcoming reflected the backpedaling of the Nixon and Ford administrations as their base became more conservative and the issue of abortion turned political. From 1973 to '74, government funding for family planning shrank by twenty percent. In 1975, President Ford vetoed the Public Health Service Act, which contained critical family planning funds. We also received meager US political support for our family planning efforts in the Third World, where the effects of overpopulation were most devastating.

Teenagers in the seventies needed good contraceptive information and care more than any generation before them. The sexual revolution had hit and women were purportedly liberated, but sex education had not kept pace with those seismic social changes. In 1974, an estimated 750,000 unmarried girls under age nineteen became pregnant—up 75 percent from 1970. A third of people seeking Planned Parenthood services were teens.

A 1975 Johns Hopkins study showed that only one in ten boys and one in five girls learned about sex at home. Sex education was taught in high school—too late—using outdated books and films. Most young people still learned about the birds and bees like I had in the 1930s—from their friends—often receiving inaccurate information.

Our efforts to provide birth control information in public schools caused an uproar in some parts of the country, despite studies showing that pregnant teens had less knowledge of reproduction and contraception than their less sexually active peers. Occasionally the urge to confront our faith-based opposition compelled me to advocate for the church to get involved in sex education. "Sunday school is the right place for sex ed, since sexual decisions are tied closely to one's basic life principles. Like President Ford, the church has chickened out," I said in several speeches.

Another major push was promoting the development of birth control devices that were safe, cheap, dignified, and reversible. In July 1975, I testified before the President's Panel on Biomedical Research, accusing the government of shortsightedness in spending three times more money researching allergies than investigating human reproduction. I also criticized the lack of research into male contraception: "It's time for the man to share the burden of family planning."

•••

Needing a breather from the crises and controversies of my job, I flew with Leftie and our young son, Jack, to Panama in the summer of 1976. We were paddling around the pool of the Punta Paitilla Holiday Inn when a man motioned me to the side. He said General Torrijos wanted to see me at my earliest convenience. Wondering what had taken him so long to find me, I towel dried and went to meet my favorite dictator. He was staying in a high-rise apartment building nearby and claimed to have looked over the balcony and spotted me. I find it more likely that his people had been keeping tabs on me since my departure from Miami International.

Canal-treaty negotiations were on Torrijos' mind that day. It had become clear to him that the Pentagon would delay treaty negotiations indefinitely through the ponderous Interoceanic Canal Commission, which endlessly analyzed sea-level canal routes lending themselves to nuclear excavation. Nixon and Ford's position was that no serious treaty talks with Panama could take place until the commission had spoken.

Failing to connect with the US executive branch and dismissing the State Department out of hand, Torrijos cleverly switched his attack to the legislative branch. He had learned that US politicians can't resist populist foreign leaders who talk like farmers. Through careful planning, persuasion, and lobbying during uncounted visits by US senators to his Farallón beach house, Omar personally set the stage for a treaty that would give the canal to Panama.

Given the solicitous way Torrijos sought me out to vent his frustrations and ask my advice, I now felt comfortable speaking frankly with him. I came down very hard on the way he had abdicated to Manuel Noriega, letting that ogre torture and kill so many peasants in Chiriquí province. I told him that as a proud populist, such behavior made him look like a phony. I asked Torrijos several times why he let Noriega intimidate him, and his response was always evasive.

In the mid 1970s, Panama was becoming a dual Torrijos/Noriega government as Noriega's rank, power, and wealth grew. Like so many couples reluctant to deal with their real differences, Omar and Manuel argued endlessly about money. On one especially drunken occasion in Farallón, Torrijos dwelt on his finances. "I am worth maybe ninety-five or ninety-six million balboas (dollars). But *mi ganster* (Noriega) is the really rich *hijo de puta* (SOB). I am sure his net worth must be in excess of a billion balboas—ten times mine. Can you believe that little mother is skimming a percent and a half of all the drug money laundered in Panama?" It was during this conversation that I first heard the name BCCI, the European bank that achieved a near monopoly laundering money in Panama.

•••

During the 1976 campaign between President Ford and Jimmy Carter, abortion rights became an indelible part of presidential politics. Trading sound bites with Carter on the campaign trail, President Ford said the Supreme Court had gone "too far" with Roe v. Wade, and he believed abortion laws ought to be made by the states. Ford saw a need for "flexibility in circumstances where the woman is raped or other unfortunate things happen." I wondered what would constitute unfortunate: if the mother already had six children; if she was living in poverty; if she was in poor health; if she was thirteen years old?

One bright spot on the national stage was Betty Ford, who openly disagreed with her husband on abortion rights during an interview with *60 Minutes*, calling Roe v. Wade a "great, great decision." Asked by reporters for a comment, I said, "Gerald Ford is not our kind of guy—Betty is."

The conservative coalition on the Hill, dominated by middle-aged white men, attacked federal funding for contraception and abortion. Federal law now required people seeking free care at family planning clinics to provide proof of household income. The rule unfairly—and intentionally—affected teenagers. Teens often came to the clinics for treatment precisely because they couldn't approach their parents. The new law caused such a decline in visits to our clinics in Hawaii that we were forced to close fourteen of fifteen family planning centers there and lay off hundreds of employees. Other centers had to cut back on education programs and public relations.

In 1976, Representative Henry Hyde, a Republican from Illinois, introduced the "Hyde Amendment," which prohibited the use of federal Medicaid funds for abortions. Although we fought hard against it in the courts and Congress, the bill passed, making it impossible for poor women to receive federal financial assistance for abortions. Incredibly, this amendment has survived in various forms until today. Our poorest constituents were now forced to take more desperate measures. In 1977, Planned Parenthood sadly released the story of Rosie Jimenez, a single mother who became the first known casualty of an illegal abortion after the Hyde Amendment went into effect.

Along with congressional blocking and political rhetoric about abortion, we also dealt with increasingly aggressive public opposition. Friends of the Fetus, old acquaintances of mine from my Peace Corps days, regularly picketed our headquarters in New York City. I found their presence almost comforting.

The more rabid members of the antiabortion movement turned to violence. The worst case during my tenure occurred in suburban St. Paul, Minnesota, at the Highland Park Clinic. When the Minnesota board voted to allow abortions at the clinic, vandals cemented the front doors shut and splashed them with red paint. Shots were fired through the windows and bomb threats made. The names, addresses, and phone numbers of Planned Parenthood board members and sponsors were published in the local paper.

On February 23, 1977, two months after abortion services at the clinic began, an arsonist set fire to the building, causing $300,000 in damage and shutting it down for six months. We raised $10,000 for Kit Briggs, the chairperson of Minnesota Planned Parenthood, as she battled lawsuits trying to put the clinic out of business. With the Highland Park building condemned, abortion services were relocated to the private office of Planned Parenthood's courageous state medical director, Dr. Mildred Hanson.

Another case that held special interest for us was that of Dr. Ken Edelin, a Boston City College OB-GYN convicted of manslaughter in 1975 after he performed a legal abortion for a teenager with a twenty-two-week-old fetus. Planned Parenthood contributed $21,000 to his defense and established a Medical Rights Fund to support physicians and other medical personnel who faced similar charges. Dr. Edelin was exonerated in December 1976.

In October 1976, shortly before Jimmy Carter narrowly won the presidency, Planned Parenthood celebrated its sixtieth birthday in New York City. All the VIPs of the movement were there as well as legions of our affiliate directors and staff. The weekend kicked off with a dinner party at the newly opened Windows on the World restaurant in the World Trade Center's North Tower. When that event sold out, overflow guests attended a party at the Rainbow Room atop Rockefeller Center.

The next day in my comments to the assembled family planners, I lauded our perseverance and passion but faulted us for the "fear and passivity" we showed toward our opposition. I also took aim at the immense time and energy we spent on organizational maintenance: "These tendencies are a hazard to our spiritual health. They deflect our attention and our energies from the main job at hand."

I personally was the subject of some energy deflection that winter when the board of Planned Parenthood set up a committee to assess my performance at the end of my second year. It felt like a bad sign but didn't cause me undue worry; countering the momentum of the antiabortion movement consumed all my energy.

As one politician and administration official after another announced his opposition to abortion, I stressed the wisdom of redirecting the conversation. Rather than lash out as pro-choice in reaction to every pro-lifer, I urged that we focus on making abortion unnecessary. The best way to accomplish that was to reach the millions of poor women without access to quality reproductive care and education. I also pushed the idea of establishing a legislative office in Washington DC to make us more relevant and available for the relentless maneuvering in Congress around abortion and contraception.

In March, I appeared before the board of directors to recap our progress and put forward my thoughts for the future. Reflecting on the last year, I gave myself a grade of C, knowing that I had failed to rally and shore up our disparate affiliates to the extent the board had hoped and that I had not made significant national policy inroads. My humor usually fell flat at these board meetings, and my ideas sparked virtually no discussion. It became clearer every time we met that I had developed little with the board members except hostility toward me.

The committee to assess my performance apparently graded me even lower than I had modestly graded myself, and I was asked for my resignation. I had never been fired by such a large and distinguished group, and never after having worked so hard. Someone at Planned Parenthood leaked the story to the *New York Post*. The article read, "Ousted again is Jack Vaughn, the stormy ex-director of the Peace Corps, ex-Assistant Secretary of State, ex-Ambassador to Colombia, and now ex-president of Planned Parenthood Federation of America."

I was delighted to have been referred to as "stormy" and grateful they hadn't included any more of my "ex's."

Always classy, Tenny Marshall sent me a warm letter after I left. She served as the interim president until the appointment of Faye Wattleton, executive director of the Miami Valley, Ohio, affiliate, and the organization's first female president since Margaret Sanger. She struck me as a perfect choice.

Recently fired and with a new family to support, it was déjà vu all over again. *The Washington Star* reported that I was at the top of Secretary of State Henry Kissinger's list to head the Sinai task force for peace, a group of two hundred Americans without military or intelligence connections who would be sent to monitor the desert battleground between the Israeli and Egyptian armies. As enticing as that sounded, it never came to anything, maybe because Kissinger caught wind of all my unflattering comments about him.

After putting feelers out in Washington, I got a call from my old friend John Macy, former head of patronage at the White House. He was working for the legendary David Lilienthal, former head of the Tennessee Valley Authority. Lilienthal now chaired Development and Resources Corporation, which managed large-scale engineering and economic development projects overseas. I had long admired Lilienthal and liked him very much after our meeting. He wanted to hire me as the company's resident manager in Iran, where a major water resources project was underway in Khuzestan Province.

My first call was to Peace Corps veteran Bob Steiner, who had been the regional director for North Africa-Near East-Asia and was born and raised in Iran. He urged me not to go to Iran at such a perilous juncture, when the Shah's empire seemed to be faltering. I didn't take Bob's good advice. I accepted the job, totally intrigued by the work and excited to be part of Lilienthal's innovative group.

11

1977–1980

Building on the theme of "Yes! We Have No Bananas," we can apply that to almost every common noun in town.

—Letter to Leftie, 1979

My reasons for taking a job in Iran in 1977 were both personal and professional. I admired David Lilienthal and his team at Development and Resources Corporation (D&R). After spending a dozen years running the Tennessee Valley Authority, Lilienthal had served as the first chairman of the Atomic Energy Commission. In the third and final chapter of his impressive career, Lilienthal had founded D&R, a broad-gauged consulting firm that had served the Peace Corps well in the 1960s with real-world agriculture training for volunteers.

I was intrigued by Lilienthal's approach to achieving accelerated growth in Third World countries: integrated resource management, the same method used by the Tennessee Valley Authority. The TVA brought not just dams but also navigation, electricity, improved farming practices, and jobs to the Tennessee Valley during the Great Depression. Likewise, D&R not only solved water and power problems but also implemented sustainable resource management, expanded employment opportunities, and improved conditions for workers.

In the 1960s, D&R worked its brand of development magic in countries as diverse as Puerto Rico, Peru, Nigeria, Italy, and Australia. During my Peace Corps years, I visited one of D&R's most successful projects, a hydroelectric plant at Calima in the Cauca Valley of Colombia, and I became a believer. I am still convinced that the D&R approach could work in most Third World settings; I have spent years making the case that it is the only solution to Haiti's problems.

D&R's project in Khuzestan Province, Iran, began in 1956 and was its longest-running and most lucrative contract. The company undertook an enormous amount of work centering on a system of dams on the Dez River providing flood control, irrigation, and electricity. The project also included the creation of sugarcane farms, fertilizer plants, and public health programs. The Iranian government eventually created the Khuzestan Water and Power Authority (KWPA) to manage the hydroelectric dams.

The Shah of Iran implemented a series of national development plans in five-year increments; the Fifth Plan began in 1974 and was characterized by tremendous, unwieldy growth. The country had grown 11.5 percent per year between 1973 and 1976, placing enormous strain on housing, water resources, railways, and roads.

Creating the infrastructure to handle Iran's growth fell mostly to foreign contractors like D&R. Iran was brimming with competing foreign engineering companies in the 1970s: Americans, French, Japanese, and Soviets dominated the building of dams, steel mills, copper mines, and petrochemical plants. The country's institutes of higher learning also experienced a boom, as the number of universities tripled to fifteen during that decade. Crucial to Iran's academic expansion was the advice and assistance of American schools like Georgetown, Harvard, and the University of Pennsylvania.

In the early seventies, D&R signed another round of contracts with the Iranian government for projects in the fertile Khuzestan region. What gave D&R an advantage over other foreign contractors during this frenzied period of infrastructure development was twofold: the company's long history in Iran and its full-service approach. The company offered engineering services along with a growing array of programs to help the government manage resources, administer public programs, and cultivate manpower.

In April 1977, when I became the resident vice president for D&R Iran, the company had an ongoing contract with KWPA to supervise its home office, manage the Dez irrigation project, design and construct power transmission lines and substations, draft a national water plan, and create an agricultural research program. We had also launched a major effort in public management aimed at helping Iran with the task of decentralization, parliament's new buzzword and a theme that would be at the heart of the Shah's Sixth Plan, beginning in 1978.

Key to the decentralization process were improved efficiency and management. Efficiency, I gathered from my conversations with D&R President John Macy, was not the Iranian government's strong suit. Government agencies regularly delayed contract negotiations and, more crucially, payments. Almost inconceivable layers of bureaucracy tied up major decisions, and shortages of trained manpower caused slowdowns in construction.

Complicating our role in Iran was KWPA, the agency that D&R had helped to create, which faced enormous problems: huge debt, lousy contractors, and poor management. Some leaders at the agency still held a grudge from the days when D&R ran the show; appeasing them required fancy footwork along the lines of my signature hesitation Shorty George dance moves. D&R often began urgent engineering projects for KWPA with a verbal agreement, then was ordered to stop all work several months later to negotiate a contract with an elaborate web of bureaucrats. KWPA always used the delay to argue for a price reduction.

Given this background and having heard warnings about Iran from my friends in the know, I questioned the wisdom of my decision to join D&R. During my May orientation in Tehran, I glimpsed a changed environment from what I remembered as Peace Corps director in the late sixties. The attitudes of Iranians I met had not reached the point of hostility, but there was an unmistakable reserve and sullenness, even among veteran D&R Iranian staff. Despite my misgivings, I stayed the course; Lilienthal was counting on me, and I needed the job.

•••

Fully loaded with the requisite vaccines, Leftie, our son, Jack, and I arrived in Tehran on August 2, 1977, joining an estimated forty thousand other Americans in Iran. A bustling city of five million, not including its vast suburban sprawl, Tehran was hot, dry, and heavily polluted. The city is bordered by mountains to the north and desert to the south and experiences all four seasons, though summer is the most extreme.

After several weeks of scouting, we found a house in Farmanieh, a mishmash of shoddily constructed homes interspersed with vacant lots like many areas of Tehran. At the end of a dead-end street, *Bombast Hasheminejad*, the house was a duplex we shared with our landlord next door and a young Iranian couple who lived above him.

Its small, overgrown yard was bursting with purple and yellow irises, to which I added pots of tomatoes and marigolds for pest control.

Foreigners did not drive in Tehran, because no laws protected us from being sued into bankruptcy in the likely event of an accident. The driver assigned to us by D&R was an affable if dim young fellow named Mehdi. He picked me up in the morning and maneuvered the office Paykan car through the crush of traffic that clogged Tehran's streets at all hours of the day. Once Mehdi parked and jumped out, leaving his door wide open; I watched wide-eyed as a car whizzed by, shearing the door off.

We arrived at the tail end of a power crisis that had plagued Iran all summer. The important Reza Shah Kabir Dam reservoir had become critically low, and the construction of generators was behind schedule. As a result, the country had suffered rolling blackouts during the hottest months of the year. During my first few months in Tehran, our office went without power for four hours each day. The Iranian government blamed foreign contractors for the blunder; Harza International of Chicago and the French Alsthom were singled out and blacklisted.

In the wake of the power disaster, the Shah appointed a new prime minister, Cornell-trained engineer and former Minister of Oil Jamshid Amouzegar. He also replaced most of his cabinet. To cap off his show of outrage, the Shah ordered the prosecution of his former minister of energy, along with other high-ranking officials from Tavanir, the Iranian power company. It was a classic witch hunt to cover up the real problem: Iran's impenetrable bureaucracy getting in the way of progress. In the assessment of D&R Executive Vice President John Silveira, "in setting up the means, sight of the end is completely lost."

In early September, I took my first trip south to Khuzestan to tour KWPA and visit the Dez irrigation project at Andimeshk. A small group of D&R civil engineers headed by the very capable and affable

John Silveira lived in Ahwaz in a military-style housing compound. Silveira was an old hand in Iran and managed a contingent of engineers from the University of California system who came to Iran in shifts to work on a variety of projects. While Tehran's atmosphere hung heavily with pollution, Ahwaz's air was almost too hot to inhale.

Silveira provided invaluable expertise as I encountered complaints or accusations from our Iranian clients. In one case, the prime minister himself had become agitated about the rapid rate of sedimentation in the Dez River reducing the lifespan of its dams, and he felt this justified a halt to construction. Since my knowledge of sedimentation was limited to urinalysis, I called on Silveira to smooth it over, which he capably did by explaining that our watershed rehabilitation program, if properly funded, would offset destructive deposits.

Just what a political mess our contracts could become crystallized for me shortly after my trip to Ahwaz. I had been trying unsuccessfully to set up a meeting with the new minister of energy, Ahmad Tavakoli, when our Khuzestan project manager, Bill Price, alerted me to a recent TV show being buzzed about at KWPA. A televised meeting of the Imperial Commission, economic advisors to the Shah, had included the false accusation that D&R had performed faulty foundation work for KWPA. Minister Tavakoli had appeared on the program and harshly criticized D&R; now I knew why he wasn't returning my calls.

To assess our PR damage, D&R senior staff met with the new managing director of KWPA, Ahmad Aleyasin, who alternately asked for our help and blamed us for creating the problems. Ultimately, his goal for the meeting was the aim of all savvy Iranian managers: to establish a baseline of preexisting problems in order to avoid future blame. At KWPA, there was a loaded baseline of problems and not enough fingers for all the blame. The agency had fifty-eight contracts with fourteen engineering firms; twenty-five percent were running over budget, and virtually all were behind schedule.

With KWPA we walked a fine line between emphasizing our history with the organization and distancing ourselves from its dysfunction. Each time a new minister or manager was put in charge, we reassessed our strategy for winning new contracts based on that official's experience with D&R, his grudges against any of our engineers, and his opinion of Americans generally. David Lilienthal attended many lunches and dinners at the homes of these officials trying to establish rapport, and I transmitted many flowery thank-you notes on his behalf.

After a couple of months on the job, I had learned how to say "Roto-Rooter" in Farsi, eaten two kilos of pistachios in one sitting, and generally settled into the comfortable chaos of the capital city. My biggest challenge was starting off without any professional or personal contacts; I was a complete unknown. Cultivating associates in this highly political environment, where grudges were nurtured and passing the buck was the national sport, became even more difficult with Iran's growing anti-American mood.

Foreseeing the disadvantage of being an American company in Iran, David Lilienthal had created an Iranian affiliate, Development and Resources Iran (DRI). Iranians managed the company and owned the majority of stock; D&R and its principals held forty percent of shares. At first, DRI's role was limited to resource development like staff training for D&R projects. Then when Iran's energy ministry announced that new development projects would be granted only to Iranian companies, DRI hit the big time with a major project in the Karkheh River Basin in Khuzestan. A favorite of the Shah, the project had the potential for development work on the scale of the Dez irrigation project.

Unfortunately, despite the promise of the arrangement, D&R and DRI had developed a Hatfield-McCoy relationship. DRI resented what it saw as shortchanging by D&R, and we were exasperated by DRI's squabbling and inefficient management. The Karkheh project was seriously behind schedule, over budget, and looking more like a liability than an asset to D&R. DRI Managing Director Houshang Vessal had also been sorely critical of the D&R chief engineer assigned to Karkheh.

A man as averse to confrontation as he was to work, Vessal decided to leave in January 1978 rather than face the mounting management challenges at DRI. He blamed his departure on his son's poor academic performance at college in Sacramento, saying he needed six months to pry the boy's attention away from his girlfriend and back to his studies. I described Vessal's resignation to John Macy as "another chapter of the popular series entitled, 'Can a middle-aged Middle Eastern engineer find fulfillment in substituting for his son's Chinese girlfriend in a Sacramento rooming house?'"

DRI's new managing director, Shahriar Mortazavi, gave us a glimmer of hope when he demonstrated a hard-nosed approach and a genuine interest in greater cooperation with D&R. With the current antiforeign contractor kick at the energy ministry, I told Macy and Lilienthal that I found it "not inconceivable" (a favorite State Department term) that Mortazavi could turn out to be a winner in getting new business. But, I said, D&R would also have to take some responsibility to hammer out a legitimate relationship with DRI in place of the Chinese fire drill we had lived with so far.

•••

Iran was my first overseas tour in a business capacity, outside the realm of diplomacy. My new seat on the sidelines of political drama was both a relief and a frustration. My frustration grew when I began to realize that my information was better than my government's. Bob Steiner had first clued me in to the perilous position of the Shah, and what I witnessed within just a few months in Tehran confirmed his warnings.

Mohammad Rezâ Shah Pahlavi had been installed by the CIA and British intelligence thirty-six years earlier after a coup toppling the democratically elected Prime Minister Mohammad Mosaddegh. The Shah, Iran's self-proclaimed "King of Kings," made strides in westernizing Iran through land reform and social and economic modernization. Most notably, he granted women the right to vote, allowed non-Muslims to hold office, nationalized the country's forests, and started a literacy campaign. But the Shah lived extravagantly and ruled corruptly; as his popularity waned he relied heavily on Iran's CIA-trained secret police, SAVAK, to snuff out his opposition.

As a secular Muslim, the Shah was unpopular with Iran's Shi'a clergy. The most notorious opponent of the Shah was Ayatollah Ruhollah Khomeini, a Shiite leader from Qom, a holy city southwest of Tehran. The Shah's western, secular bent outraged Khomeini, but nothing set his beard quivering like the Shah's cozy relationship with the United States. Khomeini's outspoken condemnation of the Shah got him deported to Turkey in 1964, but he continued to communicate and foment from his new home base in Najaf, Iraq.

In the fall of 1977, a few months after we arrived in Tehran, the first serious anti-Shah protests erupted. They were sparked by the death in Najaf of Khomeini's son, Mostafa, thought to be the work of SAVAK. In November, when the Shah and his wife, Shahbanu Farah Diba, visited President Carter at the White House, a large, spray-painted scrawl appeared on the wall opposite my office in midtown Tehran: *Marg Bar Shah* (Death to the Shah).

The next month, Jimmy and Rosalynn Carter came to Tehran to celebrate New Year's Eve. Carter effusively toasted the Shah: "Iran, because of the great leadership of the Shah, is an island of stability in one of the more troubled areas of the world. This is a great tribute to you, Your Majesty, and to your leadership and to the respect and the admiration and love which your people give to you.

"The cause of human rights is one that is also shared deeply by our people and by the leaders of our two nations. Our talks have been priceless, our friendship is irreplaceable, and my own gratitude is to the Shah, who in his wisdom and with his experience has been so helpful to me, a new leader." The following week, there was new graffiti on the wall opposite my office: *Marg Bar Jimmy Carter*.

•••

In October 1977, David Lilienthal and John Macy, my immediate supervisor, visited Iran to review our programs and call on the long list of high-ranking officials in need of hand-holding. We were particularly interested in winning our bid for continued development in Khuzestan Province. In the southwest corner of Iran bordering the Persian Gulf, Khuzestan contained five major rivers and 1.2 million hectares of cultivatable land. We felt there was still a great need for land and water planning, energy production, and improved living and working conditions.

With the government's new bent on decentralization, the Khuzestan project would be administered not by the ministry in Tehran but by the Ostan, or province. The Ostandar (provincial governor general) in Khuzestan was His Excellency Bagher Namazi, who saw himself as progressive. He wanted to use the development project in his Ostan as a pilot demonstration of decentralization. We spent significant time cultivating Namazi and felt confident about our chances to win the contract.

To our surprise, a request for proposal for the Khuzestan development project arrived in mid November from the Oil Service Company of Iran (OSCO). Namazi had decided to subcontract with the powerful OSCO to select the contractor for his important test case in government efficiency. Lilienthal hit the roof. In a Telex from New York, he described the OSCO letter as "setting out in detail the scope of work and detailed bureaucratic control and procedural complexity as great as any ever devised." So much for all of our advance work with Namazi. "What the hell is this all about?" Lilienthal wrote.

Lilienthal had also met with the Shah during his visit and come away concerned. He saw a leader in poor health and in a tenuous political position. Lilienthal shared his impressions with US Ambassador to Iran William Sullivan. Sullivan assured him there was no political problem. What we had here, claimed the ambassador, was a devastating slowdown in the construction industry that had negatively impacted the economy. As a result, there were gangs of unemployed construction workers roaming the city and causing havoc.

Lilienthal was convinced. He reported to his board of directors that "heartening things are happening in Iran." He was particularly encouraged by Tehran's interest in provincial government reform. Soon after Ambassador Sullivan had reassured Lilienthal, the Israeli ambassador to Iran called Tehran "another Entebbe." Cutting his staff by 75 percent, he sent all dependents home to Israel.

As street violence increased and a curfew was imposed, our family focused on small pleasures: playing honeymoon bridge at night, walking to the local bakery for sangak bread, and eating delicious chelow kebabs with yogurt and berenj at our favorite Iranian restaurant (later bombed because of its popularity among foreigners). An especially joyful distraction was the birth of our daughter, Jane, in July.

•••

Later that July, I had a revealing encounter with Peter and Lynn Russell, former Peace Corps volunteers who had intimate knowledge of the growing revolution. The Russells had served during the mid sixties in Qom, "City of Ayatollahs," and gotten to know several ayatollahs (of the roughly thirty in Iran), all of them devotees of Khomeini. The exiled ayatollah stayed in constant touch with his legions of followers in Iran through videotaped lectures in which he gave the impression of a disciplined intellectual.

Peter, who had returned to Iran as resident vice president for Manufacturers Hanover Trust Company, told me that the revolution was a done deal. Khomeini had circulated his marching orders right after President Carter's New Year's toast to the Shah. Conflicts among the religious leaders had been resolved, the *bazaaris* (merchants) were on board, key officers of the Shah's army had agreed to switch sides at the crucial time, and senior Baha'i leaders had been targeted for execution.

I asked Peter to share his information with our ambassador and made an appointment for him at the embassy. Ambassador Sullivan let Peter speak for no more than five minutes before cutting him off: "You Peace Corps people see things only through the eyes of the locals." Peter was politely ushered out of the embassy, and Sullivan's head remained buried in the Iranian desert sand.

Around that time, I received a letter from David Lilienthal congratulating me on the way John Macy and I had been "bucking the forces that make your task so formidable. I comfort myself with the thought that such as you two are made for the tough and consequential tests of manhood." As much as I appreciated Lilienthal's flattery, I knew by this time that these forces could not be bucked, and there was much more at stake in Iran than my manhood.

On September 7, 1978, a rally of more than one hundred thousand protesters demanded the Shah's ouster and a return to Islamic rule under Ayatollah Khomeini. The next day, the Shah instituted martial law in Tehran. Antigovernment protesters gathered in Jaleh square, pulling down statues and setting fire to anything that would ignite. The opposition claimed that tens of thousands were killed by the Shah's army, while media reports put the death toll at around one hundred. Black Friday, as it would be called, put Iran on the fast track to radical revolution.

In a Telex from Tehran to David Lilienthal in New York on September 11, John Macy wrote, "Reports of these developments naturally prompt concern and curiosity here. Media coverage extensive, but actual facts elusive. Impact on D&R current and future operations frequent topic of speculation with conclusion that no change in direction is warranted at this time. Rely on your continuing interpretation and judgment."

As if things weren't shaky enough, on September 16, Iran's biggest earthquake in ten years hit the town of Tabas, southeast of Tehran. Registering 7.7 on the Richter scale, the quake lasted a devastating three minutes. More than fifteen thousand people were killed, including all of the town's doctors. The dead were burned, and for weeks the survivors lacked water, power, and phone service.

As part of our public sector management contract, D&R was hard at work on Iran's disaster relief plan, unfortunately not ready in time for the Tabas quake. In November, when we presented the plan to Dr. Amin Alimard, secretary general of the State Organization for Administration and Employment, it sparked little interest. The threat of political disaster had already eclipsed the forces of nature.

The ongoing projects under our wide-ranging public sector contract included a computerized system for corporate taxation, a national salary reform initiative, manpower planning, and a revision of state employment law. Our progress slowed considerably that fall when ministry employees went on strike. They came to the office but refused to work until they received salary increases. Our reports to the Plan and Budget Organization, which oversaw the contract, became thinner each week.

Other projects stalled before they even got off the ground. One was an idea of mine to package D&R's orientation for new employees and offer it to other American companies. We had just begun marketing the program when American companies stopped bringing new workers into Iran. Most absurdly, we were on the verge of launching a "Two-Way Citizen's Communication Project" to help the government and the Iranians find ways to effectively exchange ideas and information using methods like town hall meetings and public service announcements. Meanwhile, the general public and the government had already found new means of communicating that involved vandalism, arson, tear gas, and murder.

Americans in Tehran left in droves as the violence escalated, but my bosses at D&R clung to the belief that the unrest would blow over. I took the family to Cyprus in late September, hoping that Lilienthal would tell us not to return to Tehran. We vacationed in Paphos, a wine-producing area where road signs warned: "Caution: Roads slippery with grape juice." It could not have been a more idyllic place to wait out a revolution.

Two weeks later, with no word from D&R, we returned to Tehran. Despite a state of martial law, violent demonstrations continued and the opposition grew in number and fervor. A petroleum workers strike in October further weakened the Shah's empire. Still, there remained a consensus among the top US diplomatic brass that the Shah was secure. With a newly installed military government, his half-million-man army, and the brutal SAVAK, he was considered too strong to be toppled.

Determined to get Leftie and the kids out, I purchased tickets for us on an El Al flight to Tel Aviv. We watched from the terminal as our plane circled overhead and departed; Israel had just broken relations with Iran. We slunk back to our dark house, which now had no electricity or water at night and no gas.

I went to work each day, but there was less and less I could do in a city under siege. My employees in Ahwaz stopped coming to Tehran for meetings because of the violence. John Macy left Iran at the end of October, as did our American contractors, who remained on optimistic standby in the US. Our family packed up again for an Al Italia flight to Rome. The scene on the plane was so jubilant that the flight attendants, with my assistance, forcibly seated and buckled many exuberant passengers so we could take off.

I left the family at Leftie's parents' house in Washington and flew to New York for an emergency board meeting at D&R. When I had finished telling the directors that our company's future was past—as it was for all other American businesses in Iran—Lilienthal seemed skeptical. "If you closely examine those large signs demanding 'Yankee Go Home,' down in one corner in small print you can usually make out 'and take me with you.'" He sent me back to Iran to check the fine print.

Back in Tehran in December, all I found was a smaller American presence and bigger signs of revolution. Marauding gangs roamed the streets, greatly increasing the threat to foreigners, especially Americans. An angry group of about twenty jostled my car one evening; when I cracked my window and shouted at the group in French, they backed off. France at the time was the only western country admired by the Iranians. (Under pressure in Iraq, Ayatollah Khomeini had moved to a village outside Paris in October.)

I decided the French act would be good insurance during the rest of my time in Iran. My driver, Mehdi, who had worked for a French company, gave me some suggestions: wear a beret, tighter pants, and a pack of Gauloise cigarettes in my breast pocket. I finessed Mehdi's ideas, but I did change my dollars into francs and begin gesturing more dramatically as I rolled my r's.

Even before the revolution, Iranians dealt exclusively in cash. We lugged a suitcase full of rials to our landlord each month. Around the time that I brought my family back to the States, Iranians frantically began withdrawing their money from the banks, and D&R's liquid assets disappeared. I returned from the US bringing suitcases stuffed with dollars, which would have felt more nerve-racking if not for all the cash carrying I had done since I moved to Tehran. With my cash reserves, I was able to make payroll for my remaining employees until the bitter end.

In early December, I received notice from Dr. Alimard that he was terminating our public sector management contract. The balance due would not be paid and no more work would be conducted. Alimard recommended that John Macy cancel his January trip to discuss the project. In a sense it was a relief: we had sent forty Iranian managers to the University of Southern California for training, and upon their return they had disappeared—we couldn't locate even one of them.

With gas scarce and electricity spotty, I kept the office open on alternate days. The day before gasoline supplies were predicted to run out, I bought Mehdi a forty-liter can that he filled and stowed in the office for our final run to the airport. On December 31, Ambassador Sullivan called all remaining resident Americans to the embassy. Some two hundred business people were there to hear that our embassy and most others were recommending that all dependents leave. Pan Am would be adding extra flights and several charters would start flying Americans to Athens. Most of the dependents of D&R employees had already left.

On January 2, I had lunch with Dean Brelis of *TIME* at the Intercontinental Hotel. He was awaiting the first big press conference of Dr. Shapour Bakhtiar, Iran's new prime minister. A moderate liberal who had opposed the Shah, Bakhtiar was appointed as a last-ditch effort to appease the Shah's critics. Among other insights, Brelis said that the foreign press thought Ambassador Sullivan was a complete horse's ass.

By the first week of January, D&R employees were beginning to show signs of stress. Staff I usually didn't see began dropping by my office regularly, hoping for some news. The wife of one of our project managers who had decided to stay in Tehran with her husband went off the deep end. She called me three and four times a day about nothing in particular; complaining of an ulcer, she stopped eating for a week.

When John Macy finally made the announcement that decisions on staff were mine, I told all my American employees to go. They left with varying degrees of swiftness depending on their ability to get plane reservations and fuel to the airport. All twenty-seven D&R employees in Khuzestan left on January 5 on a KLM flight to Amsterdam. The exception was one engineer who decided he couldn't leave his $9,000 VW camper behind. He drove to the Turkish border with his wife and teenage son; we never heard from them again.

In the Tehran office, I set January 15 as the deadline for disposing of all our office furniture, phones, and equipment. I spent five hours a day in the bitterly cold office going through files dating back to 1962. At home, I spent long days packing up the few household effects we wanted to keep and trying to find buyers for the rest. Our upstairs neighbors brought over a plate of chelow kebab, and it cost them dearly; they bought dining room chairs, a bookshelf, a folding table, and a vacuum. Every day I felt more like a used car salesman.

With all city workers on strike, Tehran became one gigantic garbage heap. Farmanieh Street, a major road into our neighborhood, was no longer passable from all the cars burned there during the night. There were no taxis running, so I was at the mercy of Medhi's ability to scrounge black market gas. One day he waited in line from 5:00 a.m. to 7:30 p.m. to get gas and then was too weak to drive. Gas on the black market cost about ten times the regular price.

On January 16, Shah Pahlavi and his family were forced into exile, and the exodus of the Iranian upper classes peaked. That day I was at a meeting of DRI in Tehran to discuss formalizing a split from D&R. As early as July, Macy, Silveira, and I had recommended to Lilienthal that we cut ties with DRI. Despite the promise of new managing director Mortazavi, our relationship with the company had continued its downward spiral. Macy wrote that our Iranian counterpart was "exploiting our name and draining our resources, with only token compensation or recognition" for D&R. Lilienthal was adamant that we withdraw from the company and take our name with us.

DRI management, seeing the writing on the wall, was hedging to maximize its financial gain. Problems on the Karkheh project, which had expanded to include dam construction, irrigation, flood control, and hydroelectric power, had multiplied since the onset of the revolution. It had become virtually impossible to continue the work or collect payment. At our meeting, Mortazavi accepted his fate, and we agreed to hire Coopers & Lybrand to determine the net value of the company before it dissolved.

Having set the wheels in motion to extract D&R from the DRI mess, and with all my American staff now out of the country, my focus quickly became getting myself extracted from Tehran. I booked an Iberia flight to Barcelona on January 20 and a backup flight on January 22.

Mehrabad Airport had a skeleton crew and no electricity at the gate. Boarding took hours, and it was after dark by the time we were ready for takeoff. The captain announced that the control tower had ordered the plane to a parking area for the night; without runway lights, they wouldn't allow departures until dawn. Our Quixote-like pilot grumbled in Spanish, "That's what the tower thinks," then taxied his plane to the runway and gunned it. Barcelona, a great city, had never seemed so inviting.

I flew to New York City for a Development and Resources board meeting, the agenda for which could have been titled *Unfortunate Developments and No Resources*. Iran had canceled all ongoing projects with us and defaulted on outstanding payments. The Iran contracts represented the lion's share of D&R's income; our remaining projects consisted of a handful of flood insurance studies and a couple of power-plant designs in the US. Lilienthal and Macy resigned, and the board voted to dissolve the company.

On February 1, Ayatollah Komeini made his triumphant return to Tehran. Known for his expert turban wrapping and daily use of Christian Dior's Eau Sauvage cologne (my own brand, although applied every other day to spare expense), Khomeini spoke at the Cemetery of Martyrs on the day he returned. Before a crowd of 250,000 devoted supporters, he made his case for taking the country back to the thirteenth century.

•••

In November, after President Carter allowed the Shah to enter the US for surgery, Iranian students stormed the US embassy in Tehran, taking sixty-six Americans hostage. Despite being heavily armed, our embassy in Tehran, like those around the world, was limited to the use of tear gas and requests for local assistance to defend itself. When those mild measures didn't succeed, embassy employees started shredding documents before being overtaken.

As ambassador to Panama and Colombia, both violent countries at the time, I had my own ideas about protecting my embassy and staff. I made a point of advising the ministers of interior that if attempts were ever made to take the US embassy, and their governments refused to come to our aid, my instructions to the Marine guards with their M-16s would be: "Firing line, lock and load, commence firing."

With the number of weapons and US military at the Tehran embassy, I am sure we could have successfully defended our property long enough for outside help to arrive. Holding off the attack would have created the opportunity for a cease-fire dialogue with Iran's new regime. By surrendering the embassy, we sent the wrong message, jeopardized American lives, and lost communication with Iran for twenty-five years.

It would be a stretch to suggest that Jimmy Carter helped start the Iranian religious revolution, but less far-fetched to conclude that he provided enormous impetus to the movement by publicly gushing about the Shah at a time when the leader's empire was crumbling from corruption and human rights abuses. That the CIA didn't twig to the obvious signs of trouble in Iran ranks high in the annals of gross bureaucratic incompetence.

As for Development and Resources, it fought to regain some of what it lost in the revolution. Like other foreign companies in Iran, D&R argued before the International Court of Justice in The Hague for payment of the money it was owed when the Iranian government collapsed. I testified as a primary witness. The company did recoup some funds, but I never asked for restitution of my wages, which were cut in half during my last months in Iran. Getting my family out alive was good enough for me.

•••

In late January 1979, I joined my family in Washington. We shook off the desert of Tehran on the sandy beaches of Contadora, an island off the Pacific coast of Panama. We had such a relaxed, good time that we returned in March 1980. To our surprise, we found ourselves there with another Iranian refugee, the Shah of Iran. Bribing all the right people, President Carter's good ol' boy chief of staff, Hamilton Jordan, had brokered the ailing despot's stay in Panama.

Before we left Contadora, General Torrijos requested my presence, and I caught an Isla Del Rey flight to Panama City to catch up with the Maximum Leader of the Panamanian Revolution, whom I hadn't seen since I left for Iran. Torrijos was feeling especially cocky since signing the Panama Canal Treaty with President Carter in September 1977. Panama's ownership of the canal would become effective on December 31, 1999. It was a huge achievement for the Panamanians, especially my friend Fernando Eleta, who had been fighting for Panamanian control of the canal since World War II.

Torrijos' populism played beautifully alongside Jimmy Carter's bumpkin naïveté. "Nixon hated Latins, but Carter hates to say no to us," Torrijos said. Angling to win back the canal since the moment he had assumed power in 1968, the dictator boasted on several occasions, "The first time I saw President Carter at a news conference talking about Panama, I knew I had my patsy."

In order to keep the US off balance during canal-treaty negotiations, Torrijos had periodically played his "Castro card," publicly cozying up to the Cuban Communist. Torrijos did not get along well personally with Castro ("He is the most boring man I ever met") and considered this tactic a necessary evil.

The real turning point in treaty maneuvering had come, according to Torrijos, when he took his plight to the United Nations Security Council. Concerted lobbying of the UN had culminated in a security council meeting in Panama and a vote to send the US to the negotiating table. Four years later, after Torrijos had charmed countless senators and members of Congress with the Farallón treatment, he had sealed the deal with Carter.

Torrijos' victory made him no less critical of US foreign policy in Latin America. He found our embargo against Cuba grossly ignorant and ineffective. "Ever since the Bay of Pigs *bochinche*, Fidel has been able to import any western-made commodity from Spain, Mexico, Canada, or the Colon Free Zone in Panama." He likened our Cuba policy to our drug policy: "out of date and out of control, and they both make the US look stupid."

When I asked Torrijos whom he thought was behind the assassination of the Kennedy brothers (something I did both when he was drunk and sober), he always responded decisively: "Fidel. It is such a logical conclusion for the Latin mind. The Kennedys were the only political leaders we know who were relentlessly trying to eliminate Castro. How many moves did *Robertito* (Bobby) make on Fidel—ten, fifteen? There comes a time when even the wimpiest man must turn on his pursuers. Fidel got both."

•••

BACK FROM IRAN IN 1979 without prospects at the shuttered Development and Resources, I filled the void with a couple of board memberships that had come to me in the revolutionary summer of 1978. In June of that year, I had been named a director of a new international merchant bank launched by my friend, John Pierce Clark. Pierce International and its savvy group of principals financed projects around the world and consulted with American companies doing business in developing nations. Pierce was my steadiest employment for the first year and a half after I returned to the US.

Clark was a financial wiz with a Latin American bent who had worked at the Inter-American Development Bank (IDB) in Washington when I was assistant secretary of state and director of the Peace Corps. On the small senior team was T. Graydon Upton, the former assistant secretary of the treasury under President Eisenhower, and the well-connected international banker David Gregg.

We invested in Pingon, a tower crane company based in Spain. I traveled there frequently, flying into Madrid and taking the overnight train to San Sebastian near the French border. In Spain, I also pursued a sausage-casing venture. In Latin America, we arranged financing for low-cost housing in Venezuela and developed working capital and trade financing for industrial operations in Chile, Ecuador, and Mexico. We syndicated loans for these projects, sending them out in Eurodollars to regional American banks and institutions in Europe or Japan.

My trips to South America for Pierce in 1979 and '80 allowed me to resuscitate an old money-making pipe dream in Colombia. The dream began at Florida International University when I received a call from Russell Law, a Miami insurance salesman who wanted to salvage the Spanish galleon *San José*. An aficionado of the shipwreck, Russ had visited the national libraries in Madrid and Panama, finding the bills of lading for the *San José*. They revealed upward of $3 billion worth of gold and silver.

Sunk by a British frigate off the coast of Santa Marta, Colombia, in 1708, the *San José* rested seven hundred feet below the ocean's surface. Just before the attack, the ship had taken on a massive cargo of pieces of eight and gold doubloons at Portobelo, Panama. There were also around a hundred leather trunks aboard, the kind of containers used by returning colonists to store their Incan treasures. Russ asked if I, with my experience and contacts in Colombia, would join his salvage effort.

He had me at "doubloon."

Russ and I hired a three-man ore-hunting submarine owned by the Aluminum Company of America to locate the ship. The tiny sub, named the *Alumina*, found the *San José* the very first day by going right to the place Russ said she was: four miles off Santa Marta. Now we had proof of the bounty but no legal means to retrieve it; litigation over Colombian treasure, antiques, and patrimony had always lingered indefinitely in Colombian courts. We tried for years, approaching various Colombian politicians, Navy officials, and lawyers, to convince the government to enact a modern and equitable salvage law. In the absence of such legislation, our efforts had been awash in legal fees, *mañanas*, and broken promises.

On a business trip for Pierce to investigate a Chilean gold mine investment, I stopped over in Bogotá to visit Diego Asencio, my old State Department staffer and friend, now US ambassador to Colombia. We reminisced about Bobby Kennedy and discussed my latest treasure hunting frustrations. Diego had good news: the US government had just made available to the Colombian Navy six high-speed frigates for the escalating cocaine wars along Colombia's coasts. Diego felt confident that given this new development, the Navy could be motivated to push through a rational salvage law to help out its gringo friends : "The admiral owes me one."

I left Bogotá for Santiago, Chile, the next day on a cloud, tourist class. After three days at the gold mine north of Valparaiso, I returned to my hotel in Santiago to find in bold letters on the *Miami Herald*'s front page: "US ambassador held hostage in Bogotá." The article detailed the capture by Marxist M-19 rebels of fifty diplomats from fourteen countries at a reception hosted by the embassy of the Dominican Republic (another reason to eschew those dreary cocktail parties).

The terrorists' biggest catch was Diego Asencio. As any friend of Diego's could guess, the gifted and personable ambassador became the hero of the M-19 hostage drama, which lasted sixty-one days. He kept a running dialogue with his captors and eventually out-negotiated them. Of course, Diego could never return to Bogotá, and the salvage-averse admiral was never pressured. Russ and I let our idea drop, a bit poorer and wiser, and I fell back on my get-rich-slowly schemes. The value of that mother lode, still resting on the ocean floor, is now estimated at around $10 billion.

•••

A SECOND BOARD OPPORTUNITY surprised me in August 1978 when my friend Herbert Allen managed to get me appointed to the Columbia Pictures board of directors. After Fred Harris for President folded, Herbert had consoled himself with the purchase of a controlling stake in the movie studio.

I joined the board during a lively time of sparring with Kirk Kerkorian, owner of Metro-Goldwyn-Meyer and a minority shareholder of Columbia Pictures. Attempting a hostile takeover, Kerkorian called a meeting with board members John McMillian, Dwayne Andreas, Ed Bloustein, and me to try to divide us from Chairman Herbert Allen and Columbia President Fay Vincent. McMillian, a tough oil man who dished out Texas-style intimidation, brought his chair up to Kerkorian's so they sat knee to knee. Leaning forward and speaking in a low growl, McMillian said that he didn't like Kerkorian or his company and would never turn Columbia Pictures over to a mobster like him.

It was a bad day for the MGM chief on several fronts. While Kerkorian sat locking horns with McMillian at the Regency Hotel in New York, his Las Vegas hotel, the MGM Grand, was burning. The blaze was one of the worst hotel fires in history, and for a time that morning no one could find Kerkorian to give him the terrible news. A few months later, he declared a truce and sold his Columbia stock back to the company. Allen & Company sold Columbia Pictures to Coca-Cola in 1982.

•••

IN THE SPRING OF 1980, my name began circulating for the position of administrator for Latin America and the Caribbean at the US Agency for International Development (USAID). My connection to Vice President Walter Mondale through our mutual friend Herbert Allen probably nudged my name to the top of the list. Having held this position in the Johnson administration when I ran the Alliance for Progress, I approached the job possibility with a certain confidence. It was misplaced.

President Carter nominated me to be assistant administrator of USAID on June 16, 1980. During the weeks before my Senate Foreign Relations Committee hearing that August, the Capitol was inundated with letters, mailgrams, and telegrams passionately denouncing my nomination. Northern Catholics and Southern Baptists had united behind Senator Jesse Helms of North Carolina to derail my confirmation. My tenure with Planned Parenthood was coming back to haunt me.

USAID funded a number of family planning projects in the Third World, a fact that had riled Senator Helms for years. In 1973, he had pushed through the Helms Amendment to the Foreign Assistance Act, which ensured that no AID money ever paid for abortions. The idea of putting the former president of Planned Parenthood in charge of those funds launched Helms into the stratosphere.

Facing such fierce opposition, I was comforted to find that my Senate confirmation hearing was chaired by my friend Senator Paul Tsongas. He led me through a series of questions related to US support of dictators in Latin America and the current situations in Cuba, Haiti, and Mexico. I still believed what I had told the members of Congress at my contentious confirmation as assistant secretary of state in 1965: we should provide economic aid to Latin American countries regardless of their government du jour. I urged a long-term commitment of assistance despite the sometimes wild pendulum swings between leftist and right-wing regimes.

The hearing went smoothly and amicably for the first thirty minutes because Senator Helms was late. The suspense grew as we waited for the senator, whom I had never met. In the weeks leading up to this meeting, he had set the stage for a fight, calling me "the world's leading abortionist" and even "the most hated American in Latin America."

When he finally arrived, Helms immediately took the floor to ask me about Planned Parenthood of New York's lawsuit to nullify the Helms Amendment. "In light of your recent association with the effort to overturn congressional policy in this matter, do you believe you can ably carry out the congressional intent with respect to the nations of Latin America?" I assured him I could.

Continuing in this vein and becoming louder as he went, the senator asked, "Do you, as one who has argued in this country for abortion on demand as a matter of equal rights, believe that the posture of the US government ought eventually to be one of encouraging developing nations to permit liberalized abortion?"

"I believe a policy more attuned to our nation, where we come from, and what we stand for, would be to urge a system where there was freedom of choice among the peoples of all nations of the hemisphere in terms of what they did with their life and how they planned their families." I had seen firsthand the enthusiastic reception of USAID's family planning programs in the mostly Catholic countries of Latin America.

Helms argued to the contrary. "The nomination of Mr. Vaughn has already created great concern in Latin America. Earlier this month, Bishop Dario Castrillion, Secretary of the Family Life Department, Consejo Episcopal Latino Americano (CELAM), stated that the Latin American bishops opposed the nomination of Mr. Vaughn and that his nomination is viewed as a threat to the families in their countries. CELAM represents more than seven hundred bishops and more than ninety percent of the people of Latin America."

Helms had amassed a great quantity of ammunition against my nomination, including many out-of-context quotes from my speeches as president of Planned Parenthood. But that was nothing compared to the mail coming in from across the country, described by USAID's Bureau for Legislative Affairs as "unprecedented." Some members of Congress had received as many as fifty letters both to their district and Washington offices.

One particularly compelling mailgram came from Anna Smelser of the Fort Wayne-South Bend Council of Catholic Women: "Planned Parenthood is famous for circulating blasphemous caricatures of the Blessed Virgin Mary all over Latin America in order to promote sexual practices which are abhorrent to the religious and moral convictions of the people there. We consider Vaughn's nomination a personal insult to every Catholic in the US."

Despite Helms' best offense, the Committee on Foreign Relations voted seven to five to report my nomination favorably to the Senate. In losing, Senator Helms promised to filibuster my nomination. The Ad Hoc Committee in Defense of Life vowed to make my confirmation "the toughest abortion vote of the year."

In congressional limbo, I began work as USAID administrator for Latin America in an "acting" capacity, meaning that I couldn't sign anything intimidating. My boss was the enormously gifted USAID administrator, Doug Bennet. A couple of weeks after I started work, Bennet received a lunch invitation from John Carbaugh, a known hatchet man for Jesse Helms and one tough, unctuous *hombre*. The invitation included me and a professor from North Carolina.

When the four of us met at an expense-account restaurant on M Street, Bennet and I knew what might be coming, but we expected greater subtlety. Carbaugh said my nomination could sail through the Senate for $60,000. That was how much Senator Helms needed to send two professors to China to study female infanticide. Bennet in effect told Carbaugh to go to hell. Not just anyone in Washington could get away with telling Jesse Helms to go to hell, even indirectly.

My nomination never did see the Senate floor. It became clear that neither Carter nor Mondale was prepared to go to bat for me in the twilight of their administration. I enjoyed my seven months as acting director, traveling to all my favorite places and working with seasoned professionals like Bennet, who went on to become president of National Public Radio and then Wesleyan College. Among my projects were a $9.5 million loan for agrarian reform in Costa Rica and a training program for Third World nurses run by Florida hospital administrators.

In November, I traveled to Panama with Bennet. It seemed that about half of US foreign aid for the western hemisphere had been earmarked for the tiny isthmus, which in 1980 was fast becoming cocaine heaven. Our first stop was Torrijos' beach house in Farallón. We found him asleep between palm trees, halfway installed in a large hammock, one arm and leg dangling out. It was mid morning, and the bar was open.

Greeting us warmly, Torrijos blurted out, "You gringos are crazy!" He was referring to our haphazard and confused Latin American policy, which had been spotlighted recently in El Salvador, where a brutal civil war was underway. President Carter, that champion of human rights, had once again backed a leader responsible for the worst atrocities against humanity. He provided aid to the abusive right-wing government and then supported agrarian reform at a tumultuous time when it was virtually guaranteed to fail.

"Don't you know that land reform is the most destabilizing thing you can do in a rural society? And you push this while brothers are fighting brothers?" Torrijos had a soft spot for El Salvador, where he had attended military school on a scholarship. He knew our approach there would do more harm than good—and he was right. Thirty-five years later, El Salvador is still trying to recover from Carter and Reagan's ignorant policies.

That visit with Bennet was the last time I saw Torrijos. He was killed on July 31, 1981 when his plane crashed into a cloud-covered hill in central Panama. Speculation flew about the possible assassination of Panama's "*Supremo Supremo*," still in his prime at fifty-two. Most fingers pointed at the CIA, but some suggested Manuel Noriega had planted a bomb or that American businessmen with interests in the canal had arranged the crash.

During a congressional hearing on Panama in 1986, I was questioned about Torrijos' death by California Rep. Bob Lagomarsino. Having had some experience with plane crashes in Latin America, I told the congressman I felt confident we could take the accident at face value. Torrijos had always been a wild risk-taker and usually employed cowboy pilots. Anyone is his right mind would not have flown in the weather that day.

Soon after his death, evidence of his corruption tarnished Torrijos' image. The passage of time and the favorable comparison to his successor, Manuel "Pineapple Face" Noriega, has healed much of the ill will. Shining through any Torrijos ugliness is the glory of getting the canal—for free. It was no surprise that Omar's son Martín won the May 2004 presidential election in Panama.

12

1980–1997

If anyone calls, tell them I'm at the Beltsville Ag Research Center studying winged beans.

—Note on the refrigerator, circa 1988

IN THE FALL OF 1980 at my office in USAID headquarters, I received a call from Spencer Beebe, the director of The Nature Conservancy's new international program. Spencer remembered me from a speech I had given as Peace Corps director in 1968 at Puerto Rico's Camp Crozier, where he had been a volunteer recruit preparing to work with fishermen on the Honduran coast. He had come to Washington to create The Nature Conservancy's roadmap for protecting the great expanses of tropical rainforests throughout Latin America.

A bespectacled, soft-spoken young man with a mop of brown hair and the look of a rugged outdoorsman out of his natural habitat in

Washington, DC, Spencer had an infectious passion for conservation. I sensed immediately that this graduate of the Yale School of Forestry possessed the right instincts for conservation in the Third World.

Challenges in the hemisphere were significant: a paucity of pristine wilderness and privately owned land, and a general resistance to gringo meddling. For centuries, indigenous people had lived off the land, cutting trees for heat, drinking from rivers, washing in streams, and farming on subsistence plots. The Nature Conservancy's model—finding untouched wilderness, then buying and protecting it—didn't translate well.

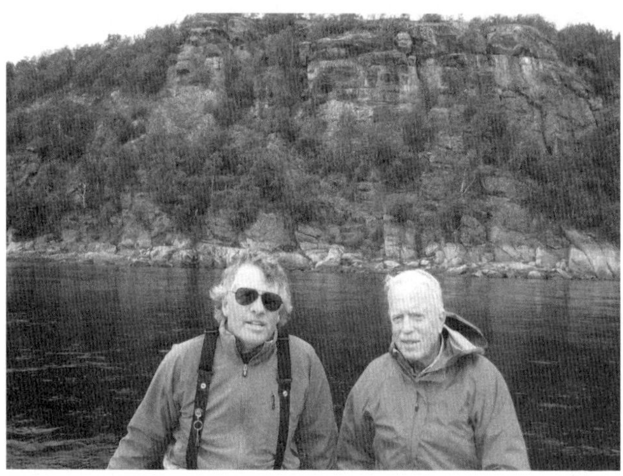

Spencer Beebe

Meeting Spencer marked the beginning of the last and most important chapter of my life. It introduced me to a lifelong friend and mentor in conservation and to a cause bigger and more consequential than any I had worked on before. I became Spencer's informal Latin America advisor as he navigated the politics and government bureaucracies of Central and South America. Before long, I joined the board of The Nature Conservancy, where I chaired the volunteer committee.

Conservation was my avocation in the 1980s: Spencer and I traveled to Panama, Colombia, Bolivia, Chile, Venezuela, Costa Rica, Guatemala, and Mexico visiting my contacts and making new ones. As Spencer toured the hemisphere brokering deals and working with local conservation groups, he determined that the only way to make a lasting and meaningful impact in Latin America was to let countries tackle problems in their own way. In Spencer's view, the need to preserve and improve the land had to be balanced with the right of native people to sustain themselves off the land.

In 1983, Spencer's team negotiated its first big deal in one of my favorite places, Bolivia. The Beni River lowlands were the holy grail of conservation in Latin America: pristine, cheap land—and lots of it. The Nature Conservancy's international program purchased a five-thousand-acre ranch in the Beni called El Porvenir, which became a base for research, education, and tourism. In partnership with the Academia de Ciencias Nacional de Bolivia, it grew into a three-hundred-thousand-acre protected area.

In Bolivia, I introduced Spencer to Minister of Planning Gonzalo Sánchez de Lozada, who would become president twice, in 1993 and 2002. Bolivians called him "El Gringo" because he spoke heavily accented Spanish, the result of growing up in the American Midwest as the son of a Bolivian politician in exile. He was helpful to us in many ways, not the least of which was the loan of his twin-engine airplane.

Spencer, an adventurer *sans frontières*, waxed rhapsodic about camping in Bolivia's Beni River lowlands among five hundred types of mammals and one thousand species of birds. He saw the opportunity to expand our reach into this Amazonian basin and wanted me to experience the possibilities firsthand. Fellow board member Peter Stroh of the Stroh Brewery Company and I agreed to go.

Our trip stalled early when Gonzalo's plane, too small to take us all in one trip, ferried us separately to different dirt strips in the Bolivian rainforest. It was an easy mistake; the Beni, a prime cocaine-producing hub, was home to roughly seven thousand airstrips. Spotty communications from our respective grass hut airports delayed our reunion for a day or two, but we finally gathered at the same dirt strip in San Borja, where a boy wearing an old Stroh Brewery baseball cap emerged to greet us.

That auspicious sign was followed by a less promising one: a three-hundred-pound man bouncing toward us on a Honda 50. As he approached we saw that his face was puffed up to the size of a basketball. The man introduced himself as the mayor of San Borja and the recent victim of a bee attack. He bid us a gracious if slurred greeting through swollen lips. After a few pleasantries, Spencer, Peter, and I began the trek to a remote campsite being set up for us by a team of local hires.

Then the rains came, and the trail flooded with knee-deep muddy water. After a few miles we arrived at an unexpected, gushing river. We fashioned a very wobbly raft from tree branches and made it across, feeling like triumphant Amazon explorers. Shortly after fording the river, we encountered our advance team fleeing the campsite. They explained that prowling jaguars the night before had accelerated their departure.

When we arrived at camp, we found it partially erected and fully soaked. Without solid ground for tents, we set up hammocks between the trees and covered ourselves with blankets and tarps for the night. As we got settled and darkness descended, Spencer commented casually that anacondas, not jaguars, were the real threat out there. As Spencer promised, Peter and I got a real feel for the Beni lowlands—and how low they were.

In more upscale *hazañas*, I traveled with Spencer to Costa Rica, which had outshone its neighbors in virtually every sector thanks to good leadership and a robust democracy. We helped the National Park Service there develop opportunities for ecotourism, which we were convinced could replace agriculture as the country's largest source of income. Today, of course, that idea has played out almost too well, as tourists pour in from all northern climes and Americans settle there at a great clip.

•••

My work with The Nature Conservancy was thrilling, but it didn't bring home the responsibly sourced bacon. With the incoming Reagan administration in January 1981, my job at USAID ended. I returned to Pierce International as senior vice president, but after masquerading as a banker for a couple of years, my roots in international development drew me back in.

My old friend from the Peace Corps and State Department, Leveo Sanchez, had started a consulting firm that specialized in evaluating and advising USAID programs overseas. One of his vice presidents was Jack Sullivan, who had worked as assistant administrator for USAID's Bureau for Asia and the Pacific during my time at USAID in 1980. Jack suggested that Leveo and I get together; with a gentle persuader like Leveo, such a meeting could have only one outcome.

Joining Development Associates in 1983 felt like old home week. Leveo had started the company with Jean Rogers, the daughter of my mentor in international development, Vance Rogers. I had known Jean when she was a child, and had worked for her dad at Point Four in Panama. I became a vice president at Development Associates during a time when increasingly large sums of US foreign aid were being funneled to Latin America, and Leveo's services were in high demand.

Development Associates conducted projects in more than 120 different countries, primarily Africa and Latin America. I immediately jumped into a project in Bolivia to provide technical assistance to the Food for Peace program. I led a small group of consultants into the remotest reaches of the Altiplano, which had been suffering from a severe draught, to assess the food distribution system for hundreds of thousands of people in need.

In many cases, our teams went into countries to perform general assessments of USAID missions—their staff, contractors, and programs. With a team of seasoned economists and MBAs, I evaluated the missions in Liberia, Upper Volta, Niger, Mali, Guatemala, and Honduras, among others.

In El Salvador, I worked with Peter Fraser, an economist and former Peace Corps volunteer and staff member in Colombia, to advise USAID on its support of small enterprise and rural economic projects. We recommended that AID partner with the *Fundación Salvadoreña de Desarrollo Económico y Social* (FUSADES), a start-up founded by Salvadoran entrepreneurs to improve the plight of those at the bottom of the economic ladder. FUSADES has since grown into the premier development nonprofit in El Salvador.

Honduras

The advantage of USAID programs working *with* rather than above their local hosts had been clear to me for decades, even before the Peace Corps—since the time I worked in Bolivia and Panama. Especially in a situation like El Salvador's, where a civil war raged and suspicion of outsiders ran high, it always proved most effective to let the local experts run the show. Unfortunately, the concept of partnership in foreign aid continued to elude top US policymakers.

Leveo Sanchez and I argued our case for international cooperation in testimony before President Reagan's National Bipartisan Commission on Central America, informally known by the name of its chairman, Henry Kissinger. We suggested the reintroduction of the *servicio* system in US foreign aid, where each sector, from education to agriculture, was administered through a jointly managed and funded program with the host country. During the 1950s, the *servicios* produced fine local leaders who had worked shoulder to shoulder with their American counterparts and went on to become governmental ministers with strong ties to the American aid community.

Instead of recommending the partnership that Leveo and I touted, the Kissinger Report issued in January 1984 warned of the "domino effect" of Communist uprisings in Central America, with El Salvador and Nicaragua generating the most panic. The report essentially affirmed the disjointed approach the US had taken for years: provide military support to counter leftist revolutions while funneling aid for economic development. Predictably, the report glossed over the delivery system for economic aid, and the *servicios* remained a dusty relic of our past successes.

Considerably more satisfying than testifying before Kissinger's cronies was working with the smart, experienced Development Associates staff. We had the often delightful task of telling AID bureaucrats, among whom I had toiled for years, exactly what they were getting wrong—and right. We answered the questions that officials in Washington asked themselves constantly: is the money being spent effectively? Are the people in most desperate need really being helped? Will there be a lasting impact? In my role as an evaluator for Development Associates, I never minced words, even when our findings of incompetence or dysfunction in AID programs made Leveo pale.

One example of such a project was our assessment of Appropriate Technology International (ATI), a company contracting on a large scale with USAID to grow small businesses in the Third World using innovative technology. I visited their sites in Bolivia, Senegal, Zimbabwe, and Nepal with Peter Fraser and Bob Flick, another economist who specialized in small enterprise development.

Getting a treadle pump lesson in Senegal

Our first stop was Bolivia, where ATI was working with an alpaca and vicuña yarn factory to implement a process that took wool from spinning and weaving to the customer using sophisticated equipment.

In Senegal, treadle water pumps designed by ATI scientists were being introduced to irrigate gardens previously watered by bucket. In Harari, Zimbabwe, ATI's sunflower oil factory used an efficient and user-friendly seed press developed at a machine shop in Vermont. Continuing east we visited the Nepal program, where ATI scientists were cloning seeds through potato tissue culture production as a better way to deliver root stock to farmers in the hinterlands.

Each project was an attempt to create, through the subsidized inventions of ATI, a value-added chain benefiting local entrepreneurs and improving the quality of life in those communities. Peter, Bob, and I wondered what all this new technology would really change for subsistence villagers, especially once the ATI subsidies and technical assistance were gone and the cost of the equipment and maintenance fell to the locals. And where was the booming local market for alpaca yarn and sunflower oil? We concluded that the programs were not cost-effective or self-sustaining, which is what we told a high-level USAID audience when we returned to Washington.

The AID brass, who had been divided in their opinions of ATI, seemed grateful for our assessment. Not so the head of ATI. Shortly after our report to AID, I received an irate call from him at my home at three in the morning. It was no wonder he was angry; ATI and its romantic notions of microtechnologies making macro improvements for the Third World had taken USAID by storm. By 1985, ATI had amassed $38 million in USAID grants for projects all over the world; within two years of our report, AID had defunded its projects in those four countries.

In 1984, Development Associates received several contracts as a result of the Caribbean Basin Initiative (CBI), a carrot in the United States' typical stick approach to battling communism in Latin America and the Caribbean. The initiative gave tariff breaks and trade benefits to reward countries resisting the clutches of leftist forces.

In July 1984, Leveo sent me to advise Haiti's special presidential commission, whose goal was to maximize the development impact of the CBI. Leveo and I both had a special interest in Haiti, which had been in such desperate straits for so long. When we worked together in the State Department in 1965 and aid to Haiti had been temporarily suspended, Leveo and I figured out a way to funnel money through back channels to their minister of health, who had gone to college with Hubert Humphrey's physician and close advisor, Dr. Edgar Berman. Haiti used the secret funds to start a large-scale family planning program.

On the six-month presidential commission project, my team was responsible for the overall leadership of the commission, which developed public-private partnerships and export strategies and created a new labor code. The work went well as we lobbied business leaders and ministers with daily phone calls and meetings to convince them of the benefits of new laws and expanded cooperation. I drove a tiny rental car in the kamikaze traffic of Port-au-Prince with quiet desperation, my slow pace giving the locals a chance to sharpen their tailgating skills.

Our work took place during the reign of Jean-Claude "Baby Doc" Duvalier, the son of former longtime president Dr. Francois "Papa Doc" Duvalier. Papa and Baby, who became president at nineteen when his father died in 1971, were both profiteers who made millions off the backs of Haitians and used the brutal *Tonton Macoutes* paramilitary troops to suppress their opposition.

Public disenchantment with Baby Doc was gaining momentum during our project in Haiti. By the time we delivered our trade recommendations and rewritten labor code to the president, we knew they were barely worth the green paper they were written on because the Haitian revolution had passed the point of no return. In 1985, rioting broke out in Gonaïves and spread quickly to other major cities. Baby Doc fled to France in 1986, courtesy of the US Air Force. He maintained an opulent existence until 1993, when he lost his fortune the old-fashioned way, through divorce.

•••

I KEPT MY HAND in Panama during the eighties, when the corrupt and brutal reign of Omar Torrijos' successor, Manuel Noriega, made that county a growing source of intrigue and outrage. In 1983, Noriega arrived in Washington aboard the cocaine-running Learjet of his friend, Colombian drug lord Pablo Escobar. He came as a newly self-promoted brigadier general to visit with President Ronald Reagan to discuss, among other awkward hypocrisies, Noriega's selection to win Panama's upcoming democratic elections.

Set for May 1984, these would be the first open presidential elections in sixteen years, and US officials wanted to make sure the winner was someone they could live with. The lucky pick was Nicolás (Nicky) Ardito Barletta Vallarino, a former vice president of the World Bank and economics student of Secretary of State George Schultz—a perfect candidate in every sense but political. Barletta would never be able to defeat the popular Panameñista Party candidate and three-time former president, Arnulfo Arias Madrid, unless the elections were rigged. In this case, they were.

That May, I went to Panama as an election observer with Freedom House and could smell fraud before clearing customs. Soldiers voted early and often at any precinct, whether registered there or not. The military took custody of the ballot boxes and the vote count was conspicuously delayed for ten days. Nicky Barletta won by a small but reliable margin. US Ambassador Everett Briggs dutifully appeared before Panama's Electoral Tribunal to congratulate its director on a good, clean election.

When the Freedom House team attempted to share its evidence of massive electoral fraud, Ambassador Briggs refused to see us, as did both the assistant secretary of state and George Schultz. Appealing as far up the ladder as we could, we encountered only complicity and arrogance. The election was a travesty for the Panamanians, who had thriving, well-led political parties—upward of fourteen of them—that were denied a chance for true democracy.

Barletta served as president for a year, until he began asking questions about the torture and beheading of former Vice Minister of Health Dr. Hugo Spadafora, a vocal critic of Noriega. In September 1985, Noriega's heavies had intercepted Spadafora at the Costa Rican border in Chiriquí Province and later dumped his headless body in a river. When Barletta announced a commission to investigate the murder, which had received attention in the United States, he was forced to resign. His successor, First Vice President Eric Arturo Delvalle, projected an even weaker aura of legitimacy.

In the spring of 1986, Congress and the media were stirred by two groundbreaking articles in *The New York Times* by Seymour Hersh describing the extent of General Noriega's involvement in drug trafficking and money laundering. Hersh had the guts and analytical ability to report what old-time Panama hands knew had been going on for decades. Congress responded to these alarming reports the best way it knew how—with hearings—and I was invited to several before the House Committee on Foreign Affairs.

At a hearing in 1986, I explained to Chairman Gus Yatron that while in most of the Western world drug-running and gun-running were handled by the mafia, in Panama organized crime was the purview of the military. "The Panamanian military hold us hostage because they say, in effect, 'if you close in on us, there's nothing stopping us from going to the Russians or the Cubans for our training and weapons.' That's a pretty strong deterrent for us; it's been the Panamanian military's secret weapon."

When questioned about Noriega, I was particularly candid because someone had to be. “General Torrijos used to refer to him in English as ‘my gangster.’ In Panama, those who agree with me say that Noriega ‘*es capaz de todo*,’ meaning he is capable of anything. When you look at recent events—the stolen election, the torture and murder of Hugo Spadafora, and people being pushed out of airplanes, it is quite obvious that a lot of Panamanians are right that Noriega is *capaz de todo*.”

My comments on the general were picked up by the Latin American media, and the next day Noriega was prepared for a Panamanian television reporter’s question: “General, how do you respond to Ambassador Vaughn’s referring to you as a gangster before the US Congress?”

“I think three things about Mr. Bond. First, he was a lousy boxer. Second, he was a bad ambassador. Third, and in general, *es un mal hombre*.”

The same House committee reconvened two years later on the same subject, now convinced that Manuel Noriega had to go but unsure how to do it. Rep. Robert Lagomarsino opened by explaining that “we are well into the second month of severe economic pressure against the Noriega regime, but we have seen little evidence that it is having any real effect on the political situation in Panama...the question remains what form further US pressure should take.”

I reminded the members of Congress that while we complained about the military regime of the Panamanians, the United States had run a military government in the Panama Canal Zone for eighty years. I argued that in order to win the confidence and good will of the Panamanian people and unify our foreign policy, we must remove our military leadership from the Canal Zone. “I have never heard any US military officer criticize any Panamanian Defense Force officer.” Until we eliminate US-Panamanian military camaraderie and the buddy system, “we are going to lack clarity.”

Secondly, I said, we must confront the narcotics issue. The head of the DEA had been sending letters of commendation to Noriega for his work in curbing cocaine traffic; that kind of nonsense had to stop. Drugs were the core issue in Panama. "Noriega is a rapist, a murderer, and a perpetrator of fraudulent elections, but our most credible cause for seeing his overthrow is that he is a drug lord."

Remembering the lessons of the Dominican Republic invasion of 1965, I urged Congress not to take on Panama alone. "We must seek allies…if we don't have allies we don't have much except the blame." I suggested Colombia's impressive president, Virgilio Barco, would be a smart choice. However we neutralized Noriega, it should be with the input and cooperation of our Latin American friends, whose help we needed desperately.

Shortly after that hearing, I served on President George H. W. Bush's delegation to observe Panama's 1989 presidential elections. The group of fourteen observers was led by Rep. John Murtha of Pennsylvania and included Sen. John McCain of Arizona. Jimmy and Rosalynn Carter and Gerald Ford were also there with an international observation team. Told in no uncertain terms by Panamanian officials that our delegation would be unwelcome, we circumvented the visa process by landing at Howard Air Force Base in the Panama Canal Zone. We expected the worst; Panama's Electoral Tribunal had already released "data" showing an increase of 160 percent in registered voters since the last election.

On the first day, I was asked to ride in the Carters' car to brief them on the history of Panamanian elections. By way of providing some background and local color, I told them the story of the presidential candidate accused of being impotent (roughly translated from the Panamanian expression for watery sperm), rendering him less than a man and unfit for office. The candidate's response was to run off to Paris with a sixteen-year-old girl in the weeks before the election. He returned to a decisive victory. Jimmy and Rosalynn were appalled by

my story. They stopped talking and didn't make eye contact with me for the rest of the car ride.

A lighter moment with Jimmy Carter in 1996

In subsequent trips to Central America, I have often been mistaken for Jimmy Carter, just four years my junior and possessing similar jowls and gummy smile. So many times did this happen that eventually I began giving autographs and even brief commentary to reporters who insisted I was *Presidente* Carter.

The elections of May 1989 were perhaps the most inelegantly rigged under Noriega's control. When it became obvious that opposition candidate Guillermo Endara would crush Noriega's man at the polls, the election was nullified, Noriega blaming "foreign interference." The next day, Endara and his two vice presidents boldly led a protest march through historic downtown Panama City, where Noriega's thugs pulled them from their motorcade and beat them to a pulp. Noriega installed his puppet president, Francisco Rodríguez, but the US recognized Endara, despite his scars.

Panama continued its downward trajectory until President George H. W. Bush unilaterally overthrew the government by military force in December 1989. Noriega was sentenced at the US District Court in

Miami to forty years in prison for drug trafficking, racketeering, and money laundering.

For future reference, it may be helpful for Congress and taxpayers to remember that all those Panamanian military officers who became so corrupt were trained by the US military. Most were students at one of the half dozen military programs in the US and at bases in the Canal Zone. I doubt the Pentagon has ever trained the armed forces of any nation as extensively as it did those in Panama. Something important was missing at the core of that curriculum.

•••

For the first six years, The Nature Conservancy benignly neglected its international program, giving the staff autonomy to conduct business its way. The program had its own senior management structure and five-member subcommittee on the board. Spencer Beebe eventually pushed for nonprofit status as an independent entity, but headquarters insisted on treating its international arm like a dependent subsidiary. Giving the program autonomy, Nature Conservancy executives feared, would split the donor base.

Building on its successes, the international program tested and refined its alternative approach to conservation and began to develop donors of its own. The program was fueled by a talented and mostly Latin American female staff dispersed among ten countries in Latin America. The Nature Conservancy management in DC began to sweat over their start-up program that was taking over the hemisphere.

Into this power struggle stepped Frank Boren, a former football coach and lawyer who was elected from the California chapter to preside over The Nature Conservancy worldwide on January 1, 1987. In theory, Boren said he supported the plans and strategy of the international program to become more independent. In practice, he panicked.

Warned by Spencer that putting the international staff under Washington management would trigger a mass exodus, Boren asked them to sign loyalty oaths. That move went over badly as you might expect among a bunch of idealists. In the face of the international team's resistance, Boren threatened to remove Spencer and his colleague, Peter Seligmann, from their leadership roles, turn over the seven conservation data centers in Latin America to The Nature Conservancy's domestic science chief and place the rest of the program squarely under headquarters control.

My international committee colleagues Peter Stroh and Chuck Hedlund and I made a last-ditch effort to persuade Frank of the doomsday outcome of his decisions. We got nowhere. I told Spencer, "I've seen this story unfold again and again. They leave you alone when you're struggling. When you create a success, they take over and botch it every time." The international staff needed no encouragement from me; they started a revolution and never looked back.

Spencer drew up a letter of resignation signed by thirty-five staff members. The number resigning ultimately rose to fifty-five out of sixty-three international employees. The five board members on the international committee—Stroh, Hedlund, Jean Vollum, Sophie Engelhard Craighead, and I—also resigned. Pete Seligmann and Spencer delivered the letter on January 30, and then we crowded into our makeshift headquarters at Washington's Tabard Inn to officially ratify the articles and bylaws of our new organization. Murray Gell-Mann, a Nobel Prize-winning physicist and chair of the MacArthur Foundation's World Resources and Environment Committee, joined us there with great applause from the staff.

The Nature Conservancy reacted in all the predictable ways: placed a guard at the building, locked the international staff out of its offices, and confiscated Spencer's hard drive to prove a conspiracy (they couldn't). Spencer and Seligmann, both gifted fundraisers, managed to sustain all staff salaries and overhead from day one. It was a new day and a new organization founded with a common philosophy by staffers from Washington to Bolivia. Today, Conservation International is among the largest and best known environmental groups in the world.

After the tsunami at The Nature Conservancy, it was all hands on deck at Conservation International (CI), and I was only too happy to come aboard. I left my job at Development Associates in 1987 to become a very involved founding chairman of CI. We moved out of the Tabard Inn to offices near Farragut Square on eighteenth Street. Spencer and I went back on the road, visiting Mexico, Guatemala, Costa Rica, Colombia, and Bolivia to reassure nervous or confused partners and donors that our good work would continue under a new name.

We met with some partners who were concerned they were no longer affiliated with a major institution in the US; others had been warned against working with CI on projects funded through The Nature Conservancy, even though Spencer and his team had raised that money. I explained the shift as "*un divorcio*" after an unhappy marriage, and most people were reassured that they had sided with the right spouse.

Our Latin American counterparts didn't have to wait long for CI to prove itself. In the 1980s, Latin American countries were accruing debt at a great clip, and inflation was through the roof. Bolivia's annual inflation rate was 2,000 percent, and its debt was trading at a small fraction of its value. With the Beni River lowlands again in Spencer's sight, CI hatched a plan to buy Bolivian debt and allow the country to make good in a novel way.

We approached a Swiss bank holding $650,000 of Bolivian debt. Never expecting to be repaid, the bank accepted our offer of $100,000 for the note. The Bolivian CI staff then presented the Banco Nacional de Bolivia with a deal: pay off your $650,000 debt to Conservation International by giving $500,000 in pesos to the Academia de Ciencias Nacional for its endowment of the research and education center, El Porvenir, and proposing a UNESCO Man and the Biosphere Reserve of almost three million acres around the center. It was an easy decision for the Bolivian bank, which would not have to pay the full amount of the loan or repay anything in dollars.

This first "debt-for-nature swap" in July 1987 took the conservation movement by storm. Conservation International appeared on the front page of the *Wall Street Journal* in an article about a new way to solve the global financial crisis. Soon thereafter, the MacArthur Foundation awarded CI a $3 million grant for general support. Since then, more than $1 billion of debt-for-nature swaps have taken place throughout the hemisphere; even The Nature Conservancy has gotten into the act.

As CI settled into its place at the forefront of the international environmental scene, I found a little excitement of my own in Washington. I left work early to take the family on an overseas vacation. As I walked from the Sixteenth Street bus stop to our house on Upshur Street, a carload of young men pulled up beside me. Several of them jumped out and surrounded me, one jamming a sawed-off shotgun in my ribs. Knowing when to fold, I quickly handed over my bulging wallet, wishing I had purchased American Express Travelers Cheques. They also got my roll of Tums.

That experience prepared me for my next mugging, this time in New York City. In town for a meeting, I left my hotel around midnight to pick up the first edition of *The New York Times*. As I trotted back to the hotel in the rain, holding the newspaper over my head, a bulky figure stepped out of the shadows, grabbed me from behind, and pinned my arms while he tried to extract the wallet from my back pocket.

I hit my robust assailant in the throat with my elbow. He dropped his arms for a moment, and I turned and kneed him in the groin before landing my famous left hook to the liver. He let out a small grunt, and I continued to pummel him with a dozen more of my best shots before he collapsed face down in the wet gutter. In classic timing, a policeman came running over. The wide-eyed newspaper vendor gave the officer his account, and the incident ended up in *The New York Times* and other papers the next day under the heading, "Pity the Mugger."

•••

After two exciting years working as a glorified Latin America program officer at Conservation International, and at the ripe age of sixty-eight, I began to think seriously about accelerating my retirement savings. In my divorce, I had cashed out my federal retirement and ceded half to my first wife. With two children still years away from college, I knew I had to get serious about returning to the Foreign Service and reclaiming my pension.

To that end, I was in Honduras investigating a job possibility with USAID when I bumped into my friend Gordy Straub at the bar of the Honduras Maya Hotel. I had met Gordy in a Washington elevator when we both worked for USAID in 1980. He had introduced himself as a former Peace Corps volunteer in Guatemala, and we had kept in touch. Over a couple of Cokes, I told him about my interest in rejoining the ranks of the Foreign Service, and he suggested I come work for him at the Regional Office for Central America and Panama (ROCAP).

A little-known offshoot of USAID created in 1964, ROCAP was born from the progressive but bureaucratically contentious idea that Latin America would benefit from a regional approach to solving its economic and other development challenges. During my brief time at AID in 1980, I had pushed for more funding for the regional organization, but because ROCAP money came from the AID honey jar, that idea found no traction among Washington bureaucrats.

In 1988, USAID was finally beginning to get serious about the environment, and ROCAP seemed the logical vehicle to deliver that aid. The Central American mountains, rainforests, and rivers were not contained within sovereign borders; it made little sense for our aid to be parceled out to individual countries. ROCAP added "natural resources" to the title of its agriculture program and began allocating funds for conservation projects.

Gordy pitched me to his boss, and I applied to be the senior environmental advisor for ROCAP, based in Guatemala City. The job seemed a perfect match for my consuming interest in conservation, Latin America, and retirement planning. Once the hiring committee got over my propensity for switching jobs every two years, they hired me. We moved to Guatemala City in January 1989.

Guatemala, the most populous country in Central America, is also one of the poorest. Its checkered past follows the pattern of many of its neighbors, although the US military played an especially large role in Guatemala's drama. A 1954 coup backed by the US overthrew a progressive, left-leaning government and installed a military leader. Subsequent years of rigged elections and suppression of the indigenous population spurred the formation of antigovernment guerilla groups, and a civil war began in 1966 that lasted thirty-six years.

The most appealing aspect of Guatemala is its indigenous people, descended from the Maya, who account for almost half the country's population. (Their numbers would be much higher if the US-trained Guatemalan military hadn't slaughtered so many of them.) While the capital, Guatemala City, is a smoggy urban sprawl with little native flare, the rest of the country is dotted with vibrant, colorful villages perched on steep green hillsides. The markets are picturesque and bustling, the churches charming and well-worn, and the smell of burning incense permeates everything.

ROCAP headquarters in Guatemala City had a most unusual mission director. Nadine Hogan was a nurse turned Republican political operative who had endeared herself to the Coors family of Colorado in the 1970s. After helping Ronald Reagan get elected in 1980, Nadine was hired as a White House staffer; then she became an associate director at the Peace Corps. In 1985, President Reagan appointed her head of ROCAP. Nadine was a larger-than-life character with genuine affection for Latin American people and great political instincts. We liked each other very much, and she left me to my own devices.

Shortly after I arrived, Gordy Straub moved to a position with USAID and Ron Curtis replaced him as my immediate boss, ROCAP's chief of agriculture and natural resources. With a PhD in economics and lengthy experience in rural development, Ron was salt of the earth seasoned with an Irish temper that kept things interesting. Gordy, Ron, and I, the old USAID retreads (and I much older than they), met for coffee every morning.

Although I was based in Guatemala City, my bailiwick included all seven Central American countries: Belize, Costa Rica, El Salvador, Guatemala, Honduras, Nicaragua, and Panama. I was on the road constantly, trying to bolster private, government, and nonprofit support for conservation across the region.

At ROCAP, Ron and I created the Regional Central American Environmental Program (RENARM), an environmental strategy that initiated and funded regional organizations and supported conservation projects already in progress. RENARM was ambitious in both funding and scope, including forest preservation, watershed rehabilitation, and pest management for farming operations through a partnership with the Zamorano Pan-American Agricultural School.

The six-year, $60 million project created national parks and nature reserves throughout Central America. At these very beginning stages, an influx of cash and support from AID made a huge impact. I added a matching program to entice major US environmental nonprofits to invest in Central America and made it my responsibility to shepherd the groups through the process.

Because we had included in RENARM's objectives that it would support and cooperate with USAID programs, Ron and I traveled constantly to AID outposts throughout Central America to bring them into the fold. Shifting perspectives and allegiances within the AID bureaucracy was an uphill battle. AID disdained ROCAP "as a religion," as Ron would say. We were the Johnny Come Lately agency competing for limited funds. Eventually we made some inroads, and by the end of my tour I felt we had added a hint of respect to all the resentment.

I had an easier time jollying up Guatemalan President Vinicio Cerezo and Vice President Roberto Carpio, who occasionally lent their weight to our environmental causes. Cerezo, a Christian Democrat, was the first democratically elected president in seventeen years when he took office in 1986. He faced all the usual struggles of a Latin American leader, especially a military that he couldn't fully control. The military's genocide campaigns and human rights abuses fueled antigovernment guerilla activity that destabilized most of the country.

Cerezo's army twice tried to overthrow him. In his effort to appease them, the president proved very reluctant to prosecute human rights violations. Our tough and candid ambassador to Guatemala at the time, Tom Stroock, had the guts to publicly criticize Cerezo for his failure to act after a string of assassinations and kidnappings. Ambassador Stroock famously withheld a $2 million check in US aid until the soldiers responsible for killing American Michael DeVine were arrested. Cerezo's greatest achievement was hanging on: he withstood his challengers to serve a full five-year term before turning the presidency over to his democratically elected successor, Jorge Serrano.

Nadine Hogan and Ambassador Tom Stroock

Cerezo's twenty-three-year-old son, "Maco," whom the president put in charge of environmental issues, was a supporter of ROCAP's projects. Maco and Vice President "El Vice" Roberto Carpio, both quite familiar with pyramid schemes, were working to create a green pyramid in which small farmers were encouraged to plant trees and recruit others to do the same. By happy coincidence, ROCAP's forestry advisor, an impressive young fellow named Henry Tschinkel, had just completed a research project identifying tree species with the greatest potential for reforestation by small farmers in Central America.

I took Henry to the presidential palace to meet Carpio, introducing him as the foremost authority on Central American reforestation. Henry and El Vice hit it off, despite Carpio's insistence on calling him "Dr. Tinkle." *Proyecto Pirámide* was launched with Henry's expert guidance. Like many honorable efforts in conservation, this one never received adequate funding, but it did yield Henry a great nickname that stuck.

•••

Despite the political instability, military violence, kidnappings, and coup attempts during our time in Guatemala, we were fortunate to have had few problems. During one coup attempt, I was in Washington at a White House meeting when Leftie got an early morning phone call from Ron Curtis telling her to stay indoors. She turned on CNN hoping to follow the coup's progress; instead she saw coverage of my meeting, including footage of me chatting with National Security Advisor Brent Scowcroft. While Leftie was unable to get any news about Guatemala, in DC Scowcroft was telling me that the coup would amount to nothing. He was right—life quickly returned to Guatemalan normal.

On another occasion, Leftie and I volunteered to chaperone our son's earth science class on a field trip to the top of the local volcano, Pacaya. Its cone made for a majestic if ominous sight from the city, occasionally emitting puffs of billowing smoke. On the trek were about twenty students and the science teacher—a former Peace Corps volunteer, naturally.

After a long morning of hiking, we stopped for a snack on a grassy plateau about half a mile below the peak. The group forged ahead while I stayed behind with my daughter and two of her friends who had hiked as far as they could. I had just drifted off to sleep with a fishing hat over my face when a man appeared in the tall grass about ten yards away. The girls jostled me to attention and I looked up to see Billy the Kid; he had a bandana over his nose and mouth and was pointing a gun at us. He announced unnecessarily, "*Este es un asalto.*"

I greeted him warmly and told him that we had lots of food to share; he said money was more important to him than food. Keeping my wallet in my back pocket, I pulled a wad of small bills out of my shirt pocket, a ruse that had worked well for me in previous hold-ups. I threw the money and an enticing selection of bologna sandwiches and trail mix toward him. I wished him *buen provecho*, and he disappeared back into the brush. The girls giggled in relief, and I told them to wake me again if another gunman came by. The next month, a group of Dutch hikers on Pacaya was surrounded by several gunmen, robbed and assaulted, and the US embassy added the volcano to its long list of destinations off-limits to Americans.

The bureaucratic limits put on our mobility in Central America for reasons of safety or protocol left me cold. I regularly traveled where I wasn't supposed to or took trips without the formal permission required by US embassies, and usually I pulled it off. In one case, however, I took it too far. A day after an unapproved trip to Managua, ROCAP received a fiery missive from the AID director in Nicaragua. "Ambassador Jack Vaughn was seen last night live on local television at a signing ceremony with the Central American presidents. He did not have country clearance and this is not the first time that this has happened." It wouldn't be the last, either.

•••

I LEFT ROCAP AFTER three years and moved to Tucson, the perfect home base for my protracted semiretirement. I interrupted my gardening to attend board meetings at EARTH University in Costa Rica and Cypress Bioscience in San Diego. I also remained on Conservation International's Advisory Committee. In 1990, I shifted my environmental attention northward, following Spencer Beebe's star. Through extensive mapping work with Conservation

International, Spencer had discovered that North America was home to most of the world's temperate rainforests, and half of them had already been destroyed or developed.

With my friend Fernando Eleta at the EARTH University commencement, 1998

Spencer's interest in North American rainforests solidified during a visit to the Kitlope in British Columbia for a meeting with its native inhabitants, the Haisla First Nation. Along the banks of the milky blue Kitlope River is the largest virgin temperate rainforest watershed in the world—eight hundred thousand acres from glaciers to estuary. Spencer's effort to help the Haisla prevent logging in their tribal territory brought unprecedented attention to the area and ultimately both preserved the rainforest and gave birth to a new organization called Ecotrust.

Leaving Conservation International in the capable hands of Peter Seligmann and a wonderful board, I became founding chairman of Ecotrust, completely captivated by what Spencer calls "the rainforests of home." I liked the idea that Ecotrust would be more than a conservation outfit; it would be a catalyst, advocate, and enabler for conservation-based development. This was an idea grounded in the real world to help local businesses sustain their resources and reap the rewards of their natural bounty—their trees, fish, and shellfish. It seemed the definition of win-win.

Ecotrust made its headquarters in Portland and began campaigns on many fronts to preserve, rehabilitate, and invest in the temperate rainforest ecosystems that extend from the Pacific Northwest into Canada. Among the many innovative things Ecotrust has created over the years are an environmental bank, a for-profit forest management company, and an organization and movement called Salmon Nation. The entire Northern Pacific region, including parts of China, Eastern Russia, Japan, Alaska, British Columbia, Washington, Oregon, and California make up Salmon Nation, a place where year after year the salmon return to spawn.

With Spencer in Chile in 1998

Looking at the world through pink lenses, Spencer explains that salmon are a fabulous measure of health in an ecosystem. "When twenty thousand to thirty thousand healthy fall Chinook salmon die within days of entering the Klamath River, as they did in 2006 due to excessively low water flows from agricultural diversion, we know our governance, our economy, our politics are failing. Politicians may deny this, but salmon don't lie."

Ecotrust has been nimble, dynamic, and daring in its endeavors over the last twenty-six years. I have more fun working with groups that need to be reined in rather than prodded along, and Ecotrust's inventive staff certainly falls into the first category. With Ecotrust I traveled to Clayoquot Sound and the Kitlope region in British Columbia, Alaska, Willapa Bay, Washington, Chile, and the Kola Peninsula west of Murmansk, Russia.

As the son of a farmer and businessman, I have always understood the link between natural resource management and economic prosperity. It surprises me that I took so long to become an environmentalist, but it was well worth the wait. I don't yet belong to every green group in the world, but I am on their mutually reinforcing mailing lists. The highlights of every year are trips into beautiful and remote wilderness with friends. On rugged expeditions with Spencer we pass the eagle feather and catch only what we can eat; on Alaskan fishing trips with my friends at Allen & Company we pass the *Wall Street Journal*, smoke our fish, and bring it home.

•••

HAITI, THE POOREST COUNTRY in Latin America, shares the island of Hispaniola with the Dominican Republic, whose economy is 800 percent larger. For many of us working in international development, Haiti has been a challenge and a calling. At various times in my career, I introduced programs in family planning, reforestation, tourism, and job creation there, none of which had lasting impact.

I fantasized for years about bringing David Lilienthal's TVA approach to the Artibonite watershed on the border between Haiti and the Dominican Republic. The area covers nine thousand kilometers, with the majority in Haiti and about a quarter in the DR. It is the heart of Haiti's agricultural production area but also includes some of the most degraded land in the country.

Poor development and management had resulted in massive erosion problems; in 1998 the United Nations estimated that Haiti was losing thirty-six million tons of topsoil annually. That same year, Hurricane Georges delivered a stark warning: Haiti suffered devastating mudslides throughout its deforested areas and lost a huge share of its agricultural land, including eighty percent of the banana plantations. Thousands of head of small livestock and more than four hundred people died.

My TVA pipe dream grew legs when I linked up with Mike Palmbach, a former Peace Corps volunteer who became a soils man and a public finance expert. We put together a proposal for sustainable, integrated development of the Artibonite Watershed through the creation of a binational authority to manage the region's resources. The authority copied the TVA model, investing in new hydroelectric capacity, reforestation, diversified agriculture, housing, basic infrastructure, and public education.

Our calls and visits to philanthropists, international NGOs, the Organization of American States, the World Bank, and members of the House and Senate generated a commitment of $500 million. Potential partners were moved not only by the desperate need and the broad scope, but also by the prospect of a first-time collaboration between Haiti and the DR. The biggest hurdle was buy-in from the Dominicans, who were loath to engage in joint efforts with Haiti; they lived in terror of mass Haitian immigration.

We saw our opening in 2000 when Dominican President-Elect Hipólito Mejía called for universities in his country to welcome Haitian students. With an introduction made by my old Peace Corps friend Jerry DuPuy, Mike and I met with Mejía at his home. Also present was Mejía's future minister of environmental resources, Frank

Pons Moya, the foremost historian in the DR. We explained our approach, passed around a storyboard depicting the rehabilitation of dead soils, and were received most enthusiastically.

During our phone conversations, Haitian President Jean-Bertrand Aristide yielded his full support. We needed to seal the deal with both parties, but neither president would agree to meet together in public. Finally we settled on a rendezvous at a secluded, private resort in Haiti. The meeting went well, until President Mejía began talking about the effort as a project within Moya's ministry. Apparently my concept of a sovereign, binational authority to govern the watershed had failed to take root. Despite the backslapping and handshaking around the table, Mike and I understood immediately that the meeting had taken the wrong turn. We commiserated with a line from the Jimmie Lunceford song, "'Tain't What You Do (It's the Way That You Do It)."

Follow-up phone calls to Mejía describing the benefits of a binational authority produced little beyond canceled meetings. Our concept had been too big for the presidents to latch onto, and big was the only way it would work. As I like to say, the road to hell is paved in pilot projects. Our funders understood and graciously withdrew.

My failed attempt at TVA-style watershed rehabilitation was a sidelight to my more regular participation in Democratic election oversight. My old Peace Corps Colombia friend Rich Meganck got me involved with the International Foundation of Electoral Systems (IFES). I was an election observer in Equatorial Guinea (grossly fraudulent), Nicaragua (surprisingly honest), Panama, the Dominican Republic, Honduras, and El Salvador, among other countries.

•••

In November 2001, Congress was gearing up to confirm a new director of the Peace Corps, a political appointee named Gaddi Vasquez. A group of returned Peace Corps volunteers asked if I would testify against the nomination, and, after looking over Vasquez's record, I was happy to oblige.

A former Orange County supervisor, Vasquez had presided over the county's bankruptcy in 1994. With no international experience, he seemed to have nothing to show for himself besides a record of poor management. I told the Senate Foreign Relations Committee, chaired by former Peace Corps volunteer Chris Dodd, "As they say on the racing tout sheet for a horse that is not in the running: 'nothing to recommend.'"

At a Peace Corps Colombia I reunion, circa 1985

If Vasquez applied to become a Peace Corps volunteer, I testified, he wouldn't make the cut. He did, however, make a $100,000 contribution to the Republican Party. "It's clearly a political payoff, and it would be a shame to see him approved." Dodd had become considerably more submissive since I first met him as a feisty Peace Corps trainee; he and the committee weren't prepared to vote against President George W. Bush. They approved Vasquez's nomination by a vote of fourteen to four. I was heartened by a thank-you note from Sargent Shriver.

I stay involved with the Peace Corps because I love the volunteers and am convinced they are critical to our success at home and abroad. My greatest pleasure of the last fifty years has been engaging with past, present, and future volunteers. I meet them everywhere and I am honored to be invited to reunions, graduations, and Peace Corps Fellow events.

Robert Gelbard, appointed US ambassador to Bolivia in 1988, was the first Peace Corps volunteer to return to his host country as ambassador. (Parker Borg, our wonderful ambassador to Mali from 1981 to 1984, was the first volunteer to become an ambassador.) I asked one of the Bolivian ministers what it was like working with a former volunteer as ambassador. "It's tough; we can't put anything over on that guy! We don't know if Ambassador Gelbard is representing the Altiplano Indians or the United States government." I can't imagine a finer compliment.

We who engage peacefully with others have the chance to change the world in small but powerful ways. Peaceful engagement despite our differences, be they religious, racial, national, or philosophical, trumps all other options. Those who don't agree with me haven't experienced the madness of Pacific Island trench warfare or the magic of an Ivy League grad learning basic economics from a single mother in Zimbabwe.

•••

To my surprise, I am occasionally asked for career advice, and my answers are as varied as my career has been. I often say it's a gift to be fired at least once, and it's wise to pursue what you're good at and drop what you're not. Also, in one's career it is always better to be rumored to work for the CIA than to actually be employed there.

As some of my more distinguished colleagues would tell you, there were areas where I excelled and others where I came up dismally short. Fine, sharp guys from Brent Ashabranner at the Peace Corps to Rufus Smith at the embassy in Panama picked up my slack, buckling down with the bureaucracy while I stayed up in the clouds. Knowing my weaknesses and finding talented people to compensate for them has been just as important as following my passions.

The unwavering goals of my boyhood were to become lightweight champion of the world, a West Point graduate, and a professor of French literature. Let the record show that I fell short of all three, falling hardest in the boxing ring. I have spent no time regretting my divergence from those goals but many hours reminiscing about the great fun I had diverging.

At some point in my life I developed the habit of calling every job "the best job I ever had," until I found my next one. The older I get, the more I believe that attitude is everything, or at least eighty-five percent. It's the twinkle in your eye, the hesitation in your Shorty George, and the off color of your jokes that make the difference between a humdrum life and one worth telling stories about. In my case, it helped that I took the road less traveled. It was paved with good luck, marked with mixed reviews, traversed by great friends, and dotted with assassins—none of whom succeeded in killing this gringo.

AFTERWORD

by Jane Constantineau

My dad, Jack Vaughn, died on October 29, 2012 at the age of ninety-two. He spent his last summer enjoying his grandchildren in Tucson and salmon fishing in Yes Bay, Alaska, with friends from Allen & Company. Dad began work on his memoirs in 1992, when he moved from Guatemala City to Tucson for semiretirement.

After Dad's death, the family decided that the book should be finished to honor Dad and his many friends and fans who had waited so long to read it. Dad had written chapters by subject, leaving some gaps in the chronology of his life. Also, because of Dad's interest in storytelling rather than record-keeping, many stories were missing details and context.

From audio tapes of my mom's interviews with Dad in the early nineties, interviews with his friends and colleagues, and many primary sources including news articles, speeches, and letters, I filled in the narrative gaps and organized the book chronologically. I felt that one of the most interesting aspects of his life was how he got from point A to point B, and beyond: How does a French instructor who moonlights as a prizefighter become ambassador to Panama? I kept much of Dad's original writing, especially his wonderful humor and turns of phrase.

I am hopeful there are stories in this book that even Dad's close friends haven't heard, just as there may be some stories that friends find are missing. My rule was to include only the stories Dad wrote or recorded and those told firsthand by people who were there. Any other Jack Vaughn stories will undoubtedly live on through oral tradition, repeated, I hope, with Dad's signature flare.

San Diego, July 2015

Acknowledgments

If not for the support of Herbert Allen, this book might never have been written. On Jack's behalf, I would like to thank his friends who read early drafts and offered encouragement that sustained him through years of contented writing on yellow legal pads at the dining room table. Jack's typist, Evelyn Jorgensen, faithfully transcribed those longhand pages. Jack was indebted to editors who worked with him at different stages: Coates Redmond, Billie Stanton, and Jack Vaughn Jr.

I am grateful first and foremost to my mother, Leftie Vaughn, for her boundless support, advice, commiseration, memories, photo albums, letters, and expert editing. Many people generously shared with me their stories and memories of Jack, his life, and his work. Each contributed background, anecdotes, or details that made the book better. They include Herbert Allen, Diego Asencio, Brent Ashabranner, Bob Avery, Spencer Beebe, Margaret Boonstra, Ron Curtis, Jon Darrah, Mary DeWitt, Arthur Dye, Peter Fraser,

Gretchen Handwerger, Lee Hougen, Billie Johnson, Steve Knaebel, Kevin Lowther, Dan Lufkin, Rich Meganck, Tedson Meyers, Cappie Morgan, Ed Nef, Larry O'Brien, Michael Palmbach, Hugh Pickens, Leveo Sanchez, Stan Scheyer, George Schumacher, Jan Sheldon, Bob Steiner, Gordy Straub, Jack Sullivan, Ofelia Svart, Kate Swarthout, Henry Tschinkel, Carolyn Vale, Jack Vaughn Jr., Carol Vaughn, Kathryn Vaughn, and Norton Wright.

Un abrazo muy fuerte a Steve Knaebel y Katie Fabián por su ayuda con las traducciones. My thanks to the Lyndon Baines Johnson Library for interview transcripts, the William Allan Neilson Library at Smith College for Planned Parenthood documents, and the Seeley G. Mudd Manuscript Library at Princeton University for records from Development and Resources Corporation.

My mother and I are extremely grateful to the first readers of *Kill the Gringo* who offered encouragement and help. John Coyne, Chic Dambach, and Michael Keating went above and beyond. Mary Bisbee-Beek, Carolyn Holland, Lucy Cleland, and Ike Williams generously offered their literary expertise. Kelly McNees provided a thorough and thoughtful copyedit. Our agent, Jeff Berg, was our hero, turning our publishing dreams into reality. Tyson Cornell and his team at Rare Bird worked hard and honored the spirit of the book. Thanks to Alice Marsh-Elmer, Julia Callahan, Andrew Hungate, and Hailie Johnson. Thank you to Samantha Eason, who gave me peace and quiet. And, finally, love to my husband, Dan, who was my earliest and strongest supporter on this project, and to my little firecrackers Evie and Andy.

Résumé

- **1943:** *Ann Arbor, MI*—Bachelor of Arts in French, University of Michigan; Head Boxing Coach, University of Michigan (1942–43)
- **1943–46:** *Pacific, China*—Active duty US Marine Corps Captain
- **1946–48:** *Ann Arbor, MI*—Master of Arts in French, University of Michigan; Head Boxing Coach, University of Michigan
- **1948–49:** *Philadelphia, PA*—Spanish instructor, University of Pennsylvania
- **1949–51:** *La Paz, Bolivia*—Director, USIS Binational Cultural Center
- **1951–52:** *San José, Costa Rica*—Director, USIS Binational Cultural Center
- **1952–56:** *Panama City, Panama*—Program Officer, USAID
- **1956–58:** *La Paz, Bolivia*—Program Officer, USAID
- **1958:** *Baltimore, MD*—Instructor, Johns Hopkins School of Advanced International Studies
- **1958–59:** *Washington, DC*—Program Officer, USAID Europe and Africa

- **1959:** *Conakry, Guinea*—Director, USAID Guinea
- **1959–61:** *Dakar, Senegal*—Director, USAID Senegal, Mauritania, Mali
- **1961–64:** *Washington, DC*—Regional Director for Latin America, Peace Corps
- **1964–65:** *Panama City, Panama*—US Ambassador to Panama
- **1965–66:** *Washington, DC*—Assistant Secretary of State for Inter-American Affairs/Coordinator, Alliance for Progress
- **1966–69:** *Washington, DC*—Director, Peace Corps
- **1969–70:** *Bogotá, Colombia*—US Ambassador to Colombia
- **1970–71:** *Washington, DC*—President, National Urban Coalition
- **1971:** *Washington, DC*—Campaign Manager, Fred Harris for President
- **1972–73:** *Miami, FL*—Dean of International Studies, Florida International University
- **1973–75:** *New York, NY*—Director of International Development, Children's Television Workshop
- **1975–77:** *New York, NY*—President, Planned Parenthood Federation of America
- **1977–79:** *Tehran, Iran*—Resident Vice President, Development and Resources Iran
- **1979:** *Washington, DC*—Director, Pierce International
- **1980:** *Washington, DC*—Assistant Director for Latin America, Designate, USAID
- **1981–83:** *Washington, DC*—Senior Vice President, Pierce International

- **1983–87:** *Arlington, VA*—Vice President, Development Associates
- **1987–88:** *Washington, DC*—Founding Chairman, Conservation International
- **1989–92:** *Guatemala City, Guatemala*—Senior Environmental Advisor, USAID/ROCAP
- **1990:** *Portland, OR*—Founding Chairman, ECOTRUST

Boards: Columbia Pictures, The Nature Conservancy, Conservation International, ECOTRUST, Cypress Bioscience, Zamorano Pan-American Agricultural School, EARTH University, Inter-American Development Foundation